Envision

WRITING AND RESEARCHING ARGUMENTS

THIRD EDITION

Christine L. Alfano and Alyssa J. O'Brien
Stanford University

Longman

Boston • Columbus • Indianapolis • New York • San Francisco
Upper Saddle River • Amsterdam • Cape Town • Dubai • London • Madrid • Milan
Munich • Paris • Montreal • Toronto • Delhi • Mexico City • Sao Paulo • Sydney
Hong Kong • Seoul • Singapore • Taipei • Tokyo

Executive Editor: Lynn M. Huddon
Senior Development Editor: Virginia L. Blanford
Senior Marketing Manager: Sandra McGuire
Senior Supplements Editor: Donna Campion
Media Supplements Editor: Stefanie Liebman
Production Manager: Stacey Kulig
Project Coordination, Text Design, and Electronic Page Makeup: PreMediaGlobal
Senior Cover Design Manager: Nancy Danahy
Cover Designer: Nancy Sacks
Cover Image: Official White House Photo by Pete Souza; Iain Crockart/Getty Images; © Alex Segre/Alamy
Photo Researcher: Julie Tesser
Senior Manufacturing Buyer: Roy Pickering
Printer and Binder: R.R. Donnelley and Sons
Cover Printer: Coral Graphics, Inc.

For permission to use copyrighted material, grateful acknowledgment is made to the copyright holders on pp. 309–310, which are hereby made part of this copyright page.

Library of Congress Cataloging-in-Publication Data

Alfano, Christine L.
  Envision: writing and researching arguments / Christine L. Alfano and Alyssa J. O'Brien.—3rd ed.
    p. cm.
  Includes bibliographical references and index.
  ISBN-13: 978-0-205-75847-0 (alk. paper)
  ISBN-10: 0-205-75847-9 (alk. paper)
    1. English language—Rhetoric.   2. Persuasion (Rhetoric)   3. Visual communication.
  4. Report writing. I. O'Brien, Alyssa J. II. Title.
  PE1431.A55 2010
  808'.042—dc22

                                                                        2010026410

Longman
is an imprint of

ISBN-10: 0-205-75847-9
ISBN-13: 978-0-205-75847-0

3 4 5 6 7 8 9 10-DOC-13 12 11

www.pearsonhighered.com

Contents

PART II: RESEARCH ARGUMENTS   103

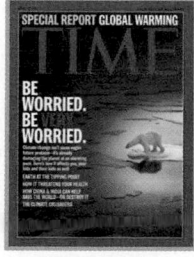

Chapter 6 **Organizing and Writing Research Arguments 160**

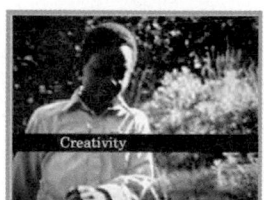

PART III: DESIGN AND DELIVERY   235

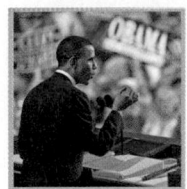

Preface

This book emerged from our practical need as writing instructors for an engaging textbook that would teach students core skills in analysis, argument, research writing, document design, and presentations—but that would do so in a way that captured student interest by using contemporary examples while building on a solid rhetorical foundation.

Our hope is that this text will accomplish two goals: first, to give teachers the confidence and resources to lead students in an appealing and rhetorically sound pedagogy focused on accessible writing instruction, and, second, to capture the interest of students while empowering them to become knowledgeable and skilled writers, researchers, and producers of well-composed rhetorical texts.

To develop students' understanding of texts of all kinds—and, along the way, move from written analysis to complex tasks such as argumentation, research writing, and presentation of those ideas—we seek to instruct students in time-honored writing techniques based on classical rhetoric. We walk students through interactive lessons on crafting thesis statements, structuring argumentative essays, developing research topics, evaluating sources, integrating quotations, revising papers, and, finally, designing and presenting effective presentations and writing projects. At the same time, we emphasize key rhetorical concepts for effective communication: attending to audience, understanding rhetorical appeals and fallacies, practicing the canons of rhetoric, differentiating levels of decorum, and using branches of oratory.

What's been most exciting about *Envision* as a project is how our students have collaborated with us: they have provided suggestions for examples, extensive feedback on each chapter, unfailing support and enthusiasm, and the ultimate gift of sharing their own writing in this book as well as on the Companion Website: http://www.pearsonhighered.com/envision.

What's New in the Third Edition

We have made a number of exciting changes in this edition of *Envision* based on feedback from instructors and students. These include:

- Significantly expanded guidance for integrating quotations, paraphrases, and summaries (Chapter 6), because students often find this particularly challenging
- A new section on the Toulmin model for analyzing arguments, in Chapter 3
- A new placement for the material on avoiding plagiarism and documenting sources, which now appears as Chapter 7, an integral part of

Part II on Research Arguments, and which includes current MLA guidelines for documentation
- Closing advice at the end of each chapter with a section called "The Writer's Process," in which we return the focus to the student's own work and writing process
- Helpful activity prompts for launching student writing at the end of each chapter with a new section called, "Prewriting with the *Envision* Website," where we point to specific resources available through our extensive Companion Website
- New and updated student writing samples as well as and professional readings, all of which have annotations and explanations.
- Revised content to address the most current issues, using captivating and relevant visual rhetoric to engage student writers

Our mission with this book is to teach students how to understand, analyze, conduct research on, and compose arguments about all kinds of texts. We hope to enable students to develop the skills, confidence, and enthusiasm for writing, research, and effective communication about issues that matter to them.

Structure of the Book

Although chapters are designed to stand alone, so that instructors may use this book in any order, *Envision's* three-part structure will help students develop the skills to become confident, competent, and effective writers.

Part I: Analysis and Argument

Chapters 1 through 3 encourage students to become proficient, careful readers of rhetorical texts and to learn practical strategies for writing thesis statements, rhetorical analysis essays, and synthesis essays incorporating various perspectives. Students learn how to analyze the forms of persuasion in verbal and visual texts—from short articles to political cartoons, ads, and photos—with an emphasis on rhetorical conventions.

Part II: Research Arguments

Chapters 4 through 7 focus on strategies of research argument for sustained writing projects. The writing lessons in this section of the book take students through the research proposal; techniques for keeping a research log; locating sources; integrating visuals; methods of outlining, drafting, and revising; best practices for integrating sources in writing; and the complexities of evaluating and documenting sources. Students can consult sample proposals, outlines, and drafts as well as examples of articles, propaganda posters, and film trailers. They learn how to locate, evaluate, and incorporate research into their own arguments while avoiding plagiarism and accomplishing successful documentation of sources.

Part III: Design and Delivery

The final chapters encourage students to present their writing in effective ways. Students learn about document design—both for academic papers and for visual arguments such as op-ads and photo essays—as well as how to translate written work into effective oral and multimedia presentations. Students gain guidance on how to design memorable and compelling writing projects for a range of academic and professional purposes, including service-learning courses.

Sequence of Assignments

Throughout this book, we base our writing assignments on lessons from classical rhetoric. This edition retains our particular media theme for each chapter—analyzing a range of textual examples, from cartoons, ads, and news photos to propaganda posters, film trailers, and student presentations. Yet our goal is to teach writing skills in analysis, research, and argument. To that end, we've devised our assignments to meet the learning objectives specified by the Council of Writing Program Administrators (WPA), as shown in the accompanying table.

MAJOR ASSIGNMENTS AND LEARNING OBJECTIVES

Chapter Title	Chapter Learning Goals	Major Assignments	Media Focus
1: Analyzing Texts	■ Understanding the rhetorical situation ■ Considering relationships between audience, text, and purpose ■ Textual analysis ■ Developing thesis statements	■ Personal narrative essay ■ Rhetorical analysis essay	Cartoons, comic strips, and editorial cartoons
2: Understanding the Strategies of Persuasion	■ Strategies of argumentation ■ Understanding rhetorical appeals: *logos, pathos, ethos* ■ Abuses or exaggerated uses of rhetorical appeals ■ Importance of context and *kairos*	■ Contextual analysis essay ■ Analysis of rhetorical appeals and fallacies ■ Comparison/contrast essay	Advertisements

(continued)

Chapter Title	Chapter Learning Goals	Major Assignments	Media Focus
3: Composing Arguments	■ Introductions and conclusions ■ Arrangement and structure of argument ■ Considering various perspectives on argument ■ Developing persona and rhetorical stance ■ Addressing opposing opinion in an argument ■ Effective titles	■ Position paper ■ Multiple sides of argument assignment ■ Argumentative essay incorporating diverse viewpoints ■ Synthesis Essay	Photographs, photo essays
4: Planning and Proposing Research Arguments	■ Generating and narrowing research topics ■ Prewriting strategies ■ Developing a research plan ■ Drafting a formal proposal	■ Research log ■ Informal research plan ■ Research proposal	Propaganda posters
5: Finding and Evaluating Research Sources	■ Research strategies ■ Evaluating sources ■ Distinguishing between primary and secondary sources ■ Locating sources ■ Conducting field research ■ Best practices for note taking	■ Critical evaluation of sources ■ Annotated bibliography ■ Field research contact assignment	Magazine and journal covers, Websites
6: Organizing and Writing Research Arguments	■ Organizing and outlining arguments ■ Importance of multiple drafts and revision ■ Writing and peer response ■ Quoting from sources	■ Formal outline ■ Peer review and response ■ Using visual evidence ■ Integrating Sources ■ Writing the Research argument	Film and movie trailers
7: Documentation and Plagiarism	■ Best practices in documenting sources ■ MLA style rules ■ Avoiding plagiarism	■ Ethical note-taking exercises ■ Citation practice	
8: Designing Arguments	■ Understanding the conventions of academic writing ■ Writing abstracts ■ Adopting appropriate voice and tone ■ Considering different genres of argument ■ Relationship between rhetorical situation and types of argument ■ Formatting and genre considerations	■ Writing an abstract ■ Visual argument—opinion advertisement or photo essay ■ Creating electronic arguments using multimedia (audio and visual)	Op-ads, photo essays, Websites, and multiple media

Chapter Title	Chapter Learning Goals	Major Assignments	Media Focus
9: Delivering Presentations	■ Using technology to address a range of audiences ■ Transforming written arguments into visual or spoken texts ■ Strategies of design and delivery ■ Conducting field research	■ Conversion assignment—written to oral rhetoric ■ Fieldwork assignment ■ Multimedia presentation ■ Collaborative conference presentation	Presentations, poster sessions, PowerPoint and other slide software, Multimedia Writing

Resources for Teachers and Students

Envision Companion Website

Envision is designed around the pedagogical philosophy that students learn more when they interact with the course material and when they are challenged to teach each other than when they simply implement the lessons taught to them. To complement this book we have designed a comprehensive, multilayered Companion Website that contains an extensive collection of materials designed to facilitate learning, including links to writing, research, and rhetoric resources, supplemental readings, additional writing activities, and over 250 student writing projects.

Instructors will find resources on the Companion Website designed to help you with everyday instruction in the classroom including lessons plans, classroom activities, sample syllabi, assignment guidelines, annotated classroom readings, and resources for teaching students with disabilities.

An Interactive Pearson eText in MyCompLab

A dynamic, online version of *Envision* is available in MyCompLab to create an active learning experience for students.

MyCompLab, an eminently flexible application, empowers student writers and teachers by integrating a composing space and assessment tools with multimedia tutorials, services such as online tutoring and exercises for writing, grammar and research. Students can use MyCompLab on their own, benefiting from self-paced diagnostics and a personal study plan that recommends the instruction and practice students need to improve their writing skills. Teachers can recommend MyCompLab to students for self-study, set up courses to track student progress, or leverage the power of administrative features to be more effective and save time. The assignment builder and commenting tools, developed specifically for use in writing courses, make managing assignments and evaluating papers more efficient and put power-ful assessment within reach. Students receive feedback within the context of their own writing, which helps them develop skills based on their individual needs. Learn more at www.mycomplab.com.

A CourseSmart eTextbook

Envision is also available as a CourseSmart eTextbook (www.coursesmart.com). Students can subscribe to and search the text, make notes online, print out reading assignments that incorporate lecture notes, and bookmark important passages for later review.

Instructor's Manual

The Instructor's Manual for *Envision* provides teachers with pedagogical advice including chapter overviews, teaching tips for working with the main concepts and reading selections in each chapter, suggestions for classroom exercises and writing assignments, and strategies for integrating the resources on the *Envision* Companion Website and in MyCompLab into your class-room. The Instructor's Manual also offers sample syllabi and suggested ways of organizing the content according to days of the week.

A Note of Thanks

In our chapter on documentation, we emphasize the importance of acknowl-edging your debts as a writer to those who made your ideas and work possi-ble. We'd like to offer our own note of thanks to those who made possible the writing of this book. We are grateful to the reviewers whose comments informed our decisions about this revision: John C. Gooch, The University of Texas at Dallas; Katherine Heenan, Arizona State University; Rebecca B. Hewett, California State University, Bakersfield; Jodie L. Marion, Mt. Hood Community College; Stephanie Mood, Grossmont College; Patricia E. O'Connor, Georgetown University; and Margaret Price, Spelman College.

In particular, we extend our greatest appreciation to those who envisioned our accomplishment and rallied us all the way through: from our friends and families, to our professional colleagues and those who reviewed the book, and to our publication team at Pearson who made the book possible. Thank you.

Lastly, thank you for your interest in *Envision*; we hope you find the book as useful to your teaching as it has been rewarding for us to use in our own classes.

Christine L. Alfano and Alyssa J. O'Brien

Part I

ANALYSIS AND ARGUMENT

CHAPTER 1
Analyzing Texts

CHAPTER 2
Understanding Strategies
of Persuasion

CHAPTER 3
Composing Arguments

Rhetoric's classic definition as the art of persuasion suggests a power. So much of what we receive from others—from family and friends to 30-second blurbs on TV—is intended to persuade. Recognizing how this is done gives greater power to choose.

—Victor Villanueva, Jr.

Analyzing Texts

Chapter Preview Questions

- How do we read and analyze texts rhetorically?
- How do we write about visual texts?
- How can we generate thesis statements for arguments?
- How can we draft rhetorical analysis essays?

Everywhere around us, words and images try to persuade us to think about the world in certain ways. From "Got Milk?" ads to political campaign posters, words and images combine to move us, convince us to buy something, shape our opinions, or make us laugh. Living in such a world requires us to pay attention and to think critically and analytically about all the texts we encounter every day. We can see this persuasive power especially in visual texts, such as the political cartoons and comics you might find on your favorite Weblog or in the campus newspaper.

Consider the political cartoon by Nate Beeler shown in Figure 1.1. How do the words and the images work together to persuade audiences to think, feel, or act a certain way? Beeler's cartoon conveys through words and images the atmosphere around the first presidential debate between Barack Obama and John McCain. With the collapsing columns and the twin towers in the background, the cartoon offers a

FIGURE 1.1. Beeler's cartoon from the 2008 election uses visual references to classical catastrophes to make a point about the climate facing the candidates during the election.

Source: © 2009 Nate Beeler, *Washington Examiner,* and PoliticalCartoons.com powerful message about how America today struggles under many issues or "calamities." Notice that the presidential candidates don't say anything—their faces show consternation while their silence suggests they are overwhelmed by the issues. The cartoon is ironic since when we think of rhetoric, we often think of political rhetoric—or "empty rhetoric." Indeed, rhetoric began as a skill men learned in order to speak in public, often in courts of law where they had to represent themselves. The falling classical columns in the cartoon evoke this history while showing us how "rhetoric" today has expanded to mean any communication that seeks to persuade a specific audience in a certain situation, whether the text be written, visual, auditory, or multimedia.

We can understand how this cartoon works by asking questions about its argument, audience, and author. We can analyze its elements carefully and then come up with our interpretation of the text. When we ask questions and make our own argument about how a text works, we are analyzing how texts can be **rhetorical**, how they aim at persuading particular audiences through the careful choices made by the writer in composing the text. When we make arguments about a text—in writing or in speech or with visual compositions—we are using rhetoric as a practical art.

As you launch into the art of rhetoric and the skills of analyzing and writing in this chapter, you'll learn about comics and political cartoons. By studying these texts, you'll develop skills as both a reader and a writer, learn how to analyze rhetoric, and begin to create powerful arguments about the texts you encounter every day. In the process, you'll come to appreciate how writing as we know it is changing, causing us to approach it with a new set of eyes and a necessary set of rhetorical tools.

Understanding Texts Rhetorically

To approach texts rhetorically means to ask questions about how the text conveys a persuasive message or *argument*, how the text addresses a specific *audience*, and how the writer operates within a *specific context* or *rhetorical situation*.

You encounter many kinds of texts every day, even in just walking across campus. Once you recognize how these texts function *rhetorically*—once you see how texts try to shape your mind about the world—then you can decide whether or not to agree with the many messages you encounter on a regular basis.

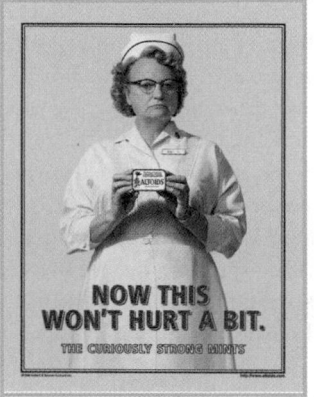

FIGURE 1.2.

To grasp this concept, let's follow one hypothetical student—we'll call her Alex—as she walks to class and note the rhetorical texts she sees along the way.

First stop: the dorm room, your average institutional room, which Alex and her roommate have decorated with Altoids ads they've ripped from magazines (Figure 1.2). There's also a large poster for the women's basketball team on one wall and a small Snoopy comic taped above the computer screen.

Alex walks down the hall, past the rooms of other students who have photos and graffiti on their doors, pausing in the lounge where several of her friends are watching a rerun of *The Daily Show* with Jon Stewart and his famous smirk and strategic gestures on a large flat-screen TV (Figure 1.3). She watches until the show breaks for a commercial for Nike shoes, then she continues, down a stairwell dec-orated with student event flyers—a charity dance for the victims of a

FIGURE 1.3.

recent earthquake, a rally against immigration laws, a dorm meeting to plan the ski trip—and she pushes her way out into the cool autumn air. Outside the student newspaper has a political cartoon on the front designed to grab her attention and she pauses to look at the image of student apathy in the past election (Figure 1.4). The cartoon argues that students prefer popular culture over politics.

She only has two minutes to get to class, so she walks briskly past the student union with its bulletin boards covered with notices of upcoming events, such as one for the Digital Action Group (Figure 1.5), which uses a mash-up of images to grab the attention of viewers.

FIGURE 1.4.

Source: © Tribune Media Services, Inc. All Rights Reserved. Reprinted with permission

Alex walks over the school crest in the walkway and past students outside the administration building, waving signs that protest the conditions of janitorial workers. She turns left, weaving along the back of a cluster of gleaming steel and brick buildings that constitute the engineering quad. She passes a thin metal sculpture called *Knowledge and Life* that guards the entrance to the library. Finally, she reaches her destination: the English department. As Alex climbs the stone steps, she stops to scan the photos and headlines on the campus paper before heading down the hall. Into the classroom she rushes, but she's late. The

Using the Internet to Increase Citizen Power!

▽ A Brown Bag Lunch with ▽
Leaders of

MoveOn.org
studentsrising.org

12 noon on Saturday, Nov. 22
202 Willard Straight Hall

Sponsored by Students for a More Just Society
and WPRk

FIGURE 1.5.

professor has started the PowerPoint lecture already. Alex picks up the handout from the TA and sits down in the back row.

Now that we've seen Alex safely to her seat, how many rhetorical texts did you notice along the way? Ads, posters, cartoons, Websites, textbooks, television shows, flyers, statues, signs, newspapers, PowerPoint slides, even architectural design: each can be seen as an example of rhetoric. Once you begin to look at the world rhetorically, you'll see that just about everywhere you are being persuaded to agree, act, buy, attend, or accept an argument: rhetoric permeates our cultural landscape.

Student Writing
See examples of several students' visual rhetoric narratives.
www.pearsonhighered.com/envision/05

The next time you walk to class, pay attention to the rhetoric that you find along the way. Recognizing the power of rhetoric to persuade is an important part of learning to engage in contemporary society. Learning how to read texts rhetorically is the first step in thinking critically about the world.

Understanding Rhetoric

In one of the earliest definitions, ancient Greek philosopher Aristotle characterized **rhetoric** as *the ability to discern the available means of persuasion in any given situation.* Essentially, this means knowing what strategies will work to

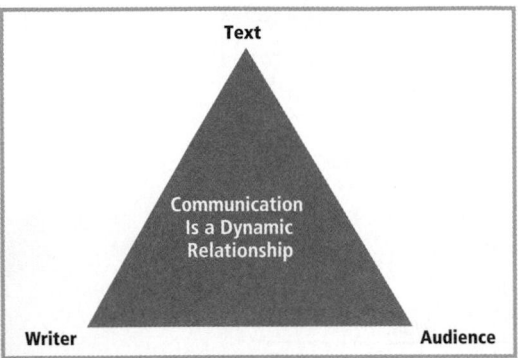

FIGURE 1.6. The rhetorical situation is a dynamic relationship between writer, text, and audience.

convince your audience in a given situation. As shown in Figure 1.6, this involves assessing and attending to the **rhetorical situation**—that is, to the relationship between writer, text, and audience. Think of

- the politician who might argue the same political platform but in strikingly different ways depending on what part of his constituency he's addressing;
- the various ways mothers, students, or police officers might convey the same antidrug message to a group of middle school students;
- the clothing retailers who adapt their marketing messages to suit the media in which they're advertising—magazines, TV, or the Internet.

In each case the *argument* has been determined by the unique relationship between the writer, the audience, and the text.

In constructing your own arguments every day, you also need to evaluate your rhetorical situation.

- When you want to persuade your coach to let practice out early, you probably make your case face to face, rather than through a formal letter.
- When you ask for an extension on a paper, you most likely do so in a well-crafted email rather than a hasty after-class appeal.
- When you apply for a job or internship, you send a formal résumé and cover letter to indicate the seriousness of your interest.

Here we see that the success of your argument depends at least in part on your choice of text (verbal plea, written email, cover letter) in relation to the audience (coach, professor, potential employer) that you're addressing. All these examples are rhetorical acts in the form of oral and written arguments.

Understanding Visual Rhetoric

Yet persuasion happens through visual means as well: how you stand and make eye contact, how you format your professional documents, even how you capitalize or spell words in an email. Moreover, when you insert an image in an essay, create a poster to advertise a club sport, or draw a cartoon spoofing university policy, you are moving into the realm of **visual persuasion**—"writing" with images. From photographs to Websites, political cartoons to advertisements, these visual texts use rhetorical means to persuade an audience. Although some images may be more aesthetic than argumentative, many convey either inherent or explicit persuasive messages. Think about brochures, movie trailers, flyers, commercial Websites, and even comics; these are all created as arguments to convince audiences.

Since such strategies of persuasion occur through images—either alone or combined with words—rather than merely through words, they are called **visual rhetoric**. Additional examples of visual rhetoric include:

- A documentary produced to suggest a point of view
- An illustration in a children's book provided to shape the meaning of a story
- Sequential cartoons of a comic strip to offer powerful commentary on society or culture

In each example, the writer chooses the best visual representation for the message of the text. In this way, the study of visual rhetoric provides you with the means to understand how and why such choices are made, and what the significance of these decisions is in the larger culture in which we live. In the process of studying such texts, you will develop an essential life skill called **visual literacy**—how to read, analyze, understand, and even produce texts that are primarily visual in nature and powerful as compact messages about culture.

Strategies for Analyzing Texts Rhetorically

Think of your favorite comic strips, political cartoons, or cartoon animations. Although they may seem merely informative about current events, or just plain funny, they do serve as an important mode of communicating ideas and making statements about society. For example, the comic antics in *Calvin and Hobbes, xkcd* (a Web comic of romance, sarcasm, math, and language), or *The Boondocks* may not appear to carry any strong arguments about human relations or political events. However, if you look closely at the details—the address to a specific audience, the words of the characters in the cartoons, and the message made through combination of image and text—then you can gain a deeper understanding of the cartoon's argument. This is what we mean by analyzing texts rhetorically.

In fact, sometimes images can be even more powerful than words at reaching audiences. This is the argument made by Scott McCloud in his book, *Understanding Comics*:

> When pictures are more abstracted from "reality," they require greater levels of perception, more like words. When words are bolder, more direct, they require lower levels of perception and are received faster, more like pictures.

McCloud tells us we need to develop "greater levels of perception," or visual literacy, in order to *read with a critical eye.* In effect, we can look to the brief passage quoted here as an example of a persuasive use of written rhetoric, in which McCloud makes very deliberate choices to strengthen his point. Notice how his words use comparison-contrast (pictures versus words), qualified language ("reality"), and parallel structure (both sentences move from "When" to a final phrase beginning with "more like") to persuade his audience of the way pictures and words can operate in similar ways. Such attention to detail is the first step in rhetorical analysis—looking at the way the writer chooses the most effective means of persuasion to make a point.

What's interesting about McCloud's rhetoric, though, is not just his written strategies but also the way he uses a combination of words and images to make his point. To fully appreciate McCloud's rhetorical decisions, we need to consider the passage in its original context. As you can see in Figure 1.7, McCloud amplifies his argument about comics by using the

FIGURE 1.7. Scott McCloud writes in the medium of cartoons to explain comics.
Source: Courtesy of Scott McCloud

form of the graphic novel, creating what we call a hybrid text—a strategic combination of words and images.

This complex diagram relies on the visual-verbal relationship itself to map out the complicated nature of how we understand both written text and pictures. The repetition and echoes that we found in the quoted passage are graphically represented in Figure 1.7; in fact, translated into comic book form, the division between word and image breaks down. It becomes a visual continuum that strongly suggests McCloud's vision of the interrelationship between these rhetorical elements. The power of this argument comes from McCloud's strategic assessment of the rhetorical situation: he, the **author**, recognizes that his **audience** (people interested in visual media) would find a **text** that relies on both visual and verbal elements to be highly persuasive.

McCloud's example is also instructive for demonstrating the way word and image can collaborate in modern arguments. Today more than ever, rhetoric operates not just through word choice but also through choice of multimedia elements—images in a TV commercial, the audio of a viral ad on the Internet, the design choices of a Website or flyer, even the layout strategies of your textbooks. Therefore, we need to develop skills of analysis for all rhetorical texts. We need to understand argument *as writing across diverse media* and in turn develop **multimedia literacy**, or a careful way of reading, analyzing, and understanding media (visual, verbal, and other rhetorical texts).

One way to develop multimedia or visual literacy is to understand how cartoonists "write" through certain tools. The cartoon in Figure 1.8a shows the writing studio of *New Yorker* cartoonist Marisa Acocella Marchetto. Notice how Marchetto shows her many drafts, her tools of recording devices, and her pens and pads (see Figure 1.8b). As this cartoon reveals, writing is changing today so that audio recordings and graphic novels or cartoon books are becoming legitimate forms of researching and writing arguments about the world.

Analyzing a Comic Strip

As you can tell from Marchetto's drawing of her writer's studio, comic strips are an important form of rhetoric. They can serve as a productive starting point for examining how the rhetorical situation and composition strategies work together to produce powerful texts.

In "The Hipness Threshold," from the *Penny Arcade*, drawn by cartoonist Jerry Holkins (Figure 1.9, p. 12) you see Gabe and Tycho as they accompany their friend Charles into an Apple Computer store. Notice the

FIGURE 1.8a. Marchetto's writing tools include a tape recorder and drafting pads—with these tools she can compose her cartoons.

elements of the cartoon: images, words, characters, layout, and action. Observe facial expression, body postures, and the changes between the panels. Now try to determine: Who might be the audience? What is the writer's message? Then put it all together and ask yourself: What persuasive statement does the cartoon convey? What is its argument? In this way, you are analyzing visual rhetoric.

Now read the following excerpt from one of the cartoonist's blog posts that accompanied the online publication of this comic. In it, Holkins makes

FIGURE 1.8b.

an argument very similar to that made in the cartoon—but this time in words. In what ways does this different rhetorical situation (blog versus Web comic) influence the way he makes his argument?

> The way Apple projects its brand, however, has nothing to do with the underlying technology. It could not be more divorced from it. So if they want to create largely empty stores staffed exclusively by young hardbodies in ill-fitting t-shirts, it's open season. It's possible that each manifestation of this chain does not resemble the others, that each one is not populated with the scrubbed, tousled young things of the sort one sees in serious teen dramas. You'll forgive me if

FIGURE 1.9. The Hipness Threshold cartoon depicts the adventures of Gabe and Tycho as they accompany their friend Charles into an Apple Computer store.

Source: Penny Arcade, Inc. www.penny-arcade.com

I don't believe that. I'd say it's far more likely that there is a single Apple Store, connected by a series of geographically distinct portals.

I don't put this out there to imply that the places I have to go to get technology or software are somehow superior, because they aren't. They're horrid. But at least I never feel underdressed.

Observe how Holkins uses visual metaphors in his writing to convey his social critique about Apple Stores. He mentions the tousled hair and hardbodies—visual signs of particular trends in society, reminiscent of Abercrombie & Fitch, for instance, and the physical "look" of Apple store staffers. His words echo the visual design of his cartoon argument. In his writing, he makes his point in the last paragraph by moving his argument to focus "the places I have to go to get technology" and ending with a sarcastic line about not worrying about being "underdressed." The sharp tone parallels the dejected stares of his characters. His persuasive writing strategies thus span both visual and verbal media. Understanding how both work rhetorically will give you the ability and confidence to analyze and produce similar texts of your own.

As these examples demonstrate, we can gather a tremendous amount of information from a seemingly simple comic strip. As we learn to develop our *visual literacy,* we can make more and better-informed interpretations of such intriguing visual texts. These skills of visual analysis will help you approach other kinds of texts rhetorically: political speeches, scholarly articles, letters to the editor about timely issues, even instant messaging and—as we just learned—blog posts. At the same time, approaching visual texts rhetorically will help you develop your skills to participate in and respond to powerful multimedia arguments shaping the world around you.

CREATIVE PRACTICE

Using the comic strip shown in Figure 1.9, create your own version. Change the symbol of Microsoft from inside the box of the panel and put in something different—words or images. Then, write down your point just as Holkins did for his blog entry. When you are done, move into a small group and share your work—both your written analysis and your hybrid text. Discuss what you have learned in producing oral, written, and cartoon texts, and how each text conveys your argument.

"[Cartoons] provide alternative perspectives at a glance because they are visual and vivid and often seem to communicate a clear or obvious message."

—*Matthew Diamond*, "No Laughing Matter" (270)

Analyzing Editorial Cartoons

In addition to comic strips, we can look at political cartoons—or **editorial cartoons** as they are also called—for another set of visual arguments to help us further develop effective strategies for analysis and interpretation. Editorial cartoons offer a rich resource for this sort of work.

From the densely symbolic eighteenth-century plates of William Hogarth, to the biting social satire of *Punch*'s illustrators, to the edgy work of political cartoonists such as Ann Telnaes, Mike Luckovich, and Daryl Cagle, the editorial cartoon has emerged as a succinct, powerful tool for writers to contribute to public dialogue on contemporary issues.

In the drawing by Daryl Cagle, for instance (see Figure 1.10), the particular face is recognizable to most twenty-first-century readers: the impish smile, the circular, black-frame glasses, and the prep-school tie identify

FIGURE 1.10. This cartoon by Daryl Cagle uses a striking symbol to make its argument.

Source: Daryl Cagle, Cagle Cartoons, Inc.

What Would Mohammed Drive?

FIGURE 1.11. Doug Marlette received death threats after publishing this cartoon.

Source: Courtesy of Doug Marlette

this figure almost immediately as the young actor who plays Harry Potter in the film series. However, through one strategic substitution, Cagle transforms this image from illustration into commentary; he replaces the famous lightning bolt scar on Potter's forehead with a dollar sign. Cagle's Potter has been branded not by his encounter with a nearly omnipotent wizard but by his face-off with American capitalism. In this way, Cagle uses visual elements in his editorial cartoon to comment on the way this children's book hero has become a lucrative pop culture franchise.

For a more politically charged example, let's look at a powerful cartoon created by Pulitzer Prize–winning cartoonist Doug Marlette.

In this cartoon (Figure 1.11), Marlette uses the strong reactions against Muslims following the September 11, 2001, attacks as a springboard for lampooning cultural prejudices and fears. His cartoon practices visual and verbal means of persuasion, both of which are important to consider when we are analyzing and writing about a text.

The words of his title, "What Would Mohammed Drive?" echo the famous Christian saying, "What Would Jesus Do?" as a guideline for behavior, even while the irony of the rewriting asks readers to challenge their assumptions about different religions. Yet, the title suggests a link between the Muslim religion and terrorism by asking what vehicle Mohammed, if fueling terrorist impulses, would drive to conduct the act. The visual drawing positions an Arab man driving a Ryder truck that contains a nuclear warhead. This image echoed fears of "truck bombs" in the wake of the airplane attacks of 9/11. But it also rudely depicts the prophet Mohammed as a terrorist, and many readers view this as blasphemy, insult, or worse. Consider how a negative, demeaning depiction of Jesus might be received by some readers.

The cartoon caused a firestorm of protest from the Muslim community in America, including death threats on the cartoonist. Marlette responded by asserting that "the objective of political cartooning 'is not to soothe and tend sensitive psyches, but to jab and poke in an attempt to get at deeper truths, popular or otherwise'" (quoted in Moore). Marlette's own words reveal that cartoons are not just humorous texts but rather, as we have seen, they are rhetorical—they intend to persuade.

Student Writing
See Jeff Enquist's analysis of a cartoonist's commentary on the media representation of Catholic priests as part of a larger social issue dealing with the place of religion in American culture.
www.pearsonhighered.com/envision/15

Look again at the cartoon and ask yourself *how* it attempts to jab or poke. What elements of composition, framing, shading, and layout suggest to you the target of Marlette's jab? How does the title set up or shape possible readings of the cartoon? How might this cartoon be read differently by an American audience, an Arab audience, and an Arab-American audience? How might it be interpreted in the United States or in the Middle East as conveying a different persuasive message?

Some might argue that the cartoon takes the announced threat of terrorists potentially using trucks to carry out nuclear attacks and reproduces it without irony. Another reader analyzing the cartoon could say that it mocks and belittles the government issuing the warning about post-September 11 terrorists. A third reader could point to the caricature of the driver and state that the cartoon makes fun of people of Arab descent. These varied ways of reading and responding to the text depend on both *audience* and *context*, bringing to light the importance of the rhetorical situation. They also reveal the importance of learning effective means of persuading others to see the text through a certain interpretative lens or way of reading the cartoon.

What we can learn from this practice with rhetoric is that the relationship between interpretation and argument is a complex one. Although the author might intend to produce a certain argument, at times the audience may offer a slightly different interpretation. Our task as readers and writers is both to study a text carefully and to learn how to persuade others to see the text as we see it.

Let's turn now to Doug Marlette's writing to see how he used the art of rhetoric to persuade his many readers to see the cartoon from his perspective. As you read this article, originally published in the *Columbia Journalism Review*, use some of the same strategies of analysis that we've used on comics and cartoons throughout the chapter. Ask yourself: Who is his audience? How does Marlette position himself as author? What is his argument? What evidence does he use to support that argument? Which parts are the most persuasive? Which are the least persuasive? What visual images does he convey with words? Are you persuaded by his argument?

I WAS A TOOL OF SATAN
Doug Marlette

Last year, I drew a cartoon that showed a man in Middle Eastern apparel at the wheel of a Ryder truck hauling a nuclear warhead. The caption read, "What Would Mohammed Drive?" Besides referring to the vehicle that Timothy McVeigh rode into Oklahoma City, the drawing was a takeoff on the "What Would Jesus Drive?" campaign created by Christian evangelicals to challenge the morality of owning gas-guzzling SUVs. The cartoon's main target, of course, was the faith-based politics of a different denomination. Predictably, the Shiite hit the fan.

Can you say "fatwa"? My newspaper, *The Tallahassee Democrat,* and I received more than 20,000 e-mails demanding an apology for misrepresenting the peace-loving religion of the Prophet Mohammed—or else. Some spelled out the "else": death, mutilation, Internet spam. . . . "What you did, Mr. Dog, will cost you your life. Soon you will join the dogs . . . hahaha in hell." "Just wait . . . we will see you in hell with all jews. . . ." The onslaught was orchestrated by an organization called the Council on American-Islamic Relations. CAIR bills itself as an "advocacy group." I was to discover that among the followers of Islam it advocated for were the men convicted of the 1993 bombing of the World Trade Center. At any rate, its campaign against me included flash-floods of e-mail intended to shut down servers at my newspaper and my syndicate, as well as viruses aimed at my home computer. The controversy became a subject of newspaper editorials, columns, Web logs, talk radio, and CNN. I was condemned on the front page of the Saudi publication *Arab News* by the secretary general of the Muslim World League.

My answer to the criticism was published in the *Democrat* (and reprinted around the country) under the headline *With All Due Respect, an Apology Is Not in Order.* I almost felt that I could have written the response in my sleep. In my thirty-year career, I have regularly drawn cartoons that offended religious fundamentalists and true believers of every stripe, a fact that I tend to list in the "Accomplishments" column of my résumé. I have outraged Christians by skewering Jerry Falwell, Catholics by needling the pope, and Jews by criticizing Israel. Those who rise up against the expression of ideas are strikingly similar. No one is less tolerant than those demanding tolerance. Despite differences of culture and creed, they all seem to share the notion that there is only one way of looking at things, their way. What I have learned from years of this is one of the great lessons of all the world's religions: we are all one in our humanness.

In my response, I reminded readers that my "What Would Mohammed Drive?" drawing was an assault not upon Islam but on the distortion of the Muslim religion by murderous fanatics— the followers of Mohammed who flew those planes into our buildings, to be sure, but also the Taliban killers of noncompliant women and destroyers of great art, the true believers who decapitated an American reporter, the young Palestinian suicide bombers taking out patrons of pizza parlors in the name of the Prophet Mohammed.

Then I gave my Journalism 101 lecture on the First Amendment, explaining that in this country we do not apologize for our opinions. Free speech is the linchpin of our republic. All other freedoms flow from it. After all, we don't need a First Amendment to allow us to run boring, inoffensive cartoons. We need constitutional protection for our right to express unpopular views. If we can't discuss the great issues of the day on the pages of our newspapers fearlessly, and without apology, where can we discuss them? In the streets with guns? In cafes with strapped-on bombs?

Although my initial reaction to the "Mohammed" hostilities was that I had been there before, gradually I began to feel that there was something new, something darker afoot. The repressive impulses of that old-time religion were now being fed by the subtler inhibitions of mammon and the marketplace. Ignorance and bigotry were reinventing themselves in the post-Christian age by dressing up as "sensitivity" and masquerading as a public virtue that may be as destructive to our rights as religious zealotry. We seem to be entering a Techno Dark Age, in which the machines

Notice the way that Marlette also condemns the "murderous fanatics" he describes based on an ongoing pattern of behavior—a rhetorical decision that makes his critique seem less reactionary and more thoughtful.

In this paragraph, he evokes the First Amendment and ends with an implicit comparison between America, with its civil liberties, and more militaristic and war-torn countries. Notice the power of the rhetorical questions that he uses at the end of the paragraph, asking readers to consider the alternatives to American freedom of speech.

that were designed to serve the free flow of information have fallen into the hands of an anti-intellectual mobocracy.

Twenty-five years ago, I began inciting the wrath of the faithful by caricaturing the grotesque disparity between Jim and Tammy Faye Bakker's televangelism scam and the Christian piety they used to justify it. I was then working at *The Charlotte Observer,* in the hometown of the Bakkers' PTL Club, which instigated a full-bore attack on me. The issues I was cartooning were substantial enough that I won the Pulitzer Prize for my PTL work. But looking back on that fundamentalist religious campaign, even though my hate mail included some death threats, I am struck by the relative innocence of the times and how ominous the world has since become—how high the stakes, even for purveyors of incendiary doodles.

One of the first cartoons I ever drew on PTL was in 1978, when Jim Bakker's financial mismanagement forced him to lay off a significant portion of his staff. The drawing showed the TV preacher sitting at the center of Leonardo Da Vinci's *Last Supper* informing his disciples, "I'm going to have to let some of you go!" Bakker's aides told reporters that he was so upset by the drawing that he fell to his knees in his office, weeping into the gold shag carpet. Once he staggered to his feet, he and Tammy Faye went on the air and, displaying my cartoons, encouraged viewers to phone in complaints to the *Observer* and cancel their subscriptions.

Jim Bakker finally resigned in disgrace from his PTL ministry, and I drew a cartoon of the televangelist who replaced him, Jerry Falwell, as a serpent slithering into PTL paradise: "Jim and Tammy were expelled from paradise and left me in charge."

One of the many angry readers who called me at the newspaper said, "You're a tool of Satan."

"Excuse me?"

"You're a tool of Satan for that cartoon you drew."

"That's impossible," I said. "I couldn't be a tool of Satan. *The Charlotte Observer*'s personnel department tests for that sort of thing."

Confused silence on the other end.

At this point, Marlette returns to describing his career as an equal opportunity offender, shifting the focus off Islam and instead discussing his troubles with evangelical Christians. By mentioning the death threats he received for his cartoons about the PTL Club (a televangelist show hosted by Jim and Tammy Bakker in the 1980s), he draws an implicit comparison here between Christian fundamentalists and what he calls Islamic "fanatics."

Although he doesn't reproduce his 1978 cartoon here, he offers a clear description to his readers.

This exchange brings humor back into the piece and demonstrates Marlette's seemingly flippant response to his critics.

"They try to screen for tools of Satan," I explained. "Knight Ridder human resources has a strict policy against hiring tools of Satan."

Click.

Until "What Would Mohammed Drive?" most of the flak I caught was from the other side of the Middle East conflict. Jewish groups complained that my cartoons critical of Israel's invasion of Lebanon were anti-Semitic because I had drawn Prime Minister Menachem Begin with a big nose. My editors took the strategic position that I drew everyone's nose big. At one point, editorial pages were spread out on the floor for editors to measure with a ruler the noses of various Jewish and non-Jewish figures in my cartoons.

Again, Marlette takes time to implicitly defend himself against claims of targeting Islam by describing how he has offended other religious groups as well.

After I moved to the Northeast, it was Catholics I offended. At *New York Newsday,* I drew a close-up of the pope wearing a button that read "No Women Priests." There was an arrow pointing to his forehead and the inscription from Matthew 16:18: "Upon This Rock I Will Build My Church." The *Newsday* switchboard lit up like a Vegas wedding chapel. *Newsday* ran an apology for the cartoon, a first in my career, and offered me a chance to respond in a column. The result—though the paper published it in full—got me put on probation for a year by the publisher. That experience inspired the opening scene of my first novel, *The Bridge.*

Here Marlette cleverly plays on the idea of cartooning by pausing to assert that the reaction of his critics is "cartoonish" and exaggerated.

* * *

But how do you cartoon a cartoon? It's a problem of redundancy in this hyperbolic age to caricature an already extravagantly distorted culture. When writers try to censor other writers, we're in Toontown. We are in deep trouble when victimhood becomes a sacrament, personal injury a point of pride, when irreverence is seen as a hate crime, when the true values of art and religion are distorted and debased by fanatics and zealots, whether in the name of the God of Abraham, Isaac, and Jacob, the Prophet Mohammed, or a literary Cult of Narcissus.

It was the cynically outrageous charge of homophobia against my book that brought me around to the similarities between the true believers I was used to dealing with and the post-modern

Marlette now comes to one of the focal points of his discussion: the way censorship is enforced not by angry critics but by a culture of "niceness" that is afraid to offend.

The reference to the Columbia journalism school would have extra force considering that this piece was originally published in the *Columbia Journalism Review*. Here, also, he clearly articulates the central point of his extended Mohammed story: that the most "disturbing thing" was that critics were able to influence his editors into refusing to run the cartoon.

Having begun his argument applauding American principles—namely, freedom of speech—he now demonstrates the way that corporate structure and an ideology of tolerance (both hallmarks of American culture) are actually operating in conflict with First Amendment rights.

secular humanist Church Ladies wagging their fingers at me. The threads that connect the CAIR and the literary fatwas, besides technological sabotage, are entreaties to "sensitivity," appeals to institutional guilt, and faith in a corporate culture of controversy avoidance. Niceness is the new face of censorship in this country.

The censors no longer come to us in jackboots with torches and baying dogs in the middle of the night. They arrive now in broad daylight with marketing surveys and focus-group findings. They come as teams, not armies, trained in effectiveness, certified in sensitivity, and wielding degrees from the Columbia journalism school. They're known not for their bravery but for their efficiency. They show gallantry only when they genuflect to apologize. The most disturbing thing about the "Mohammed" experience was that a laptop Luftwaffe was able to blitz editors into not running the cartoon in my own newspaper. "WWMD" ran briefly on the Tallahassee Democrat Web site, but once an outcry was raised, the editors pulled it and banned it from the newspaper altogether.

The cyberprotest by CAIR showed a sophisticated understanding of what motivates newsroom managers these days—bottom-line concerns, a wish for the machinery to run smoothly, and the human-resources mandate not to offend. Many of my e-mail detractors appeared to be well-educated, recent emigres. Even if their English sometimes faltered, they were fluent in the language of victimhood. Presumably, victimization was one of their motives for leaving their native countries, yet the subtext of many of their letters was that this country should be more like the ones they emigrated from. They had the American know-how without the know-why. In the name of tolerance, in the name of their peaceful God, they threatened violence against someone they accused of falsely accusing them of violence.

With the rise of the bottom-line culture and the corporatization of news gathering, tolerance itself has become commodified and denuded of its original purpose. Consequently, the best part of the American character—our generous spirit, our sense of fair play—has been turned against us.

Tolerance has become a tool of coercion, of institutional inhibition, of bureaucratic self-preservation. We all should take pride in how this country for the most part curbed the instinct to lash out at Arab-Americans in the wake of 9/11. One of the great strengths of this nation is our sensitivity to the tyranny of the majority, our sense of justice for all. But the First Amendment, the miracle of our system, is not just a passive shield of protection. In order to maintain our true, nationally defining diversity, it obligates journalists to be bold, writers to be full-throated and uninhibited, and those blunt instruments of the free press, cartoonists like me, not to self-censor. We must use it or lose it.

Political cartoonists daily push the limits of free speech. They were once the embodiment of journalism's independent voice. Today they are as endangered a species as bald eagles. The professional troublemaker has become a luxury that offends the bottom-line sensibilities of corporate journalism. Twenty years ago, there were two hundred of us working on daily newspapers. Now there are only ninety. Herblock is dead. Jeff MacNelly is dead. And most of the rest of us might as well be. Just as resume hounds have replaced newshounds in today's newsrooms, ambition has replaced talent at the drawing boards. Passion has yielded to careerism, Thomas Nast to Eddie Haskell. With the retirement of Paul Conrad at the *Los Angeles Times*, a rolling blackout from California has engulfed the country, dimming the pilot lights on many American editorial pages. Most editorial cartoons now look as bland as B-roll and as impenetrable as a 1040 form.

We know what happens to the bald eagle when it's not allowed to reproduce and its habitat is contaminated. As the species is thinned, the eco-balance is imperiled.

Why should we care about the obsolescence of the editorial cartoonist?

Because cartoons can't say "on the other hand," because they strain reason and logic, because they are hard to defend and thus are the acid test of the First Amendment, and that is why they must be preserved.

He ends this paragraph by clarifying his interpretation of the First Amendment, specifically with relation to journalism. He then uses a cliché to emphasize his point.

Notice the analogy he makes between political cartoonists and bald eagles. It operates on two levels, on the one hand emphasizing that they are endangered and on the other hand suggesting that cartoonists represent America's freedoms.

His references on this page to important political cartoonists (Herbert Block, Jeff MacNelly, Paul Conrad) underscore his message about the decline of political cartooning as a genre.

In the next paragraph he returns to his metaphor of the bald eagle, developing it into a richer analogy.

As he moves toward his conclusion, Marlette draws his essay together by echoing and slightly revising the title of the cartoon that started the controversy and demonstrating the way that images carry symbolic weight.

What would Marlette drive? Forget SUVs and armored cars. It would be an all-terrain vehicle you don't need a license for. Not a foreign import, but American-made. It would be built with the same grit and gumption my grandmother showed when she faced down government soldiers in the struggle for economic justice, and the courage my father displayed as a twenty-year-old when he waded ashore in the predawn darkness of Salerno and Anzio. It would be fueled by the freedom spirit that both grows out of our Constitution and is protected by it—fiercer than any fatwa, tougher than all the tanks in the army, and more powerful than any bunker-buster.

Marlette solidifies his connection to great contributors to American culture by referring to great American writers and trailblazers, from novelist John Steinbeck (the Joads are the family from *The Grapes of Wrath*) to cultural icon Ken Kesey and astronaut Neil Armstrong.

If I drew you a picture it might look like the broken-down jalopy driven by the Joads from Oklahoma to California. Or like the Cadillac that Jack Kerouac took on the road in his search for nirvana. Or the pickup Woody Guthrie hitched a ride in on that ribbon of highway, bound for glory. Or the International Harvester Day-Glo school bus driven cross-country by Ken Kesey and his Merry Pranksters. Or the Trailways and Greyhound buses the Freedom Riders boarded to face the deadly backroads of Mississippi and Alabama. Or the moon-buggy Neil Armstrong commanded on that first miraculous trip to the final frontier.

In his final paragraph, Marlette repeats his new catch phrase and uses it to provide a final comment on his vision of America and its inherent freedoms.

What would Marlette drive? The self-evident, unalienable American model of democracy that we as a young nation discovered and road-tested for the entire world: the freedom to be ourselves, to speak the truth as we see it, and to drive it home.

In his written argument, Marlette describes the observations he has made about the public's response to his cartoons. Notice how specific Marlette is in describing the reactions to his cartoons and how concretely he conjures up American identity through the imagery of the bald eagle and the driven vehicle. These are *rhetorical moves*, strategic choices he has made as a writer in deciding how best to persuade his readers (especially those outraged by the cartoons) to see his drawing from a different point of view. Just as Holkins picked the most appropriate words and images for inside his *Penny Arcade* cartoon, Marlette picked the most appropriate words and metaphors to use in his article.

Practicing Rhetorical Analysis

We've learned that rhetoric works as a means of persuading an audience to accept the argument of the author. This is also true for the arguments you make about a text. In other words, rhetoric also applies to the texts you craft to persuade someone to accept your interpretation of a specific cultural or political text.

Your task is to argue convincingly and persuade your audience to see the text the way you see it. Your challenge as a student of writing and rhetoric is not only to identify the argument contained by a text but also to craft your own interpretation of that text. This involves a careful assessment of the ways in which the elements of the rhetorical situation work together to produce meaning in a text. In many cases your analysis will also address the interplay of words and images. Your analysis can take many forms: a written essay, an oral report, a visual argument, or a combination of these.

AT A GLANCE

Selecting a Visual Rhetoric Image

When choosing a visual text for analysis, ask yourself the following questions:
- Does the image attempt to persuade the audience?
- Are there sufficient elements in the image to analyze?
- What do you know about the author or the intended audience?
- What's your own interpretation of this image?

Selecting Texts for Analysis

As you select a text for analysis, think back to the cartoons or comics you found most striking in this chapter—perhaps the election cartoon, Scott McCloud's strip, or Doug Marlette's cartoon. Each of these texts conveys a powerful message through words and images, verbal and visual rhetoric. When you choose your own text for rhetorical analysis, make sure you pick one that offers a persuasive point about society or an issue. It is harder to write about a text that is not meant to make a social or political point, one that is not meant to persuade.

Developing a Thesis Statement

Once you have selected the image for analysis, then the most important part of your writing will be your **thesis statement**, the concise statement of your interpretation about your chosen text. To understand thesis statements, let's work through an example. Imagine, for instance, that you want to write an argument about the editorial cartoons in Figures 1.12 and 1.13. Both

FIGURE 1.12. Cartoon by Daryl Cagle.
Source: Daryl Cagle, Cagle Cartoons, Inc.

FIGURE 1.13. Cartoon by Michael Ramirez.
Source: Michael Ramirez and Copley News Service

cartoons comment on recent debates about immigration policy. How might you develop a thesis statement that persuasively conveys your interpretation of how these cartoons contribute to the debate surrounding the status of undocumented immigrants?

Start by jotting down what you see; make close observations about these cartoons. Then use questions to bring your argument into focus and to make a specific claim about the images. The end product will be a *working thesis*. The process of developing your thesis might look like this:

1. Write down your observations.

Close observations: Both pictures focus, literally or symbolically, on the border between the United States and Mexico and on the way that we set up fences (or vault doors) to keep illegal immigrants out. Both also show holes in those barriers: one focuses on people running through a hole in the fence; the other shows a small door in the vault that looks as if it's been propped open from the inside. The words are interesting, too. In the Cagle cartoon, the big sign says "Keep out," while the smaller signs are designed to draw people in. In the Ramirez cartoon, the small sign says "Cheap labor welcome," contradicting the message of the large, high-security door that blocks access to the United States.

2. **Work with your observations to construct a preliminary thesis statement.**

   First statement: Both cartoons focus on the contradiction in American border policy.

3. **Refine your argument by asking questions that make your statement less general.**

   Ask yourself: How? What contradications? To what effect? How do I know this?

4. **Revise your preliminary thesis statement to be more specific; perhaps include specific evidence that drives your claim.**

   Revised statement: The cartoons in Figures 1.12 and 1.13 focus on the contradictions in American border policy by showing that on the one hand, the American government wants to keep illegal immigrants out, but on the other hand, economic forces encourage them to enter the United States illegally.

5. **Further polish your thesis by refining your language and asking questions about the implications of your working thesis statement.**

   Ask yourself: What do you find interesting about this observation? How does it tap into larger social or cultural issues?

6. **Write your working thesis to include a sense of the implications of your claim. Sometimes we call this the "So What?" of your claim.**

   Working thesis: The political cartoons in Figures 1.12 and 1.13 offer a pointed commentary on the recent immigration debate, suggesting ways the official government stance against illegal immigration is undermined by economic forces that tolerate, if not welcome, the entry of undocumented workers into the United States.

A strong, argumentative thesis does more than state a topic: it makes a claim about that topic that you will develop in the rest of your paper. Let's look at one more example to further consider ways to produce sharp, clear, and persuasive thesis statements. The examples that follow are a series of

FIGURE 1.14. Cartoon by Mike Thompson.

Source: Mike Thompson and Copley News Service

thesis statements about Mike Thompson's cartoon in Figure 1.14, published in 2006 in reaction to rising gas prices.

Thesis 1: Mike Thompson's cartoon is very powerful.

> *Assessment: This thesis relies too heavily on subjective opinion; the author offers no criteria for evaluating the cartoon or a context for understanding the statement.*

Thesis 2: Mike Thompson's drawing shows his opinion about SUVs.

> *Assessment: This thesis statement rests too much on a broad generalization rather than specific analysis.*

Thesis 3: In response to rising gas prices, Mike Thompson draws a powerful editorial cartoon about the relationship between driving SUVs and consuming fossil fuels.

> *Assessment: This thesis statement merely states a fact and makes a broad claim rather than offering a focused interpretation of the cartoon. It needs to explain how the cartoon was powerful.*

Thesis 4: In his 2006 editorial cartoon "Aptly Named," Mike Thompson persuasively plays with the term *fossil fuel* to suggest that SUVs and the "wanton consumption" of gasoline represent an outdated approach to transportation that needs to recognize its own imminent extinction.

> *Assessment: Of the four examples, this thesis provides the most provocative and specific articulation of the author's interpretation of the significance of Thompson's cartoon.*

A strong argument, driven by a strong thesis statement, is at the heart of any successful rhetorical analysis essay.

AT A GLANCE

Testing Your Thesis

Do you have a specific and interesting angle on your topic?

- Does it offer a statement of significance about your topic?
- Is the thesis sharp enough (not too obvious)?
- Could someone argue against it (or is it just an observation)?
- Is it not too dense (trying to compact the entire paper) or too simplistic (not developing your point thoroughly)?

Analyzing a Student's Writing Sample

Student Writing

See examples of other students' rhetorical analysis essays.

www.pearsonhighered.com/envision/27

Let's look at how one student, Cyana Chilton, combines effective strategies of analysis with a carefully crafted thesis statement to compose her own rhetorical analysis of a recent editorial cartoon.

Chilton 1

Cyana Chilton
Dr. Alyssa J. O'Brien
Rhetorical Analysis Essay

Drugs to Death in a Political Cartoon:

An Oversimplification?

As the more stable counterpart to a volatile southern neighbor, the United States has always had a wary outlook towards Mexico. In recent years, the increase in illegal immigration, the unpredictable economies in both countries, and the issues resulting from drug use and trade have added tension to the already taut relationship. Blame flows easily and lands on various subjects—each government, drug cartels, drug users, and more. However, in a recent political cartoon posted by Daniel Kurtzman (see Fig. 1), various rhetorical strategies are used to portray the cartoonist's

Figure 1. A cartoon by Nate Beeler about Mexican drug cartels and their effect on Mexican society, posted by Daniel Kurtzman Source: http://z.about.com/d/politicalhumor/l/0/e/2/mexican-pinata.jpg

Cyana's title refers to the image she has chosen.

The essay begins by setting up the context for the cartoon. Into this rhetorical situation, Cyana introduces the visual text.

By including the cartoon in her first paragraph, Cyana makes a much more powerful argument than if she had simply appended it to the end of her paper.

The actual thesis emphasizes how rhetoric works to offer an argument about the drug cartels and the government by pointing to specific concrete elements of the cartoon opinion that blame should be limited to one party: the drug cartels. Through the use of color, stereotypes, and the images of death, the cartoonist blames the violent Latin American drug cartels for Mexico's problems and undermines the legitimacy of the attempts of the Mexican government, as represented by the immobile piñata, to solve the drug issue.

In the cartoon, the drug cartels are represented by the figure on the right, with a dark black shirt and a menacing face and stance. The color scheme of the figure, as compared to the gaudy piñata and the white, ethereal skulls, makes the drug cartels an image of destruction and danger.

The sheer physical size of the figure also exaggerates the responsibility of those cartels for the destruction to Mexico. The cartoon ignores the presence of the approximately 25 million people in the United States who are illicit drug users and thus create a market for the products of the drug cartels (marijuana and cocaine, for example), instead perhaps over-simplifying the situation to portray the drug problem as a one-dimensional, clear-cut, and violent issue. This message, however, is inaccurate. It may be easier for an American audience, the original audience for the cartoon, to accept an opinion that completely ignores the blame due to the consumers of the drugs sold by the cartels or other potential recipients like corrupt police forces. The oversimplification is also dangerous because it clearly separates Mexico from the United States and does not

Cyana then develops this thesis by suggesting the significance or "so-what" of her observations—that they cast the drug cartels as dangerous.

Cyana uses background knowledge to fill in the rhetorical situation for the reader.

She refers to the term in her title several times to develop her argument.

Chilton 3

acknowledge the mutual dependence and interaction, for better or for worse, between them. By creating a foreign, violent-looking figure as "Mexican," there is no attempt to foster a sense of complicity, unity, or responsibility in the audience.

The color scheme and setup of the background for the cartoon are also strategic choices on the part of the cartoonist. The landscape is barren, marked primarily by a dead and blasé tree, two indistinct cacti, and the dry ground. Even the sky is ominous; the clouds converge over the drug cartel figure, and the colors are hazy and smoky, as if rising from the dusty ground. The infertility of the landscape and the obvious lack of abundant natural resources occurring at the same time as the drug cartel's mutilation of the piñata lends many negative connotations and associations to the drug cartel, further implicating the figure in Mexico's issues. This rhetoric, however, is a fallacy; although the barren landscape and the drug cartels coincide, the correlation does not necessarily imply causation. Although the drug cartel figure may appear to be at fault for the destruction of the piñata figure and, by extension, the environment of the political cartoon, in reality there is no evidence provided that fairly places all blame on the drug cartels.

The cartoon also, besides overtly placing blame on the drug cartels for the generalized problems and violence in Mexico, underestimates the extent and power of the Mexican government to battle the acknowledged power of the cartels.

Each paragraph takes an aspect of the visual text and analyzes it in detail. Notice how her writing becomes fluid and descriptive—matching her discussion of the landscape.

Moving to the center image, Cyana takes the time to offer her own interpretation of the piñata, using persuasive force in her own writing.

Chilton 4

The imagery associated with "Mexico," in the figure of the piñata, is the most obvious connection to belittling the effects of the Mexican government against the drug cartels. The piñata is immobile, tied to a tree. It hangs suspended in the air, as if it cannot control its own motion or defenses. Its face is blank and that of a donkey—a stupid, impotent animal—suggesting a lack of intelligence or even intense feeling like that seen in the face of the drug cartel figure. This blankness seems wrong because tiny skulls are pouring out of the figure, whose stomach has just been savagely punctured, but no reactive emotion is exhibited. Ironically, piñatas are usually used as lighthearted games at birthday parties for children. The lack of a typical mask on the drug cartel figure's face makes the destruction intentional and more malicious. The implication of the destruction being an easy, game-like pursuit for the drug cartels further attempts to persuade the audience to see the culpability of the drug cartels in comparison to the weakness of the government in Mexico.

The vacant gaze of the piñata is mirrored by the blankness of the landscape. The dead, nondescript plant life and the brown earth are seemingly disconnected from the free-hanging Mexico piñata, suggesting that the government has no control or direct connection with the country at large. In fact, however, Mexico's president, Felipe Calderón, has taken the first step against the pervasiveness of drug violence that no president has dared to take in the past. He has cracked down on drug dealers by jailing

Notice the transition— from a paragraph talking about a piñata to the Mexican countryside under President Calderón.

Her language becomes strong here as she seeks to persuade her readers to view the cartoon through her interpretation.

Chilton 5

them, sending them to the United States to be jailed, and decriminalizing small quantities of drugs in an effort to lower profits for the cartels. These efforts, while perhaps unpopular and not always effective, are the first attempts to fight back against the power of cartels and the violence that erupts as a result of the drug trade. Their reduction in this cartoon to a donkey with a flat affect suspended and isolated in midair is an exaggeration and a miscommunication of the truth.

Furthermore, Mexico is homogenized by various images in the cartoon. An overly commercialized and Americanized symbol, the piñata, deemphasizes Mexican culture's diversity and vitality. By characterizing an entire, diverse country as a small, powerless object, the cartoonist constructs *ethos*, or credibility, for himself by apparently being able to make large generalizations about complex issues, implying that he has an authoritative and encompassing grasp of the subject.

The mound of skulls further serve to homogenize the Mexican population. The skulls have a shimmering halo around them, portraying them as martyr figures and innocent deaths, pouring out of Mexico's belly without being able to stop. This imagery further demonizes the hulking drug cartel figure, but it does not acknowledge that many, if not a majority, of the deaths associated with the drug war are actually those directly involved: members of opposing cartels, policemen or hospital workers, for example. The cartoonist uses *pathos*, or an appeal to emotion, in portraying the skulls—the idea of violent death

Cyana includes a section on the writer or cartoonist.

Each paragraph ends with a strong summary line that reinforces the main point of her thesis.

Chilton 6

and the loss of one's individuality is frightening and sobering. The rhetorical device is similar to pictures of devastation from natural disasters or genocides: widespread and indiscriminate death as represented through an image. The victimized and non-individualized skulls characterize the entire Mexican population as weak and victimized. The fact that the skulls fall out of the piñata suggest that the death already existed in Mexico but was just hidden by gaudy colors and flimsy covering; this condescending criticism of Mexico has no evidence in the cartoon and thus seems unfounded. Also, there are a host of other problems at large in Mexico: a faltering economy, the swine flu epidemic, and immigration issues as always. The cartoonist's choice to ignore those issues and to focus on the inability of the government to stop just one (admittedly, a large one), is overly reducing the responsibilities of the government and the various nationwide problems that exist.

In this visually simple but subtly complex image from Nate Beeler, many stereotypes and oversimplifications are used as rhetorical strategies by the cartoonist. The color scheme of the piñata, the drug cartel figure, the landscape, and the pile of skulls all serve to place blame for Mexico's troubles solely on the drug cartels. The use, and perhaps misuse, of *pathos*, *ethos*, and logical fallacies all aid the cartoonist in refusing to acknowledge some legitimacy on the part of the Mexican government in bravely—and sometimes successfully—attempting to eradicate

As the essay begins to wrap up, Cyana broadens out to consider other problems and the larger significance of this visual rhetoric. One final point about the cartoon drives home the thesis and makes the paper a successful argument.

As she concludes the essay, Cyana restates the cartoonist's name in full and the key terms of her title and thesis. She offers a summary and then a final point for the reader to consider.

Chilton 7

drug turf wars from the country. Such a large task cannot be
accomplished quickly or cleanly, and one hulking figure cannot
possibly hold all the blame for creating a heartrending pile of
haloed skulls. The cartoonist, and the world, must look elsewhere
in an effort to truly begin to solve this international problem.

The last line offers a memorable call to action and ends the essay powerfully.

Chilton 8

Works Cited

Beeler, Nate. Cartoon. About.com.: Political Humor. *about.com*,
22 March 2009. Web. 4 April 2009.

United States Center for Disease Control. *FASTATS*. Web.
1 July 2009.

Cyana responsibly attribute the research she conducted to help her write this paper.

Referring to Images in Your Writing

When you follow this example and write about a visual text that interests you, consider the strategic placement of your image. Should you insert it in the paper or append it at the end with your bibliography? If you want to create a true hybrid composition—one that integrates words and images—include the image right in your essay. Make sure to refer to it in your writing as we do in our discussion of cartoons in this chapter. Then, below the image, include a caption and a figure number. This will show you have the proper training as a writer and rhetorician in presenting your ideas.

The Writer's Process

As you turn now to write your rhetorical analysis of a text, you'll be putting into practice all the skills you've learned so far in this chapter. You'll need to write down your observations of the text; spend time discussing them in detail, as we have done with the many examples we've worked on so far; and use these observations as evidence to make an argument that will persuade others to see the text the way you see it.

In composing your analysis of this text, you need to use the same process we have worked through for the analysis of comic strips and cartoons:

- First, look carefully at all the elements in the text. Create a list of your observations or use the prewriting checklist at the end of this chapter to help you read the text more closely.
- Then, speculate about the meaning of each element. How does it contribute to the whole?
- Next, complete the rhetorical triangle (see Figure 1.6) for the text, assessing who the author is, who the intended audience is, what form the text takes, and what the argument is, based on your observations of the details.
- Finally, put all these elements together and develop your argument about the message and meaning of the visual text.

AT A GLANCE

Visual Rhetoric Analysis Essays

- Do you have a sharp point or thesis to make about the visual text?
- Have you selected key visual details to discuss in support of your main point?
- Do you lead readers through your analysis of the text by discussing important details in sequence? These include:

    Visual composition, layout, and imagery

    Verbal elements in the text

    Color, shading, and arrangement of items

    Caption or title of the image

- Do you have an effective title, main point, introduction, body, and conclusion?
- Have you included the image in the essay?

It's crucial to remember that when you write a rhetorical analysis, you perform a rhetorical act of persuasion yourself. Accordingly, you need to include the key elements of analytical writing: (1) have a point of interpretation to share with your readers, (2) take time to walk readers through concrete details to prove your point, and (3) lead your readers through the essay in an engaging and convincing way. But of all these, the most important is your argument, your interpretation of or position on the text—your *thesis*.

In writing your analysis paper, keep in mind the need to begin with observations, but avoid simply describing the elements you notice. Instead, zoom in on specific details and think hard about their meaning. Make a persuasive argument by using *specific* evidence to support your analysis of how the text succeeds at convincing an audience to see an issue in a particular way. Spend some time working on your thesis before composing the entire draft. Make sure your angle is sharp and your interpretation takes into account audience, writer, and message as well as concrete points of visual and verbal composition. This is the key to crafting a persuasive and effective rhetorical analysis.

PREWRITING CHECKLIST

Comics and Cartoons

❏ **Topic:** What key issue is the comic or cartoon addressing?

❏ **Story:** On the most basic level, what is happening in the cartoon?

❏ **Audience:** In what country and in what historical moment was the cartoon produced? In what type of text did it first appear? A journal? A newspaper? Online? Was this text conservative? liberal? radical? feminist? How does it speak to this audience?

❏ **Author:** What do you know about the artist? What kinds of cartoons does he or she regularly produce? Where does he or she live and publish? What kinds of other writing does this person do?

❏ **Argument:** What is the cartoon's message about the issue? Is there irony involved (does the cartoon advocate one point of view, but the cartoonist wants you to take the opposite view)?

(continued)

❏ **Composition:** If this political cartoon a single frame or a series of sequential frames? If the latter, how does the argument evolve over the series?

❏ **Word and image:** Does the cartoon rely exclusively on the visual? Or are word and image both used? What is the relationship between the two? Is one given priority over the other? How does this influence the cartoon's overall persuasiveness?

❏ **Imagery:** What choices of imagery and content does the artist make? Are the drawings realistic? Do they rely on caricatures? Does the artist include allusions or references to past or present events or ideas?

❏ **Tone:** Is the cartoon primarily comic or serious in tone? How does this choice of tone create a powerful rhetorical impact on readers?

❏ **Character and setting:** What components are featured by the cartoon? A person? An object? A scene? Think about how character and setting are portrayed. What are the ethnicity, age, socioeconomic class, and gender of the characters? Do they represent actual people? Are they fictional creations? How are these choices rhetorical strategies designed to tailor the cartoon and its argument to its intended audience?

❏ **Cultural resonance:** Does the cartoon implicitly or explicitly refer to any actual people, events, or pop culture icons? What sort of symbolism is used in the cartoon? Would the symbols speak to a broad or narrow audience? How does the cultural resonance function as a rhetorical strategy in making the argument?

PREWRITING WITH THE *ENVISION* WEBSITE

For one way to begin writing about cartoons as powerful rhetorical acts, go to the *Envision* Website. Follow a link to one of the cartoon collections. Compare how different cartoon artists craft persuasive visual arguments about the same issue with remarkably divergent messages. Pick two cartoons, write an analysis of each cartoon, and prepare to share your interpretations with the rest of the class. Be sure to describe elements of the visual text in detail, present the key components of the rhetorical situation (audience, writer, message), and discuss how each contributes to the overall argument of the cartoon.

www.pearsonhighered.com/envision/36

WRITING PROJECTS

1. **Personal Narrative:** Recall Alex's observations of rhetoric on her way to class; conduct a similar study of the rhetoric in your world. Write your reflections into a *personal narrative essay.* Discuss which types of visual, verbal, bodily, or architectural rhetoric were most evident, which were most subtle, and which you found the most persuasive. Conclude with a statement or argument about these images— what do they collectively say about your culture or community? How do these texts try to shape readers or viewers with certain specific messages?

2. **Rhetorical Analysis:** Choose a political cartoon or comic strip on a current issue and write a *rhetorical analysis.* You might find an appropriate text in a recent issue of *Newsweek*, in a collection such as Charles Brooks's *Best Editorial Cartoons of the Year*, or online through the *Envision* Website resource page for Chapter 1. Use the prewriting checklist to help you write a rhetorical analysis of the cartoon. If you choose to analyze more than one cartoon on the same issue, introduce all your texts in the opening paragraph, and spend some time analyzing each one in detail. Make sure that your writing supports a thesis about elements and messages of all the texts you are analyzing.
   www.pearsonhighered.com/envision/37

3. **Comparative Rhetorical Analysis of Text and Image:** After you've begun project 2, search through recent newspapers, newsmagazines, or a library news database like LexisNexis to find an article that addresses the same issue. Write a *comparative analysis of the text and the political cartoon.* What is each one's argument, and what rhetorical strategies does each one use to effectively make that argument? You may want to use the prewriting checklist in looking at the political cartoon. If you want to take a historical approach to this assignment, choose both a political cartoon and an article that span the historical spectrum but focus on one issue, such as racial profiling, immigrant workers, or what's "hip" in the entertainment industry. Be sure to include specific details about each text, shape your observations into a thesis, and don't forget a title for your essay. Look back to the examples in this chapter on how to analyze both images and texts, and see how you can make your argument about social values.

 Visit www.pearsonhighered.com/envision for expanded assignment guidelines and student projects. Visit www.mycomplab.com for additional general writing and research resources.

CHAPTER 2

Understanding Strategies of Persuasion

Chapter Preview Questions

- What specific strategies of argumentation work as persuasion?
- What role do the rhetorical appeals of *logos, pathos,* and *ethos* play in persuasion?
- What is the effect of exaggeration in these appeals?
- How does context (*kairos*) shape texts by time, place, and culture?
- How can you incorporate strategies of persuasion in your own writing?

What convinced you to buy that new cell phone, to try that new sports drink—or even to decide which college to attend? Chances are that some combination of words and images—a printed ad or brochure, a TV commercial, a billboard—influenced your decision.

What strategies of persuasion does the iPod ad use (see Figure 2.1)? (Notice, for example, the simple design, the contrast between dark silhouette and bright background, and the placement and gleaming white color of the iPod itself, which draws your eye to the logo and slogan at the top.) Does this ad use a logical appeal, emphasizing technical features of the iPod? Or does it appeal to your enthusiasm for music or dancing?

Think of other ads you've seen. How do these ads make you pause and pay attention? Perhaps a magazine ad includes a photo of a celebrity or simply a good-looking person, someone you are attracted to or can identify with emotionally. Perhaps a TV ad

FIGURE 2.1. This eye-catching iPod ad draws the audience immediately into its argument.

Source: © Alyssa J. O'Brien, 2006

tells a compelling story or provides a memorable example. Perhaps a brochure offers impressive statistics or supporting evidence for its claims. Often it is not one but a combination of factors that we find persuasive—and often these factors are so subtle that we hardly recognize them. Techniques used to move and convince an audience are called **rhetorical strategies**.

Ads offer us a productive means of analyzing rhetorical strategies because they represent arguments in compact forms. An ad has little room to spare; persuasion must be locked into a single frame or a brief 30-second spot. Advertisements represent one of the most ubiquitous forms of persuasion. The average adult encounters 3000 of these compact, powerful arguments—that is, advertisements—every day (Twitchell, *Adcult* 2). Consider all the places ads appear nowadays: not just in magazines or on the television or radio but also on billboards and computer screens; on the sides of buses, trains, and buildings; in sports stadiums and movie theaters; on T-shirts and caps; and even spray-painted on sidewalks.

As citizens of what cultural critic James Twitchell calls "Adcult USA," we are constantly exposed to texts that appeal to us on many levels. In this chapter, you'll gain a working vocabulary and concrete strategies of rhetorical persuasion that you can use both to become a savvy reader of advertisements and also to produce your own persuasive texts.

Analyzing Ads as Arguments

By analyzing advertisements, we can detect the rhetorical choices writers and artists select to make their points and convince their audiences. In this way we realize that advertisers are rhetoricians, careful to attend to the *rhetorical situation*. We can find in advertisements specific strategies of argumentation that you can use to make your case in your own writing. Advertisers might use:

- **Narration** to sell their product—using their ad to tell a story
- **Comparison-contrast** to encourage the consumer to buy their product rather than their competitor's

- **Example** or **illustration** to show how their product can be used or how it can impact a person's life
- **Cause and effect** to demonstrate the benefits of using their product
- **Definition** to clarify their product's purpose or function
- An **analogy** to help make a difficult selling point or product—like fragrance—more accessible to their audience
- **Process** to demonstrate the way a product can be used
- **Description** to show you the specifications of a desktop system or a new SUV
- **Classification and division** to help the reader conceptualize how the product fits into a larger scheme

These strategies are equally effective in both visual and written texts. They can be used effectively to structure both a small unit (part of an ad or, in a more academic text, a paragraph or section of an essay) and a larger one (the entire ad or, in an academic paper, the argument as a whole).

Even a single commercial can be structured around multiple strategies. The famous "This Is Your Brain on Drugs" commercial from the late 1980s used *analogy* (a comparison to something else—in this case comparing using drugs and frying an egg) and *process* (reliance on a sequence of events—here, how taking drugs affects the user's brain) to warn its audience away from drug use. In this 30-second spot, the spokesperson holds up an egg, saying, "This is your brain." In the next shot, the camera focuses on an ordinary frying pan as he states, "This is drugs." We as the audience begin to slowly add up parts A and B, almost anticipating his next move. As the ad moves to the visual crescendo, we hear him say, "This is your brain on drugs": the image of the egg sizzling in the frying pan fills the screen. The final words seem almost anticlimactic after this powerful image: "Any questions?"

These strategies function just as persuasively in print ads. For example, look at the advertisement for Rusk hair spray in Figure 2.2, an ad designed to draw the viewer's eye through the visual argument. What the reader notices first are the striking pictures of the golden-haired model, somewhat flat hair on one side and voluminous curls on the other, exemplifying the powerful *comparison-contrast* strategy that is echoed in many levels of the ad. The entire ad is bisected to reflect this structure, opposing "problem" to "solution" and literally dividing the main caption—"Go from ordinary . . . to Extraordinary"—in half. What bridges the divide, both literally and figuratively, is the strategically positioned can of hairspray, tilted slighted toward the right to reinforce emphasis on the *example/illustration* of a satisfied Rusk-user. By centralizing the red-capped canister in this way, the ad therefore also establishes a persuasive *cause-and-effect* argument, implicitly suggesting that using this hairspray allowed this girl to overcome the perceived challenges of limp hair.

Within written texts, the use of such strategies provides a similar foundation for a persuasive argument. As you read the following online article from Slate.com, look carefully to see which strategies author Seth Stevenson utilizes to make his argument about recent iPod commercials.

FIGURE 2.2. This problem-solution ad for Rusk hairspray uses several strategies of argumentation.

YOU AND YOUR SHADOW
The iPod ads are mesmerizing. But does your iPod think it's better than you?

Seth Stevenson

The Spot: Silhouetted shadow-people dance in a strenuous manner. Behind them is a wall of solid color that flashes in neon shades of orange, pink, blue, and green. In each shadow-person's hand is an Apple iPod.

As part of his online series "Ad Reportcard," Stevenson uses a format not usually associated with academic writing—notice here he sets up the commercial under discussion in a separate section before even starting his essay.

Stevenson's chatty voice is very appropriate for his online audience.

Notice the way Stevenson defers his thesis, although he gives us a sense of his approach toward the ads (resentment).

In this section, Stevenson relies on description to set up the foundation for his discussion of the ads; yet, notice that he is somewhat selective, emphasizing the elements that are most important for his analysis—namely, the way the use of silhouettes emphasizes the product.

The rhetorical question here points to the turn in his piece from description to analysis, the point where the reader will come closer to understanding his resentment.

At this point in the article, Stevenson moves to description and example to set up the powerful comparison-contrast strategy that he develops further in the next paragraphs.

I myself own an iPod, but rarely dance around with it. In part because the earbuds would fall out (Does this happen to you? I think I may have narrow auditory canals) and in part because I'm just not all that prone to solitary rump-shaking. It's a failing on my part. Maybe if I were a silhouette I might dance more.

All that said, these are very catchy ads. I don't get sick of watching them. And yet I also sort of resent them, as I'll later explain.

First, let's talk about what the ads get right. For one, the songs (from groups like Jet and Black Eyed Peas) are extremely well-chosen. Just indie enough so that not everybody knows them; just mainstream enough so that almost everybody likes them. But as good as the music is, the visual concept is even better. It's incredibly simple: never more than three distinct colors on the screen at any one time, and black and white are two of them. What makes it so bold are those vast swaths of neon monochrome.

This simplicity highlights the dance moves, but also—and more importantly—it highlights the iPod. The key to it all is the silhouettes. What a brilliant way to showcase a product. Almost everything that might distract us—not just background scenery, but even the actors' faces and clothes—has been eliminated. All we're left to focus on is that iconic gizmo. What's more, the dark black silhouettes of the dancers perfectly offset the iPod's gleaming white cord, earbuds, and body.

This all sounds great, so far. So what's not to like?

For the longest time, I couldn't put my finger on it. And then I realized where I'd seen this trick before. It's the mid-1990s campaign for DeBeers diamonds—the one where the people are shadows, but the jewelry is real. In them, a shadow-man would slip a diamond ring over a shadow-finger, or clasp a pendant necklace around a ghostly throat. These ads used to be on television all the time. You may recall the stirring string music of their soundtrack, or the still-running tagline: "A Diamond Is Forever."

Like the iPod ads, these DeBeers ads used shadow-people to perfect effect. The product—in this case, diamonds—sparkles and shines on a dusky background. But what bothered me about the spots was the underlying message. They seem to say that we are all just transient shadows, not long for this world—it's our diamonds that are forever. In the end, that necklace is no over-priced bauble. It's a ticket to immortality!

My distaste for these ads stems in part from the fact that, with both the iPod and the diamonds, the marketing gives me a sneaking sense that the product thinks it's better than me. More attractive, far more timeless, and frankly more interesting, too. I feel I'm being told that, without this particular merchandise, I will have no tangible presence in the world. And that hurts. I'm a person, dammit, not a featureless shadow-being! If you prick me, do I not write resentful columns?

Like diamond jewelry, the iPod is designed and marketed to draw attention to itself, and I think (I realize I'm in a minority here) I prefer my consumer goods to know their place. If I did it over, I might opt for an equally functional but slightly more anonymous MP3 player. One that deflects attention instead of attracting it. Because I'm the one with the eternal soul here—it's my stuff that's just transient junk.

Grade: B–. Perfectly executed. Mildly insulting message.

By comparing the iPod commercials to the DeBeers campaign, Stevenson can clearly articulate his ambivalent feelings about Apple's ads.

In his semihumorous interjection, Stevenson returns to the contrast between himself and the Apple silhouettes with which he started the article.

Notice how he builds on his **comparison** by opening his concluding paragraph with an **analogy**, using a simile ("Like diamond jewelry") that reminds the reader of the connection he has established between the two campaigns.

Understanding the Rhetorical Appeals

The rhetorical strategies we've examined so far can be filtered through the lens of classical modes of persuasion dating back to 500 BCE. The formal terms are *logos, pathos*, and *ethos*.

Each type of rhetorical appeal represents a mode of persuasion that can be used by itself or in combination. As you might imagine, a text may employ a combined mode of persuasion, such as "passionate logic"—a rational argument written with highly charged prose, "goodwilled pathos"—an emotional statement that relies on the character of the speaker to be believed, or "logical ethos"—a strong line of reasoning employed by a speaker to build authority. Moreover, a text may use rhetorical appeals in a combination that produces an *overarching effect*, such as irony or humor.

AT A GLANCE

Rhetorical Appeals

- *Logos* entails rational argument: appeals to reason and an attempt to persuade the audience through clear reasoning and philosophy. Statistics, facts, definitions, and formal proofs, as well as interpretations such as syllogisms or deductively reasoned arguments, are all examples of means of persuasion we call "the logical appeal."

- *Pathos,* or "the pathetic appeal," generally refers to an appeal to the emotions: the speaker attempts to put the audience into a particular emotional state so that the audience will be receptive to and ultimately convinced by the speaker's message. Inflammatory language, sad stories, appeals to nationalist sentiments, and jokes are all examples of pathos.

- *Ethos* is an appeal to authority or character; according to Aristotle, *ethos* means the character or goodwill of the speaker. Today we also consider the speaker's reliance on authority, credibility, or benevolence when discussing strategies of ethos. Although we call this third mode of persuasion the "ethical appeal," it does not strictly mean the use of ethics or ethical reasoning. Keep in mind that ethos is the deliberate use of the *speaker's character* as a mode of persuasion.

You might think of humor as one of the most effective forms of persuasion. Jokes and other forms of humor are basically appeals to pathos because they put the audience in the right emotional state to be receptive to an argument, but they can also involve reasoning or the use of the writer's authority to sway an audience.

Since they appear so frequently in combination, you might find that conceptualizing logos, pathos, and ethos through a visual representation helps you to understand how they relate to one another (see Figure 2.3).

As you read this chapter, consider how each text relies on various rhetorical appeals to construct its message.

Logos ("Rational Appeal")

Ethos ("Ethical Appeal") **Pathos ("Pathetic Appeal")**

FIGURE 2.3. Rhetorical appeals as intersecting strategies of persuasion.

Appeals to Reason: *Logos*

As a writer, you use *logos* when you construct an essay around facts and reason; in general, an argument based on *logos* will favor the use of logic, statistical evidence, quotations from authorities, and proven facts. In the opening pages of this chapter, for instance, we used *logos*—quotations and statistics about advertising—to persuade you about the omnipresence of advertising in today's culture. Scholars often rely on *logos* in this way to make persuasive academic arguments. Consider, for instance, the way Laurence Bowen and Jill Schmid use *logos* as a strategy of persuasion in this passage from "Minority Presence and Portrayal in Mainstream Magazine Advertising: An Update":

> Some might argue that the small number of minorities featured in mainstream magazine advertising may be due to a very deliberate media strategy that successfully targets minorities in specialized and minority media. However, each of the magazines analyzed does have a minority readership and, in some cases, that readership is quite substantial. For example, according to *Simmons 1993 Study of Media and Markets,* the Hispanic readership of *Life* is 9.9%, yet the inclusion of Hispanics in *Life's* advertisements was only .8%. *Cosmopolitan* has a 11.3% Black readership, yet only 4.3% of the advertisements included Blacks; 13.3% of the magazines' readership is Hispanic and only .5% of the advertisements use Hispanics.

Notice how the authors drive their point home through reference to their research with mainstream magazines as well as to statistical data that they have both uncovered and analyzed. The inclusion of this concrete information and examples makes their argument much more convincing than had they provided a more general rebuttal to the statement that begins their paragraph. In this way, appeals to logic can take on many forms, including interpretations of "hard evidence," such as found in syllogisms (formal, structured arguments), reasoned arguments, closing statements in law, inferences in the form of statistical models, and appeals to "common sense" or cultural assumptions.

In advertising, the mode of persuasion we call *logos* often operates through the written text; significantly, the Greek word *logos* can be translated as "word," indicating the way in which we, culturally, often look to words as repositories of fact and reason.

The type of logos-based reasoning found in the Chevron ad in Figure 2.4 appears in many ads that you may also be familiar with: think, for instance, of a computer ad that juxtaposes a striking photo of a laptop with a chart detailing its processor type, memory capacity, screen size, and graphics features; a car ad that offsets a glossy showroom photo with safety ratings and positive reviews from *Car & Driver* and *Motor Trend;* or a commercial for a bank that features a smiling agent listing the reasons to open a checking account at that branch. In each case, the advertisement drives its point through facts, evidence, and reason.

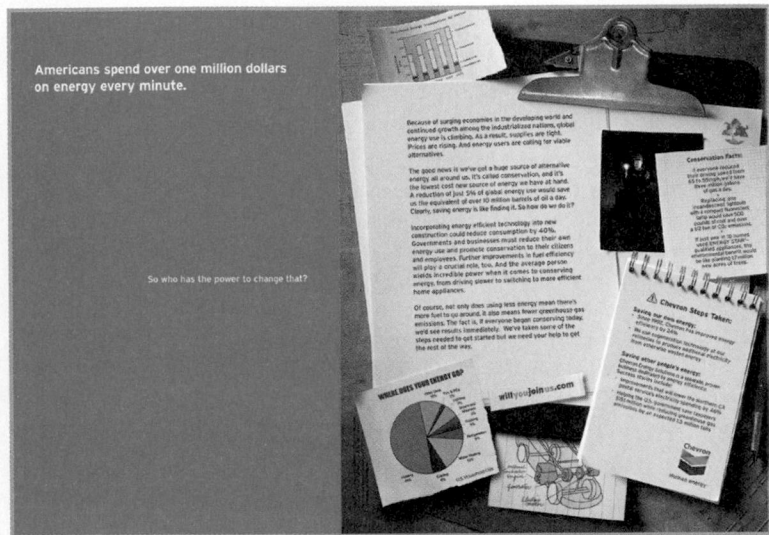

FIGURE 2.4. The Chevron ad relies on a logical argument to persuade the reader. The written text on the left side, set against a vivid background, uses a striking statistic and poses the question that governs the rest of the ad. A variety of research-based evidence on the right side, including a memo, a fact sheet, a pie chart, a schematic, and a bar chart, provides a persuasive abundance of evidence, suggesting that the ad's argument is based in fact rather than simply opinion.

In fact, some might argue that *logos* as an appeal underlies almost all advertising, specifically because most advertising uses an implicit *causal argument:* if you buy this product, then you or your life will be like the one featured in the ad. Sometimes the associations are explicit: if you use Pantene shampoo, then your hair will be shinier; if you buy Tide detergent, then your clothes will be cleaner; if you buy a Volvo sedan, then your family will be safer driving on the road. Sometimes the *cause-and-effect* argument is more subtle: buying Sure deodorant will make you more confident; drinking Coke will make you happier; wearing Nikes will make you perform better on the court. In each case, *logos*, or the use of logical reasoning, is the tool of persuasion responsible for the ad's argumentative force.

The ad for Crest Whitening Strips in Figure 2.5 offers us a useful example of how *logos* can operate in more subtle ways in an ad—through visual as well as verbal argumentation. When we first look at the ad, our eyes are drawn immediately to the model's white smile, positioned near the center of the two-page spread. Our gaze next moves up to her eyes and then down again to the two juxtaposed close-up shots of her teeth.

These two before-and-after close-ups carry the force of the argument. The contrast between the

Student Writing

Fred Chang analyzes Apple Computer's reliance on *logos* in its advertising battle with Intel.

www.pearsonhighered.com/envision/46

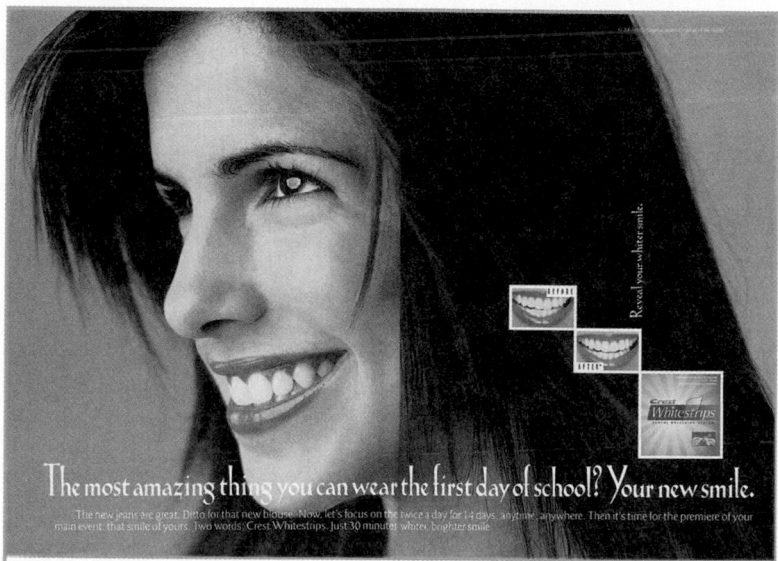

FIGURE 2.5. In this Crest Whitening Strips advertisement, inset images offer visual evidence for the ad's argument.

two images makes a deliberate *logos* appeal by constructing a cause-and-effect argument, and the captions confirm the message imparted by the images and solidify the visual promise of the ad. The final small box insert is our last visual stop; it shows the product and suggests the solution to the logical equation at work in this ad. The fact that the ad's words, "Your new smile," appear beneath the photo of the product—as the conclusion of the logical argument—reinforces the persuasive message that Crest indeed will give its users such white teeth. To put the logic plainly: if people brush with this product, then they too will achieve this result. In this way, the ad relies on *logos* to attract and convince its audience.

Logical Fallacies. When crafting your own written analysis of advertisements, be careful not to rely on mistaken or misleading uses of *logos*, commonly called **logical fallacies**. The causal strategy underlying most advertising can be seen as an example of faulty logic, for surely it is fraudulent to suggest that wearing a certain brand of clothing will make you popular or

AT A GLANCE

Logical Fallacies

• *The post hoc fallacy:* confusing cause and effect
• *The cum hoc fallacy:* interpreting correlation as causation
• *The hasty generalization:* drawing a conclusion too quickly without providing enough supporting evidence
• *The either-or argument:* reducing an argument to a choice between two diametrically opposed choices, ignoring other possible scenarios
• *Stacking the evidence:* offering proof for only one side of the issue
• *Begging the question:* using an argument as evidence for itself
• *The red herring:* distracting the audience rather than focusing on the argument itself

that drinking a certain beer will make you attractive to the opposite sex. In classical rhetoric, this fallacy of causality is called a ***post hoc ergo propter hoc fallacy***—namely, the idea that because something happened first (showering with an aloe-enhanced body gel), it is the direct cause of something that happened afterward (getting great grades on your midterms). A similar effect can be produced by the ***cum hoc ergo propter hoc fallacy***, often called a correlation-causation fallacy. According to this model, because two unrelated events happen at the same time (are correlated), they are interpreted as cause and effect. For instance, the following is an example of a *cum hoc fallacy:* (1) a teenager plays his varsity basketball game wearing his new Air Jordans; (2) the teenager makes many key rebounds and jump shots while playing the game; (3) the Air Jordans caused his success in the game. You can probably think of many commercials that rely on these two particular logical fallacies.

However, in those same commercials, we see more and more cases of advertisers guarding themselves against claims of false causality. For instance, consider the typical weight-loss advertisement. "I lost 31 pounds in 3 months using this nutritional plan!" one happy dieter exclaims on camera. The camera shows an old video clip of the subject at her previous weight, and then it moves to the newly trimmed-down version, usually with a trendy hairstyle and tight-fitting clothes—a clear before-and-after strategy. However, more and more often, you now find these images captioned with one telling phrase: "These results not typical." This disclaimer points to advertisers' recognition that they, like other rhetoricians, need to be careful in their use of logos as an argumentative appeal.

Appeals to Emotion: *Pathos*

Roughly defined as "suffering" or "feeling" in its original Greek, the term *pathos* actually means to put the audience in a particular mood or frame of mind. Modern derivations of the word *pathos* include *pathology* and *pathetic,* and indeed we speak of *pathos* as "the pathetic appeal." But *pathos* is more a technique than a state: writers use it as a tool of persuasion to establish an intimate connection with the audience by soliciting powerful emotions. For instance, consider the way the following paragraphs foster an emotional reaction from the reader:

> Dorsey Hoskins' father Bryan felt a tingling in his arm. The diagnosis—an inoperable brain tumor. Six months later, he died at the age of 33, leaving his wife to raise Dorsey and sister Hattie.
>
> Fortunately, Bryan bought life insurance when he married, and again when his daughters were born. Thanks to Bryan's foresight, Dorsey, Hattie, and their mom are taken care of.
>
> Are you prepared should the very worst happen?

This passage relies on a *pathos* appeal on many levels. Clearly, the very premise of the piece—moving from tragedy, to a sense of tempered relief, to personal identification—is designed to evoke a sympathetic response. Looking more closely, however, suggests that even the more subtle stylistic choices also contribute to the emotional appeal. Notice, for example, the power of word choice: the author initially introduces Bryan as "Dorsey Hoskins' father," establishing him from the first in terms of his daughter and, ultimately, her loss; the author withholds Bryan's age for three sentences, at which point he can disclose it to accentuate the tragedy of his early death; finally, after the powerful opening anecdote, the author uses the second person to draw the audience itself into the piece through the pointed rhetorical question.

It shouldn't be a surprise to discover that this passage is in fact taken from an advertisement for life insurance or that the pathos of the text is echoed by the emotional charge of a close-up photograph of 5-year-old Dorsey, which serves as the background for the advertisement. We encounter ads that rely on pathos all the time, and indeed, the visual composition of an ad often taps our emotions in ways we barely recognize.

Let's look closely at another advertisement that relies on creating an emotional connection with the audience to sell its product. In the spring of 2006 Volkswagen launched a new marketing campaign aimed at pitching safety rather than sportiness; the "Safe Happens" commercials revolve around an unexpected collision and its surprisingly reassuring aftermath (see Figure 2.6). In this commercial, the viewer finds herself transported

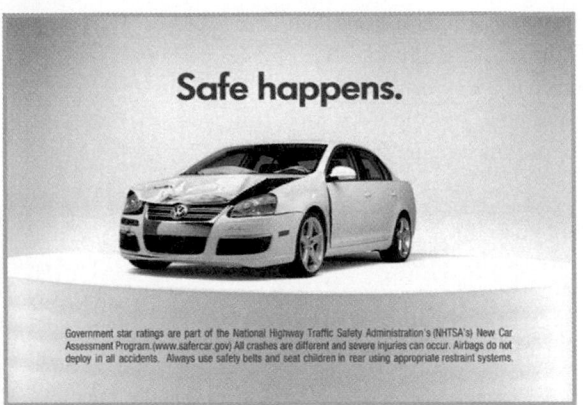

Safe happens.

Government star ratings are part of the National Highway Traffic Safety Administration's (NHTSA's) New Car Assessment Program. (www.safercar.gov) All crashes are different and severe injuries can occur. Airbags do not deploy in all accidents. Always use safety belts and seat children in rear using appropriate restraint systems.

FIGURE 2.6. The final frame from a Volkswagen commercial reinforces the audience's identification with the occupants of the damaged vehicle and extends the *pathos* appeal of the ad's narrative.

into the interior of an automobile. At this point, there is no clue as to the car's make or model; the camera shots are all of the car's occupants, a group of friends in their late twenties or early thirties in the middle of a friendly, light-hearted conversation. The camera focuses on each face in turn, creating a bond between the characters and the viewer. The exchange is informal and comfortable, the mood light.

The commercial cuts the characters off midsentence with a screech of brakes, blinding headlights, and the sound of a collision. The viewer, an invisible passenger in the car, feels the same surprise and horror as the main characters. The camera focus abruptly changes and moves us outside the vehicle; we become bystanders, watching a nondescript SUV plow into the white sedan that we identify as *our* car, the power of the collision captured with harsh accuracy. As the screen goes black, suddenly silence prevails, except for the uneven clatter of a rolling hubcap.

After a couple of seconds, the image reappears, and we see our former companions, unharmed, standing outside the battered vehicle. This first moment of product identification is captioned by an unusual voice-over; the camera zooms in on one of the female passengers, who looks with disbelief at the wreck and whispers, "Holy. . . ." The implied expletive is silenced by a quick cut to a more traditional car-commercial shot: the Jetta, in a spotless white showroom, slowly revolving on a turntable. Even here, beyond the end of the commercial's central narrative, the *pathos* appeal is reinforced. The rotating car is clearly not a showroom model; the dented driver's side door identifies it once again as *our* car, the one that kept the main characters safe. The written caption reinforces this association, proclaiming "Safe Happens" (playing

Student Writing

Cyrus Chee's rhetorical analysis reads the appeals to *pathos* in two poster ads for contemporary films about the Holocaust.

www.pearsonhighered.com/envision/50

with the female character's final words) and then announcing that Jetta has received the government's highest safety rating. This moment becomes doubly persuasive because of the viewer's emotional engagement with the commercial: we feel that we ourselves have survived the crash and look to the Jetta as the reason.

Pathos does not only operate through triggering the highs and lows of emotion in its audience; sometimes the appeals, though still speaking to the visceral more than the rational, are more subtle. Patriotism, indignation, excitement—all these effects can be linked to the pathos appeal. Consider the Porsche commercial showing a sleek red car speeding along a windy mountain road, the Ford Escape TV spot featuring the rugged SUV plowing through a muddy off-road trail, or the Mini Cooper ad using uniqueness as a selling point for the little car. Each of these ads uses *pathos* to produce a specific feeling in viewers: I want to drive fast, wind in my hair; I want to get off the beaten path, forge a new frontier; I want to stand out in a crowd, make a statement.

You are probably even more familiar with another type of *pathos* appeal—the appeal to sexuality. Clearly, "sex sells." Look at Victoria's Secret models posed in near nudity or Abercrombie & Fitch poster displays featuring models more likely to show off their toned abs than a pair of jeans, and you can see how advertisers tend to appeal more to nonrational impulses than to our powers of logical reasoning. Perfume and cologne advertisers in particular often use the rhetoric of sexuality to sell their fragrances, whether it be Calvin Klein's Obsession, Armani's Acqua Di Gio, or even Axe's cologne ads, which demonstrate the "Axe effect" by showing cologne-wearers being mobbed by bikini-clad women. Such ads work cleverly to sell perfume, not on the merits of the scent or on its chemical composition but through the visual rhetoric of sexuality and our emotional responses to it.

> "Humos is the rhetorical appeal to humor."
>
> —David Baron, Stanford student.

Looking at Figure 2.7, we can see yet another typical use of *pathos* to drive an argument: humor, or what some students call *humos*. By using a bald man as a spokesperson for shampoo, this advertisement pokes fun at the stereotype of the lush-haired shampoo spokesmodel to create a memorable and comic argument for its audience.

If you think about it, as a culture we tend to be quite persuaded by humor; against our more rational impulses, the ads that make us laugh are usually the ones we remember. To prove this point, you need only think back to last year's

"If I had hair, I'd use Vidal Sassoon for men."

Geoffrey Holder,
Actor,
New York, N.Y.

FIGURE 2.7. This shampoo ad uses humor as a *pathos* appeal to promote its product.

Superbowl ads: Which ads do you remember? Which ads did you talk over with your friends during and after the game? Probably most of those memorable commercials relied on humor. The arguments these ads make may not always be the most logically sound, but the way they foster a connection with the audience makes them persuasive nonetheless.

Exaggerated Uses of Pathos. Although these strategies of persuasion successfully move audiences, sometimes advertisers exaggerate the appeal to emotion for more dramatic effect. Many consider the "This-is-your-brain-on-drugs" commercial, described on page 40 as a classic example of the **scare tactic** in the way it builds on its audience's fears to make its argument about the effects of drug usage. The Partnership for a Drug Free America, which originally created this ad, took it one step further in 1997. In this revision, actress Rachel Leigh Cook relies on the familiar props of an egg and a frying pan to demonstrate her point. However, this time instead of frying the egg, she uses the pan to smash the egg dramatically on the counter. Holding up the pan with egg dripping from it, she says, "This is what happens to your brain after snorting heroin." She then continues, "It's not over yet." Wielding her frying pan as a weapon, she destroys the kitchen, shatters plates, glasses, and even the wall clock to demonstrate the effect of snorting heroin on a user's friends, family, and job. What we see here is a dramatic enactment of a **slippery slope** argument—one that suggests that one act leads to a chain of events that results in an undesirable conclusion. More specifically, we can see how the commercial suggests through its dramatic analogy that any heroin use will result in total devastation.

AT A GLANCE

Exaggerated Uses of *Pathos*

- ***Over-sentimentalization:*** distracting the audience from evidence or relevant issues
- ***The scare tactic:*** capitalizing on the audience's fears to make a pitch
- ***The false need:*** amplifying a perceived need or creating a completely new one
- ***The slippery slope fallacy:*** suggesting that an event or action will send the audience spiraling down a "slippery slope" to a serious consequence

You might be even more familiar with another type of exaggerated *pathos*: the creation of a **false need.** In these cases, a company exaggerates the severity of an existing problem or defines a new one (e.g., thin eyelashes; garbage bags that are difficult to close; even bad breath), then offers up their product as a solution. Take a moment to recall times in your life when you may have been motivated to purchase a product through *false need:* Have you ever bought a razor specifically designed for a man or a woman? Curved sole shape-up or toning sneakers? An angled toothbrush? Curl-enhancing mascara? A transparent Band-Aid? 'Smart' water? What other examples of false needs or exaggerated *pathos* can you recall?

Appeals to Character and Authority: *Ethos*

The last of the three appeals that we'll look at in this chapter is *ethos*—literally, "character." Perhaps you have used *ethos* in other disciplines to mean an argument based on ethical principles. But the *rhetorical* meaning of the term is slightly different: according to Aristotle, *ethos* works as a rhetorical strategy by establishing the goodwill or credibility of the writer or speaker. In fact, as a writer you use *ethos* every time you pick up a pen or proofread your essay—that is, you construct an argument in which your power to persuade depends on credibility, your word choice, your tone, your choice of examples, the quality of your research, your grammar and punctuation. All these factors contribute to your *ethos* as an author.

Ethos can be a very powerful tool for establishing trust and therefore facilitating the persuasiveness of an argument. Companies have long recognized the persuasive power of *ethos*. In fact, a brand logo is in essence *ethos* distilled into a single symbol: it transmits in a single icon the entire reputation of a company, organization, or brand identity. From the Nike swoosh to McDonald's golden arches, the NBC peacock, or the Apple computer apple, symbols serve to mark (or brand) products with ethos.

Yet the power of the brand logo as a seat of *ethos* relies on the company's overall reputation with the consumer—a reputation that the company carefully cultivates through advertising campaigns. Many companies, for instance, trade on *ethos* by using celebrity endorsements in their advertising campaigns. Although a rational appeal is at work behind some endorsements—having basketball superstar LeBron James sell basketball shoes, for instance, makes sense—many campaigns rely not only on the celebrity's suitability for selling a product but also on the person's star appeal, character, and goodwill. Consider the power of the famous "Got Milk?" campaign. Here's the argument: if this celebrity likes milk, shouldn't we? Indeed, when we see famous people sporting the trademark milk moustache, we find the ad persuasive because these celebrities are vouching for the product. We look to their goodwill as public figures, to their character as famous people putting their reputation on the line.

However, ad campaigns based upon celebrity endorsements can backfire. The various troubles that confronted Tiger Woods in the late fall of

CREATIVE PRACTICE

With a partner, look at Figures 2.8 and 2.9 below. What specific argumentative strategies and rhetorical appeals does each use to make its argument? Choose one ad and brainstorm with your partner about how the company might market the same car by using a different strategy or appeal. Sketch out your hypothetical ad—including both image and copy—and share it with the class. Talk about how the shift in appeal (audience, context) affects your understanding of the rhetorical situation and the effectiveness of the ad.

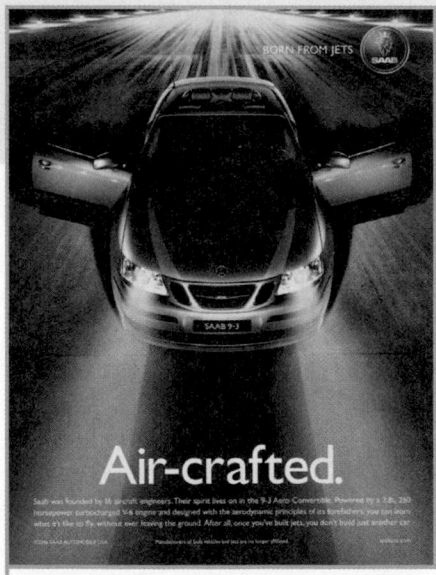

FIGURE 2.8. An advertisement for a Saab.

FIGURE 2.9. An advertisement for the Ford Escape hybrid.

2009 left advertisers from investment houses to high-end watchmakers to various golf suppliers scrambling to distance themselves from their premier spokesman.

While the impact of a celebrity spokesperson can be a powerful use of *ethos*, sometimes the *lack* of fame can be an effective strategy. The Mac/PC television ads ("I'm a Mac," and "I'm a PC") made a huge initial impression partly because the spokespeople—hip-looking Justin Long as the Mac and slightly schlubby John Hodgman as the PC—were relatively unknown but easy to identify with. It was pretty clear which one you'd like to be. But Microsoft countered with a series of ads showing "ordinary" people using PCs (and Microsoft software) successfully. The most popular of these, showing an adorable 4-year-old girl sending photos to her grandparents using Microsoft products, made us think again about who we actually are and what we want from our computers—rather than who we would like to be.

Sometimes an ad features a corporate *ethos* to establish that company's credibility. The most obvious of these are the various oil company ads that have appeared over the last few years. Battling the perception that Big Oil, heedless of its role in global warming, is motivated only by ever-increasing profits, these ads inform us endlessly of each company's "green" policies and efforts to give back to the earth.

In contrast to ads that promote a corporate *ethos*, many ads sell products through appeals to the potential consumer's character. In Figure 2.10, for example, a Longines watch ad makes its pitch through words and images: the line, "Elegance is an Attitude" suggests that both the company and the wearer of the company's product can share in elevated *ethos*. The visual image reinforces this idea through the representation of a well-dressed man standing confidently in a black jacket and pinstriped shirt. He looks directly out at the viewer, potentially catching the eye of possible viewers.

FIGURE 2.10. Longines sells its watches through appeals to character.

Misuses of Ethos. One consequence of relying on *ethos*-driven arguments is that sometimes we come to trust symbols of *ethos* rather than looking to the character of the product itself. This tendency points us to the concept of **authority over evidence**—namely, the practice of overemphasizing authority or *ethos* rather than focusing on the merits of the evidence itself, a strategic exaggeration of ethos that helps entice audiences and sell products.

The most prominent examples of *authority over evidence* can be found in celebrity endorsements; in many commercials, the spokesperson sells the product not based on its merits but based on the argument, "Believe what I say because you know me, and would I steer you wrong?" However, the American public has become increasingly skeptical of such arguments. Living in a world where rumors of Pepsi-spokesperson Britney Spears's preference for Coke circulate on the Internet, Tiger Woods's $100 million deal with Nike makes front page news, and a star like former Sprite spokesperson Macaulay Culkin publicly announces, "I'm not crazy about the stuff [Sprite]. But money is money" (Twitchell, *Twenty* 214), the credibility of celebrity endorsements is often questionable.

Often, companies deliberately attempt to undermine the *ethos* of their competition as a way of promoting their own products. You probably have seen ads of this sort: Burger King arguing that their flame-broiled hamburgers are better than McDonald's fried hamburgers; Coke claiming its soda tastes better than Pepsi's; Visa asserting its card's versatility by reminding consumers how many companies "don't take American Express"; and of course the ubiquitous, Mac versus PC commercials. The deliberate *comparison-contrast* builds up one company's *ethos* at another's expense. At times, however, this technique can be taken to an extreme, producing an ***ad hominem*** argument—that is, an argument that attempts to persuade by attacking an opponent's character. We see *ad hominem* at work most often in campaign advertisements, where candidates end up focusing less on the issues at hand than on their opponents' moral weaknesses, or in commercials where companies attack each other for the way they run their businesses rather than the quality of their products. In

Student Writing

Amanda Johnson, in her analysis of a Barbie parody ad, and Georgia Duan, in her reading of cigarette advertising, explore the construction of body image in the media and the use of parody in ads.
www.pearsonhighered.com/envision/56

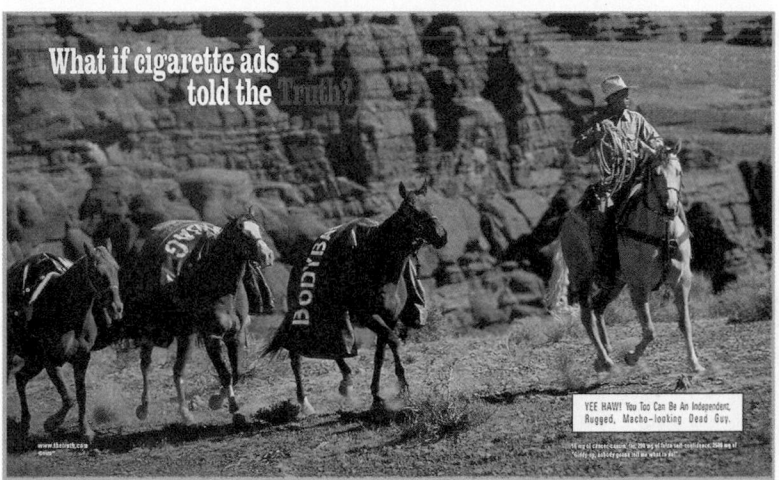

FIGURE 2.11. This TheTruth.com antismoking ad attacks ethos through parody.

other words, this strategy attempts to persuade by reducing the credibility of opposing arguments.

Another strategy of persuasion is attacking ethos through **parody**, or the deliberate mocking of a text or convention. We can see this at work in the Truth ad in Figure 2.11 that uses the conventions of a typical cigarette ad to argue against smoking. As we can see, parody can be an effective rhetorical strategy for making a powerful argument.

Considering Context: *Kairos*

As you can tell from examining ads in this chapter, a successful argument must take into account not only the *rhetorical situation* but also the context, or the right time and place. That is why promotional trailers for the ABC series *Invasion*—featuring big-budget scenes of a Florida hurricane—could captivate audiences in the early summer of 2005 but horrify and outrage that same audience two months later in the wake of hurricanes Katrina and Rita. In ancient Greece rhetoricians called this aspect of the rhetorical situation *kairos*—namely, attention to the right time and place for an argument.

In your own writing, you should consider *kairos* along with the other aspects of the rhetorical situation: audience, text, and writer. It is important

FIGURE 2.12. This Coca-Cola ad used *kairos* to create a powerful argument for its World War II audience.

to recognize the *kairos*—the opportune historical, ideological, or cultural moment—of a text when analyzing its rhetorical force. You undoubtedly already consider the context for persuasive communication in your everyday life. For instance, whether you are asking a friend to dinner or a professor for a recommendation, your assessment of the timeliness and the appropriate strategies for that time probably determines the shape your argument takes. In essence, by picking the right moment and place to make your case, you are in fact paying attention to the *kairos* of your argument.

Consider, Coca-Cola's ad campaigns. Coke has exerted a powerful presence in the advertising industry for many years, in part because of its strategic advertising. During World War II, Coke ran a series of ads featuring servicemen and inspiring slices of Americana that built its beverage campaign around the contemporary nationalistic sentiment and responded to a specific cultural moment.

Look at Figure 2.12, an advertisement for Coke from the 1940s. This picture uses *pathos* to appeal to the audience's sense of patriotism by featuring a row of seemingly carefree servicemen, leaning from the windows of a military bus, the refreshing Cokes in their hands producing smiles even far away from home. The picture draws in the audience by reassuring them on two fronts:

- It builds on the nationalistic pride in the young, handsome servicemen who so happily serve their country.
- It is designed to appease fears about the hostile climate abroad: as both the picture and the accompanying text assure us, Coca-Cola (and the servicemen) "goes along" and "gets a hearty welcome."

The power of this message relates directly to its context. An ad such as this one, premised on patriotism and pride in military service, would be most persuasive during wartime when many more people tend to support the spirit of nationalism and therefore would be moved by the image of the young serviceman shipping off to war. It is through understanding the *kairos* of this advertisement that you can appreciate the strength of the ad's rhetorical appeal.

An awareness of *kairos* likewise helps us see how a more current coke ad (Figure 2.13) is tailored to today's culture, addressing the viewer as an individual and audience of one. The visual composition of the ad includes the words "hello you" in big font reminiscent of computer type, as if the ad is

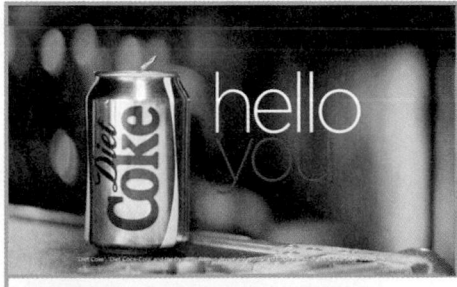

FIGURE 2.13. A 2009 Coke ad points directly to the reader.

an online dating message or IM line. In contrast to the nationalism and group solidarity of the earlier Coke ad, this one engages the viewer's attention as an individual, by appealing to *kairos*—the idea that here and now in America the individual reigns supreme. The fuzzy background and soft lighting also suggest today's spirit of fun and exploration of digital environments—our world is very different here and now than it was for the soldiers on the train in the earlier Coke ad. Attending to *kairos* enables us to attend to these differences, to learn how ads and other visual rhetoric texts make use of the present moment and place, and finally, to learn how we can optimally make use of *kairos* when composing our own arguments. Ads convey complex cultural meanings. Recognizing their persuasive presence everywhere, we realize the need to develop our ability to make more-informed interpretations. You can pursue your study of ads by conducting your own careful rhetorical analyses of these visual-verbal texts. You'll find over and over again that ads are a microcosm of many of the techniques of persuasion. From billboards to pop-ups on the Internet, ads employ *logos, pathos,* and *ethos* to convey strong messages to specific audiences. We've learned how compact and sophisticated these texts are. Now it's time to apply those insights in your own writing.

The Writer's Process

As you begin to perform your individual analyses of advertisements, consider the way your own writing, like the ads we've discussed, can "sell" your argument to the reader. Consider the rhetorical situation and the specific *kairos* of your argument. What *strategies of argumentation* and *rhetorical appeals* would be most effective in reaching your target audience? Do you want to use narration, a humorous analogy, or a stirring example to forge a connection with your readers based on *pathos*? Or is your analysis better suited to *logos*, following a step-by-step process of reading an ad, drawing on empirical evidence, or looking at cause and effect? Perhaps you will decide to enrich your discussion through cultivating your *ethos* as a writer, establishing your own authority on a subject or citing reputable work done by other scholars. It is probable that in your essay you will use many strategies and a combination of appeals; as we saw in the advertisements presented earlier, from the Crest Whitening Strips ad to the Coca-Cola campaign, a successful argument uses various rhetorical strategies to persuade its audience.

While focusing on the individual strategies, don't forget to keep an eye on the composition of your argument as a whole. Just as an ad is designed with attention to layout and design, so you should look at the larger organization of your essay as key to the success of your argument. As you approach the organization of elements in your essay to maximize your persuasiveness, even a question like "Where should I insert my images?" has profound implications for your argument. Consider the difference between an essay in which the image is embedded in the text, next to the paragraph that analyzes it, and one with the image attached as an appendix. In your writing, use the persuasive power of visual rhetoric more effectively by allowing the reader to analyze the images alongside the written explanations. Use similar careful attention to organization, placement, and purpose as you begin your own analysis and craft your own rhetorical argument.

PREWRITING CHECKLIST

Analyzing Advertisements

- ❑ **Content:** What exactly is the ad selling? An object? an idea? both?
- ❑ **Message:** How is the ad selling the product? What is the persuasive message that the ad is sending to the audience?
- ❑ **Character and setting:** What is featured by the ad? An object? a scene? a person? How are these elements portrayed? What are the ethnicity, age, socioeconomic class, and gender of any people in the advertisement? How do these choices relate to the ad's intended audience and reflect deliberate rhetorical choices?

- ❏ **Theme:** What is the underlying message of the ad (beyond "buy our product")?

- ❏ **Medium:** What medium was the advertisement produced in? Television? print? radio? How did this choice suit the rhetorical purpose of the ad and accommodate the needs of a particular audience?

- ❏ **Historical context:** In what country and at what historical moment was the advertisement produced? How do the demands of context shape the persuasive appeals at work in the ad? How does the ad reflect, comment on, challenge, or reinforce contemporary political, economic, or gender ideology? How does this commentary situate it in terms of a larger trend or argument?

- ❏ **Word and image:** What is the relationship between the word (written or spoken) and the imagery in the ad? Which is given priority? How does this relationship affect the persuasiveness of the advertisement?

- ❏ **Layout:** How are the elements of the ad arranged—on a page (for a print ad) or in sequence (for a television or Internet commercial)? What is the purpose behind this arrangement? How does the ad's organization lead the reader through—and facilitate—its argument?

- ❏ **Design:** What typeface is used? What size? What color? How do these decisions reflect attention to the ad's rhetorical situation? How do they function in relation to the ad's rhetorical appeals?

- ❏ **Voice:** What voice does the text use to reach its audience? Is the language technical, informal, personal, authoritative? Is the voice comic or serious?

- ❏ **Rhetorical appeals:** How does the advertiser use the images to work in conjunction with rhetorical appeals? For instance, does the image reinforce an appeal to reason? Is it designed to produce an emotional effect on the audience? Does the use of a certain style, such as black-and-white authority, contribute to the ethos of the ad?

- ❏ **Strategy of development:** Narration? definition? comparison-contrast? example or illustration? classification and division? process? analogy? cause and effect? How do these strategies contribute to the ad's persuasive appeal?

- ❏ **Cultural resonance:** Does the ad use famous events or places or recognizable symbols to increase its persuasiveness? If so, how does that establish audience or a relationship to a cultural moment?

PREWRITING WITH THE *ENVISION* WEBSITE

To get started writing your analysis of an ad, you might visit an online repository of commercials, such as those linked through the *Envision* Website. With a partner, browse through several commercials, selecting two or three in particular that you find persuasive. Discuss what strategies of argumentation you see at work in these visual rhetoric texts. Try to find an example of each approach listed earlier in the chapter. Write a short paragraph analyzing one of the commercials; compare your interpretation with a partner. Then share your work with the rest of the class.
www.pearsonhighered.com/envision/62a

WRITING PROJECTS

1. **Rhetorical Analysis:** Choose two or three ads for the same product and analyze the strategies of persuasion these ads use to reach specific audiences. To find your ads, you might visit an ad archive such as those linked through the Chapter 2 resources on the *Envision* Website, or look at magazines. Select ads that showcase an exaggeration of rhetorical appeals, such as logical fallacies, exaggeration of pathos, misuse of ethos, or parody. Use the prewriting checklist to help you analyze the appeals in the ads and to help you develop your argument. Be sure to address how strategies of persuasion operate and what the effects are on the audience as well as a description of context: where and when was the ad published and to whom?

2. **Contextual Analysis:** Write a contextual analysis on the *kairos* of the Coca-Cola campaign. Examine, for instance, another Coke ad from the 1940s through the Adflip link on the *Envision* Website. Do some research and read about this era: explore the time, place, and culture in which the ad appeared. How do the rhetorical choices of the ad you selected reflect an awareness of this context? How does the ad use logos, pathos, and ethos to comment on or criticize this cultural moment?
www.pearsonhighered.com/envision/62b

3. **Historical Analysis:** Working in groups, look at several ads from different time periods produced by the same company, such as ads for cigarettes, cars, hygiene products, and personal computers. Each member of your group should choose a single ad and prepare a rhetorical analysis of its persuasive appeals. Share your analyses to explore how this company has modified its rhetorical approach over time. Collaborate to write a paper in which you chart

the evolution of the company's persuasive strategies and how that evolution was informed by *kairos*.

4. **Cultural Analysis:** Write a paper in which you compare two ad campaigns and examine the ideology behind specific constructions of our culture. Does one campaign portray gender- or race-specific ideas? How do the tools of persuasion produce each message? What message is conveyed by the reliance on such cultural ideals or notions of identity? What representations of sexuality, gender roles, or class are presented by these ads? Present your findings to the class, holding up examples of the ads to discuss in support of your analysis.

Visit www.pearsonhighered.com/envision for expanded assignment guidelines and student projects. Visit www.mycomplab.com for additional general writing and research resources.

CHAPTER 3

Composing Arguments

Chapter Preview Questions

- What are the canons of rhetoric, and how do they help us to understand arguments?
- How can you create strong introductions and conclusions?
- What roles do persona and rhetorical stance play in arguments?
- How do photographs function as both visual evidence in arguments and as visual arguments themselves?
- How do writers synthesize multiple perspectives on an issue in an argument?

Imagine that it is September 2005 and the United States is still reeling from the aftermath of Hurricane Katrina. As you click through several news sites, you pause to look at the images they display. One features a striking photo of a military helicopter dropping supplies to the citizens of New Orleans (see Figure 3.1). Another shows an African-American mother clutching two small children and wading through waist-deep water. Yet another displays the image of a mob of angry people, packed together and arguing as they try to evacuate the city. A final site uses the picture of a child's dirt-smeared doll, swept into a pile of debris on the road, as its poignant commentary on natural disaster.

Based on these images, which site would you click back to? How does each image make a different argument about exactly what happened? How might the words that

FIGURE 3.1. A photograph of supplies being dropped to New Orleans survivors of Hurricane Katrina.

accompany the photo shape your interpretation of the visual texts? How does the choice of a particular visual-verbal combination present a specific point of view?

Photographs and captions on news sites or in newspapers work through the tools of persuasion that we examined in earlier chapters. In this chapter, we'll continue to explore how visual rhetoric shapes our reality in particular ways by focusing on photographs. We will also move forward in our understanding of analysis and argument by learning effective ways to create arguments. We'll become acquainted with the canons of rhetoric—five classifications of argument from ancient Greece—and we'll work through the process of creating an argument: coming up with ideas, structuring those ideas, and developing a style for your own compositions.

Understanding the Canons of Rhetoric

In ancient Greece, all communicative acts were classified into five categories, or what scholars call the **canons of rhetoric**. These are the principles by which all writing, speaking, or visual arguments operate: **invention** (coming up with ideas), **arrangement** (organizing ideas in effective ways), **style** (expressing those ideas in an appropriate manner), **memory** (accessing learned materials), and **delivery** (presenting crafted ideas to an audience).

Each of these canons is necessary for persuasive communication, whether that be through spoken word, written discourse, or, more recently, multimedia texts. For our discussion of composing arguments in this chapter, we'll focus on the first three canons (you can look to Chapter 9 for discussion of the last two canons).

AT A GLANCE

Canons of Rhetoric

- *Invention:* creating and constructing ideas
- *Arrangement:* ordering and laying out ideas effectively
- *Style:* developing the appropriate expression for those ideas
- *Memory:* retaining invented ideas, recalling additional supporting ideas, and facilitating memory in the audience
- *Delivery:* presenting or performing ideas with the aim of persuading

Invention in Argument

When you craft language with the purpose of persuading your audience, you are **inventing** an argument. That is, you are generating ideas about a topic. Aristotle defined *invention* as methods for "finding all available arguments." Methods you might use to "invent" arguments include:

- **Definition:** What does the text *mean*? What are other examples?
- **Division:** What *parts* are comprised within the text?
- **Comparison:** Does the text mean something new versus years ago? How does the text *compare* to other texts?
- **Classification:** What is the *purpose* of the text? Cause and effect? Consequence?
- **Testimony:** What do *others* say about the text?

Invention is the "discovery of valid or seemingly valid arguments to render one's cause probable."

—Cicero, *De Inventione*, I.vii

To develop ideas, you can use a range of rhetorical strategies: invoking *pathos*, using *ethos* or good character, or employing *logos* to reason calmly with your readers or listeners. Your task as a writer is to forge a powerful text that argues a point, to convince others to see a particular perspective, usually your own. In composing arguments, you can look for examples in both writing as well as verbal-visual texts all around you.

We might think a photograph provides a window on another person's reality. But in fact photographs, like written texts, are artifacts of rhetorical invention. The "reality" that photographs display is actually a *version* of reality created by a photographer's rhetorical and artistic decisions: whether to use color or black-and-white film; what sort of lighting to use; how to position the subject of the photograph; whether to opt for a panorama or close-up shot; what backdrop to use; how to crop, or trim, the image once it is printed. In effect, when we see photographs in a newspaper or art gallery, we are looking at the product of deliberate *strategies of invention*. In photography, these strategies include key elements of composition, such as selection, placement, perspective, and framing. In written texts, the same elements—selection, placement, perspective, and framing—are critical to making an argument.

Figure 3.2, an image captured by photojournalist Margaret Bourke-White, shows a line of homeless African Americans, displaced by the 1937 Louisville flood, waiting in line to receive food and clothing from a local Red

FIGURE 3.2. Margaret Bourke-White, "At the Time of the Louisville Flood," 1937.

Cross center. Does the photo merely document a moment in the history of Kentucky? Or have the choice of subject, the cropping, the angle, the background, and the elements within the frame been selected by the photographer to make a specific argument about race and American culture during the first half of the twentieth century?

In your own writing, you could look to this photograph as inspiration for invention. You could use this image to support a historically focused argument, perhaps one that examined the catastrophic 1937 Louisville flood and its impact on the local community. Or you could refer to this photograph as visual evidence in a paper that examines the link between social status, race, and disaster relief, perhaps drawing a connection to the Katrina tragedy. Either argument could draw on the power of photographs like this one, a power created by the invention strategies of the artist.

FIGURE 3.3. Dorothea Lange's wide shot gives a stark sense of the experience of migrant farmers.

FIGURE 3.4. The close-up focuses on the struggles of the migrant mother.

Let's look more closely at how invention factors into the way photographers and writers compose arguments. Consider two famous photographs by Dorothea Lange (see Figures 3.3 and 3.4), which offer very different representations of migrant workers during the Great Depression. In each case, we see a migrant family huddled inside a tent. The subjects seem to be poor, hungry, and struggling to make a living. Their material conditions are bleak.

But notice the effects of the different perspectives. In Figure 3.4, we get an intimate look inside this woman's eyes, where we can see her concern. The lines on her face, visible in this close-up, are evidence of her hard life and worries. The photograph in Figure 3.3 has a wider frame that encompasses the tent and the barren ground. This perspective makes a different kind of argument, one that addresses the condition of the soil, the landscape, the living quarters. We can hardly make out the woman huddled in the darkness of the tent. When we look for visual evidence of the living conditions of migrant workers in the American West during the 1930s, each photograph offers different angles on our argument. Which one would we use to support a thesis about the labor conditions of migrant workers? Which one would we use to argue that the human body is scarred by hardship? Depending on our purpose, we would choose one photograph over the other. Each one makes an argument that we can in turn select as evidence for our claims about the Great Depression. Each photograph uses a particular strategy of invention, creating and constructing ideas in visual form about the "reality" of life for migrant workers. We can, in turn, invent different arguments based on our starting point: which photo do we use as evidence for our thesis?

In written documents, different perspectives on the same topic can yield different arguments. Commentary on Lange's *Migrant Mother* photographs exposes the variety of perspectives not only on the photographs' status as "documentary" evidence from the Great Depression but also on the way our historical understanding of that period itself is constructed by the invention or arguments of others. For instance, the following excerpt from historian James Curtis's article "Dorothea Lange, Migrant Mother, and the Culture of the Great Depression" demonstrates the way in which Lange's photos are often interpreted as windows into that period:

> In addition to being a timeless work of art, *Migrant Mother* is a vital reflection of the times. Examined in its original context, the series reveals powerful cultural forces of the 1930s: the impact of the increasing centralization and bureaucratization of American life; the anxiety about the status and solidarity of the family in an era of urbanization and modernization; a need to atone for the guilt induced by the destruction of cherished ideals, and a craving for reassurance that democratic traditions would stand the test of modern times.

For Curtis, the images function both as what he calls elsewhere in the article "a timeless and universal symbol of suffering in the face of adversity" (1) as well as the key to understanding Lange's relationship to the evolving genre of documentary photography. For journalist Geoffrey Dunn, however, Lange's series prompts a different response:

> The photographs taken by Lange and her colleagues at the Resettlement Administration (later to become better known as the Farm Security Administration) have been widely heralded as the epitome of documentary photography. The eminent photographer and curator Edward Steichen called them "the most remarkable human documents ever rendered in pictures."
>
> In recent years, however, the FSA photographs have come under a growing criticism. Many view them as manipulative and condescending, to the point of assuming a "colonialistic" attitude toward their subjects. Still others have argued that they are misleading and disingenuous, and in some instances, fabricated.

> In a compelling essay entitled "The Historian and the Icon," University of California at Berkeley professor Lawrence Levine has argued that the FSA photographers focused their lenses on "perfect victims," and in so doing, rendered a caricatured portrait of the era.
>
> "Americans suffered, materially and physically, during the years of the Great Depression to an extent which we still do not fully fathom," Levine asserted. "But they also continued, as people always must, the business of living. They ate and they laughed, they loved and they fought, they worried and they hoped . . . they filled their days, as we fill ours, with the essentials of everyday living."
>
> With the notable exception of FSA photographer Russell Lee, and later, Marion Post Wolcott, whose largely overlooked bodies of work actually capture the dimensions of "everyday living," Lange and her colleagues focused almost exclusively on human suffering. That is most certainly the reason that people like Florence Owens Thompson [the mother in these photographs]—and many others who appeared in FSA images—resented their photographic portrayal.
>
> "Mother was a woman who loved to enjoy life, who loved her children," says Thompson's youngest daughter, Norma Rydlewski, who appears as a young child in Lange's classic photograph. "She loved music and she loved to dance. When I look at that photo of mother, it saddens me. That's not how I like to remember her."

Like Curtis, Dunn uses the photographs as the basis for an argument about Lange's practice of documentary photography; however, Dunn considers first-person accounts from other witnesses of that historical moment and arrives at a different argument. He concludes that the series exemplifies not reflection but misrepresentation.

All texts—whether written accounts or photographs—are actually shaped by individual perspective and point of view. Texts are "invented" for a specific audience. Your own writing is a text informed by your invention strategies, your purpose, and your point of view. In your writing, you are like a photographer, making important compositional decisions: What will be the subject of your text: an individual, a group, an institution? How will you pose that subject to best convey your own perspective? Should you zoom in, focusing on one particular example as a way of addressing a larger concern? Or should you take a step back, situating your argument in relation to the broader context that surrounds the issue? The choices you make will determine the ultimate impact of your argument: like photographs, effective writing persuades the viewer to look at a topic through the lens of the author's interpretation.

CREATIVE PRACTICE

Examine the picture in Figure 3.5, taken by photographer Todd Heisler, of a soldier's coffin returning home on a civilian flight into Reno, Nevada, being draped with the American flag prior to being unloaded from the plane. What argument is Heisler making about Americans' response to the Iraq war and casualties? Now consider this image as the foundation for your own process of invention: What types of arguments might you construct that would use this image as visual evidence? What other sorts of images or evidence would you use to develop your argument?

FIGURE 3.5. Photograph of the arrival of a soldier's coffin in Reno, Nevada.

Arrangement in Argument

After invention, arrangement becomes your key consideration because the way in which you present material on the page will shape a reader's response to the ideas. In many cases, attention to *arrangement* takes the form of the way you order elements in your argument—whether that be the layout of images and text on a newspaper front page or the way you structure a written argument in a more academic paper. It is the arrangement of an argument that gives it structure or that separates a free-form reaction from a carefully developed and proven argument.

Therefore, when we refer to "arrangement" in a written argument, we often are referring to the underlying structure of the essay itself. Although unifying an essay with a smooth flow of ideas is important, it is just as important that the structure of the essay not simply move from one idea to the next through the process of free association. Here are some common organizational strategies you might choose in composing your own arguments:

- **Chronological structure:** Chronology relies on examples across time, such as the transformation in the Apple computer marketing campaign from the Macintosh to the iPad.
- **Cause-effect:** Show how one event causes another. An essay confronting the issue of sexist imagery in rap music videos might start by exploring how women are represented in popular rap videos (*cause*) and then conclude by discussing the impact of this representation on the self-esteem of young girls (*effect*).
- **Problem-solution:** Define the problem, then offer a solution. A paper about violence and video games might devote the first half of the paper to exploring the *problem* of desensitization and then focus in the second half of the paper on proposing a possible *solution*.
- **Block structure:** Work your way systematically through a series of examples or case studies—such as individual James Bond films in a paper about the relationship between real-world political climates and spy narrative.
- **Thematic structure:** Focus on thematic relationships. A paper on reality TV might include sections on voyeurism, capitalism, and Darwinism (*the themes*), integrating examples from *Survivor, American Idol,* and *America's Next Top Model* as evidence in each section.
- **Deferred thesis:** Substitute a thesis question for a thesis statement at the beginning of your essay, such as "How did images featured in the news define our understanding of the impact of hurricanes Katrina and Rita?" Place your thesis at the end of your paper as a way of synthesizing the evidence explored in the paper itself.

Let's look to photography to see the way a successful argument relies on strategies of arrangement. Figures 3.6 through Figure 3.9 offer a selection of photographs from Jane Gottesman's photo essay *Game Face*, a work devoted to redefining the concept of the modern female athlete. A veteran sportswriter, Gottesman spent years accumulating photographs of amateur and professional women athletes of all ages, races, and socioeconomic backgrounds, a collection that was a museum exhibit and both a print and online photo essay. It is not surprising to find that she gave extra care to strategies of arrangement in composing her visual argument.

Looking at this version of *Game Face*, we can see from the top menu bar that it is divided into four sections: "Prepare," "Compete," "Finish," and "Achieve." Clearly, this is an example of an argument *organized by theme*. This arrangement gives a logical structure to the text: the argument moves along a continuum, from pre-game, to game play, to post-game. Within each of these sections (which roughly approximate the sections of a book or written essay), Gottesman includes several examples (which we might correlate to paragraphs in traditional academic writing). Looking at the individual images, we can see how arrangement plays a strong role in constructing an argument; each page makes its commentary on women's athletics by juxtaposing a powerful photo with a descriptive caption and a relevant quotation from a female athlete. The recurring structure gives the overall photo essay coherence and consistency, despite its variety of examples.

Let's take a closer look at the way the

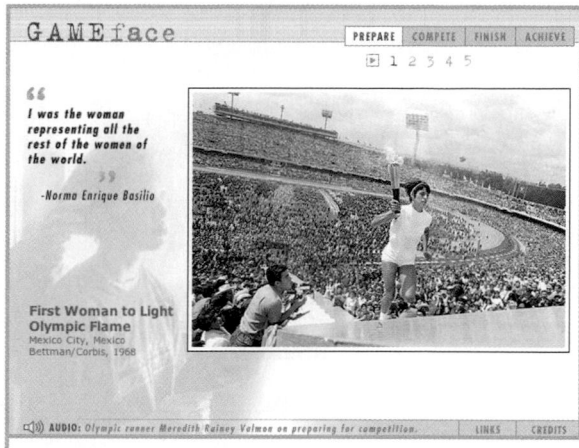

FIGURE 3.6. Picture 1 from "Prepare."

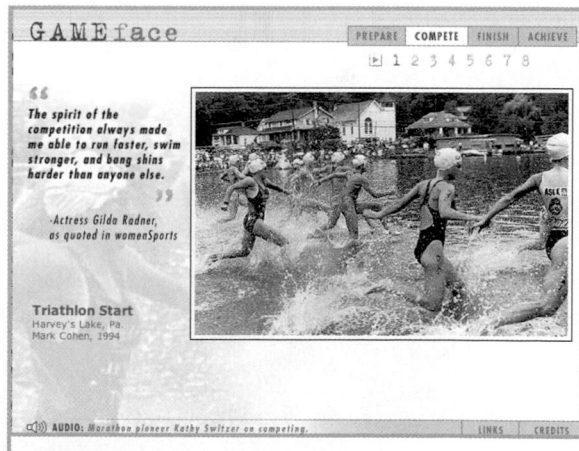

FIGURE 3.7. Picture 1 from "Compete."

pictures reinforce the underlying structure produced by the section headers; we can do so by carefully examining the lead images for the various sections. The lead image (Figure 3.6), for instance, centers on an inspirational event: the moment in 1968 when a woman, for the first time, lit the Olympic flame. As the

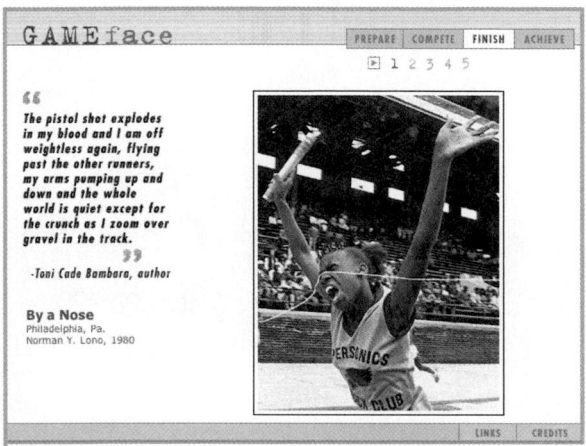

FIGURE 3.8. Picture 1 from "Finish."

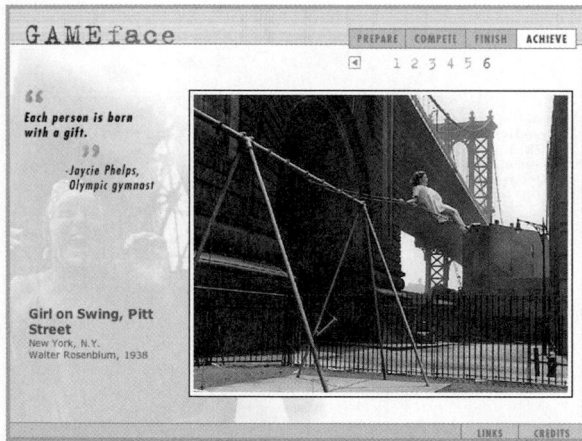

FIGURE 3.9. Final picture from the photo essay.

first image in the photo essay, this picture of Norma Basilio symbolizes accomplishment, possibilities, a global perspective, and even more importantly, an auspicious beginning to the argument, the same way in which the lighting of the flame itself marks the beginning of an auspicious event.

The next image (Figure 3.7), which heads the "Compete" section, offers a similarly strong statement but shifts perspective from the international to the local, capturing the first moments in a 1994 Pennsylvania triathlon. In this image, as much as we see individual competitors, we also see community—a theme that reappears at many different points in that particular section.

The next photograph (Figure 3.8), from the "Finish" section, moves us from the start of competition to its conclusion, focusing on the victory of the female athlete. The series of photographs in this section, from the victorious track star to the weary but triumphant soccer team, celebrate the rewards that come from following through on one's dreams. In the last section, "Achieve," the images escalate in strength, culminating with the inspirational picture of a young girl swinging powerfully toward the stars (Figure 3.9).

Using Toulmin to Arrange or Analyze an Argument

As we've seen, Gottesman makes strategic choices in structuring her photo essay to create a visually and conceptually striking argument. Another powerful way to arrange an argument is to follow the model developed by British philosopher Stephen Toulmin (*The Uses of Argument,* 1969). Toulmin suggests that a logical argument has several parts: claim, grounds, warrants, backing, rebuttal, and response. Let's look at how Toulmin's approach might help a student construct an argument about images such as the one shown in Figure 3.5. Here's the context: until 2009, the Pentagon banned the publication of photographs (and other media coverage) showing the caskets of American soldiers who had been killed in the Middle East. Coming into office, President Obama was faced with the decision about whether to lift the ban. Here's the question: should the media be allowed to publish such images?

- The **claim** is the thesis, or central argument. In other words, the claim is a statement that you are asking your audience to accept as true.

  Claim: The Pentagon should not ban publication of photographs of fallen American soldiers.

- The **grounds** are the reasons you think the claim should be believed and the evidence that supports those reasons (statistics, expert testimony, etc.).

  Grounds: The Constitution guarantees freedom of speech and of the press.

- The **warrants** are assumptions that explain *how* the grounds support the claim. If the warrants are not clear or are implied, they may also need supporting evidence, called **backing.**

  Warrants: Freedom of speech and the press imply a right to *listen* to and *read*—that is, to access information.

- The rebuttal is a listing of anticipated counterclaims, and your response. Arguments can be both written and analyzed following this model.

  Rebuttal: Publishing images of fallen Americans could negatively affect public morale during wartime.

  Response: People have a constitutional right to access information, and openness about American casualties is necessary to produce transparency in government as well as to provide opportunities to memorialize those who sacrificed their lives for our country.

As you can see, working through the Toulmin model provides a framework that helps you think through the complexities of your claim and produce a more nuanced argument. You can use the Toulmin method to compose a claim of your own, to support it with appropriate evidence, and to explain clearly how and why that evidence does in fact prove, or support, your claim. Conversely, you also will find this approach extremely useful in analyzing arguments made by others.

Style in Argument

Inventing a thesis or main idea and *arranging* the elements of your writing are two steps in completing your task of written persuasion. You need also to spend some time considering how you are going to *present* that idea to your audience. This is where *style*—the third canon of rhetoric—enters the scene. Style concerns choosing the appropriate expression for the ideas of your argument; these choices relate to language, tone, syntax, rhetorical appeals, metaphors, imagery, quotations, level of emphasis, and nuance. We'll look more closely at style and the levels of decorum in Chapter 8; for now, let's consider how this canon operates in relation to the writer's voice.

We often translate *style* into *voice* to indicate a writer's unique persona and rhetorical stance as it is manifested in word choice, syntax, pacing, and tone. To construct a successful argument, you need to be able to employ the voice or style that best meets the needs of your rhetorical situation. Consider the following two examples of style, both focused on the persona of President Obama. The first is from a *Sports Illustrated* piece:

> Obama's erect carriage and lefthandedness led me to think of Lionel "Train" Hollins, who commanded the Portland Trail Blazers' backcourt when the kid then known as "Barry O'Bomber" was making his way through high school.

Using basketball lingo ("backcourt") and casual vocabulary ("the kid" and "making his way") helps writer Alexander Wolff construct his persona as someone who speaks the language of popular readers—what classical rhetorician Cicero would have called "plain style." Moreover, the naming of famous players gives credibility to Wolff's persona as someone who knows the players and even their nicknames, and another indication of this level of style.

In contrast, a writer from the academic journal *Rhetoric & Public Affairs* uses what Cicero called high style, or elevated diction, in making a critique of President Obama's persona:

> While Obama's rhetoric of *consilience* approximates dialogic coherence, it nonetheless falls short of the discursive demands of racial reconciliation.

By using sophisticated concepts familiar only to a highly educated academic audience, such as "dialogic coherence" and "discursive demands," writer Mark McPhail forges a persona for himself as an erudite and complex-thinking member of the intellectual class. His "backcourt buddies" are the colleagues who understand that "dialogic coherence" and "discursive demands" refer to ways of speaking and writing.

Similarly, your persona and your stylistic choices contribute to building your ethos and persuading your audience. Consider your choices carefully as you will both create a persona and determine which audience will respond to you best. Therefore, if you are wondering, how do you move from invention and arrangement to developing your own style? The answer lies in careful attention to developing *persona* and *rhetorical stance* in your writing.

Constructing Persona

When you select a certain image, a set of words, or a written phrase to shape your argument and try to persuade your audience, you are constructing a **persona** for yourself as a writer and rhetorician. Your persona is *a deliberately crafted version of yourself as writer.* A public figure will often use *persona* as a purposeful rhetorical tool. President Barack Obama might choose to give a speech about war flanked by a group of military men and women, and a speech about health care surrounded by doctors, as we see in Figure 3.10.

The same principle governs the writing process. When you compose a text (written, verbal, or visual), you decide how to use language to

FIGURE 3.10. President Barack Obama talks about health care surrounded by white coated medical personnel.

present a particular persona to the audience you wish to address. You create a portrait of yourself as the author of your argument through tone (formal or informal, humorous or serious); word choice (academic, colloquial); sentence structures (complex or simple and direct); use of rhetorical appeals (*pathos, logos, ethos*); and strategies of persuasion (narration, example, cause and effect, analogy, process, classification, or definition). Creating a persona requires care. A well-designed one can facilitate a strong connection with your readers and therefore make your argument more persuasive. However, a poorly constructed persona—one that is, for instance, biased, inconsistent, or underdeveloped—can have the opposite effect, alienating readers and undercutting your text's overall effectiveness.

Choosing a Rhetorical Stance

To be persuasive, you must assume a persona that responds appropriately to your specific rhetorical situation. Wayne Booth, one of the most important revivalists of classical rhetoric, defined the writer's position in relation to the rhetorical triangle as the **rhetorical stance** and claimed that it is the most essential aspect of effective communication. He argued that communication failed between people (or a text failed to persuade a reader) if the writer assumed a position that ignored the balance of the rhetorical triangle.

We see examples of inappropriate rhetorical stances constantly: the TV evangelist who moves his congregation with a polished sermon that completely distracts them from flaws in his moral character; the used-car salesman who pads his sales pitch with offers of free gifts, rebate specials, and low percentage rates; the actor who uses her celebrity status to drive a product endorsement, rather than clearly articulating the merits of that product itself. In each case, the *rhetorical triangle*—the relationship between author, audience, and text—is out of balance, and the argument itself, ultimately, is rendered less persuasive. In your own writing, therefore, you need to pay special attention not only to the persona you create but also to the stance you assume in relation to your specific rhetorical situation.

AT A GLANCE

Three Rhetorical Stances That Lead to Communication Failure

- *The pedant or preacherly stance:* the text is paramount and both the audience's needs and the speaker's character are ignored.

- *The advertiser's stance:* the effect on the audience is valued above all, ignoring the quality of the text and the credibility of the speaker.

- *The entertainer's stance:* the character of the speaker is elevated above the text and the audience.

Titles, Introductions, and Conclusions

In writing, you signal your persona and rhetorical stance through your word choice, sentence structure, tone, and strategies of persuasion. Let's zoom in for a moment on three key elements of the written argument to see the way each operates as an important site for these stylistic choices.

Title. Your reader's first encounter with your topic and argument comes through your title; in this way, the title itself operates as a rhetorical act that provides a frame and sets up the argument. Let's return for a moment to Figure 3.1. Many newspapers featured this image on their front pages on September 2, 2005—but with different headlines. Figures 3.11 and 3.12 are two examples. Consider how each paper signals its rhetorical stance through the visual-verbal arguments contained on its front page.

How does the headline "City desperate for help" read in combination with the helicopter image suggest a different argument than "Rising rage: Descent into anarchy" coupled with the same image? The difference in tone, perspective, and rhetorical stance apparent from these contrasting examples underscores the role a headline—and, relatedly, a title—plays in forming a reader's expectations for the argument that follows. In effect, a title is often the first step in writing an interpretation or making an argument.

In writing your own papers, you should spend some time brainstorming your titles. Some writers find constructing a powerful title to be a useful brainstorming activity to start their composition process and help them with invention; others construct the title only after completing the first draft of their paper, as a way of synthesizing the argument by bringing it into sharper focus. As you work with a title, think about its role in setting up your stance on your topic, indicating to your readers not only the scope of your analysis but also

FIGURE 3.11. Front page of the *Fresno Bee*, September 2, 2005.

Source: © THE FRESNO BEE, 2006

FIGURE 3.12. Front page of the *Deseret Morning News*, September 2, 2005.

your angle on it. Try to play with language, linking the title to your main point, to a key image you discuss, to an underlying metaphor or motif, or to the larger issue raised by your argument. Test your working title by sharing it with a partner in class.

Introduction. Like your title, your introduction offers your readers insight into the persona and rhetorical stance that will characterize your essay as a whole. In these opening paragraphs (an introduction may be more than one paragraph), you establish your voice (informal? formal?), your tone (measured? firm? angry? cautious?), your persona, and your topic through careful attention to word choice, sentence structure, and strategies of development. Most introductions also provide the first articulation of your argument as well, moving from a general statement of topic to a more focused statement of your thesis.

However, perhaps even more importantly, the introduction is the moment in which you capture the attention and interest of your reader, often through a device that we call a rhetorical "hook." For instance, looking back at Jane Gottesman's photo essay, we can see how she hooks her online readers in her opening image (Figure 3.6) by framing the 1968 Olympics as a landmark event for women athletes. The reader is drawn in by the ethos of the Olympics and intrigued by the fact that it was only as recently as the late 1960s that women first participated in the torch-lighting ceremony. This hook prompts readers to wonder what other "firsts" they might not be aware of, what other facts about women athletes Gottesman might reveal. This is the hook that gets readers interested—and prompts readers to continue reading.

In written texts, you can use your introduction to hook your readers through one of several methods:

- Defining your terms (especially if you're writing on a subject that not everyone may be familiar with)

- Including a significant quotation or a startling statistic or fact
- Presenting an overview of the issue you're discussing
- Using an anecdote or narration
- Incorporating a vivid example
- Drawing on a relevant analogy or metaphor
- Using the second-person pronoun (*you*) to invite readers to make personal connections

Your choice of hook will depend to a large extent on your broader stylistic decisions about your essay and the way in which you want to develop your argument.

Let's look at how one student, Michael Zeligs, took the canon of style into consideration while composing his introduction to a rhetorical analysis of Robert Frank's photography:

> "Robert Frank, Swiss, unobtrusive, nice, with that little camera that he raises and snaps with one hand he sucked a sad poem right out of America onto film, taking rank among the tragic poets of the world."
>
> In his introduction to Robert Frank's *The Americans,* Jack Kerouac captures the photographer's responsible position as a concerned observer of his time, as the first person to sweep away dominating prejudice and expose what post-World War II America really represented. In his book, Frank pushes the limits of traditional art photography—limits that required clear foregrounds and backgrounds, clear subject and exposure and level tilt—and this enables him to focus more on scenes that dominate his eye and inspire emotional arguments. The America that Frank addresses, however, is not one of fulfilled dreams and two-car garages. It is a struggling foreground for change, founded in the two beautifully conflicting scenes of "Charleston, South Carolina," and "Trolley," where unique photographic elements merge to advance a critique of racial inequality during America's post-war crisis of identity.

What hooks the reader first is the quotation that heads the introduction: an abstract, lyrical statement that refuses to sacrifice its vision by adhering to conventional punctuation. This quote announces the essay's topic at the same time that it provides a sharp contrast for the writing style of the main body of the introduction that follows. By comparison, Michael's voice seems crisp, focused, and academic, establishing a persona that is both informed on his subject (he clearly not only has analyzed Frank's photographs but has read the introduction to the book as well) and is also able to discuss it articulately.

Michael fashions his first sentence to serve as a bridge between his opening hook and the rest of the paragraph. Rather than using the epigraph simply as a snappy device to capture the reader's attention and then abandoning it, Michael creates an ethos appeal by identifying the quotation's author (Jack Kerouac, an iconic critic of American culture) and then restates the meaning of the quote in a way that pulls it in line with his own argument about Robert Frank's photography. The rest of the paragraph moves from general (a description of the project of Frank's larger book, *The Americans,* and a definition of traditional photographic methods) to specific (clarification of the two images Michael is most interested in), ending ultimately with a clear articulation of Michael's rhetorical stance and thesis statement.

Conclusion. If the introduction offers the writer the opportunity to hook the audience's readers while articulating a personal stance on a subject, the conclusion provides the final opportunity to reinforce an essay's argument while making a lasting impact on readers. For this reason, although a conclusion by its nature should include some elements of summary (synthesizing the key points from the essay), it should also have a rhetorical power of its own. Let's look at how Michael concluded his essay on Frank's photographs:

> Robert Frank, in his images from *The Americans*, takes compelling pictures of a socially conflicted south to expose the growing struggle of race in 1950's America. His images spark from a new ideology of the photographer—a lack of concern for absolute photographic perfection allows him to document situations that really *mean* something. He chooses conflicting lives, black and white together on the page but unequal, his film subtly showing sympathy for the downtrodden worker and the weary traveler. Careful lines and deliberate tones show two opposing worlds where skin color can change the appearance of an entire backdrop, where stark white prison bars show us the walls we have erected within ourselves. These are not simple pictures of ordinary people. They are an artist's whisper about the elusiveness of equality, how in the war against bigotry, we are not done yet.

While offering a summary of his evidence, Michael takes care to make his conclusion as stylistically sophisticated as his introduction. Notice his careful use of word choice ("takes compelling pictures," "expose") that works in tandem with the subject of his essay; his return to the task of redefining American photography that he began in his introduction; his implicit reference to his analysis of the images themselves in the main body of his paper ("downtrodden worker and weary traveler," references to "lines" and "tones"); and, finally, the way he broadens his topic to touch on larger, ongoing issues of race relations. His conclusion leaves readers with more than a simple summary of points, prompting them to reflect on the ongoing state of race relations in America.

Consider ways to make your own conclusion a powerful part of your argument.

- Use a key quote, example, or reference that either epitomizes or summarizes your points.
- Return to an opening example or analogy, offering a slightly different, perhaps more informed perspective on it to connect introduction and conclusion as a frame for your argument.
- Use a chronological structure to move from the past to recent times, perhaps ending with a projection into the future.
- Use your conclusion to suggest broader implications that could increase the reader's sense of personal connection to the topic or its urgency.

No matter which strategy you choose, remember to maximize the persuasive potential of your conclusion as a means of reaffirming the strength of your argument with your readers.

Crafting a Position Paper

One way to experiment and put into practice these concepts—invention, arrangement, and style—is to draft a position paper on your topic. By definition, a **position paper** presents one side of an issue, allowing you the opportunity to construct a strong thesis statement and actively argue your main points. A position paper also can be an ideal medium for developing your own particular style, persona, and rhetorical stance. Angela Rastegar, for instance, experimented with persona during a project on photographic coverage of the war in Iraq. She tried out two very different ways of writing. First she composed an argument about the issue from the perspective of an unnamed academic or journalistic commentator. Then she revised the argument by writing a short paper representing an extreme position on the toppling of a Saddam Hussein statue by U.S. troops. Her first "position" offers the academic voice with an ostensibly objective perspective. Notice that there is no obvious "I" speaking, and yet an argument about the power of the media clearly emerges.

Rastegar 1

Angela Rastegar

Academic Position Paper

Imagine a chaotic world in which you cannot trust the media—newspapers, television reports, and magazines are full of lies about the world and politics. Picture trying to decipher current events or important situations without knowing whom to turn to or what to believe. Sounds far-fetched? Unfortunately, this is not far from the truth. Current newspapers are filled with subtle, clever methods used to deceive the public.

As you look at photographic images in widely respected newspaper articles, consider the techniques used to deceive the public. Concerning one incident—the April 9th destruction of Saddam Hussein's monument in Baghdad—the actual events of this day have been carefully concealed from the public. Although the media portrayed a "heroic" destruction of Saddam's symbol by American forces and mobs of Iraqi supporters, this event was essentially staged by the media.

We must use a cautious eye when viewing news stories and alert ourselves to subtle biases. The media has been called the "fourth branch of the government" because of the undeniable power it yields over the American public. No other source of information is so readily and unquestionably accepted. The government realizes this, and it often takes great measures to work with the media to create effective, captivating stories that not only portray Americans in a positive light but will also

Rastegar 2

sell papers. Examples of the media's influence are not by any means limited to this single event; however, wars provide the perfect opportunity for the media to influence the public. They open wounds in all Americans, leaving viewers vulnerable, easily influenced, and starving for more information. As a result, studying the media's influence on any war opens a vast field of controversy. In this time of crisis, we must read the news with a wary eye.

Finding this voice to offer too much of the "advertiser's stance," Angela then experimented with first person to shape her argument into an analysis of a specific photograph (see Figure 1 in her letter to the editor). She developed this position paper as an examination of the image and named her persona "Elizabeth Grant," a concerned media activist.

Angela Rastegar

Writing a Letter to the Editor as "Elizabeth Grant,"

Left-Wing Media Watchdog

I am writing in response to the astonishing display of deceit attempted by President G. W. Bush and the American government on Thursday, April 10th. President Bush's public address began with the words, "Iraqi citizens support overthrowing Saddam," which was illustrated by the enclosed photograph. It depicts an American marine tying the Iraqi flag around the neck of Saddam Hussein's 15-foot monument. Seconds later, U.S. troops connected the ropes

Rastegar 2

and cables to the statue's neck and brought it crashing to the ground.

The photograph, which contains a brightly colored red and white Iraqi flag in the center, focuses the viewer's attention on this emblem. Did the Iraqi citizens request to use this flag? We don't know, but we can see how the government attempted to appeal to those watching by having a soldier tie Iraq's own flag to the chains.

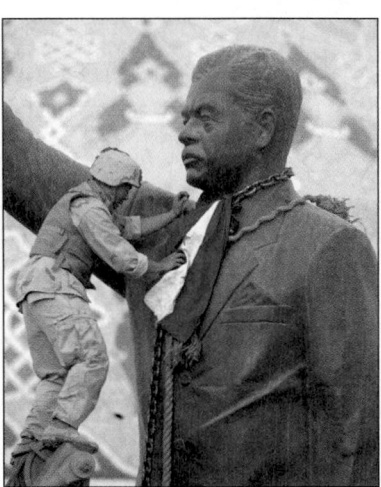

Figure 1. Laurent Rebours, Associated Press. "Scenes from Baghdad." *New York Times*. New York Times, 9 Apr. 2003. Web. 14 Apr. 2003.

The flag falsely suggests that the Iraqi people were behind the destruction of the monument and that America can work in harmony with the people of Iraq to overthrow Saddam. This message drastically distorts the truth; in fact, the soldier originally held an American flag, but his commanding officers ordered him to tie this particular flag to the chains. Thus, the government's use of logos in this photo subtly attempts to convince the public that Iraq wanted to bring down Saddam's statue—when, in reality, the citizens there had nothing to do with it.

Rastegar 3

In this photograph, the picture also appeals to the viewers' emotions by placing a rope and chains around the neck of Saddam's image. In this sense, it evokes the American hatred for Saddam and creates a clear, understandable aim. The military is able to put a noose around the neck of a symbolic Saddam, displaying the government's ability to destroy him. The government draws on these emotions from the viewers to increase patriotism. Bush applies these same tactics to his public speeches, focusing on American strength to justify our intervention.

In addition, the photo strategically includes a U.S. marine to add to the photo's visual credibility. This symbol of America— a solider in uniform—forces the viewers to place more trust in the photographer and what we see here. My greatest fear is that the average American will hear Bush speak and see this photo without realizing that their goal is to convince the world of Iraqi support for American intervention. They claim that they are fighting to "free Iraq," but in reality, our government simply ties Iraq's fate to Saddam and destroys them both.

In her first position paper, Angela writes about the power of photographs from a generalized, academic perspective, the voice of analytical assessment. But in her subsequent paper, she explores a specific point of view about media coverage of international politics. The persona of Elizabeth Grant— whose style Angela develops through careful attention to word choice, rhetorical appeals, and prose style—relies on the use of "I" and repeated use of strong language. As you can tell, the experimentation with *voice* itself was the most important product of her revisions: it allowed her both to reach into her topic and to examine differences in *style* and *rhetorical stance,* in particularly powerful ways. As she moved into the final stages of her project, she brought the power of this writing to bear on her longer researched argument; although she wrote the final paper from her own perspective, working with the pro and con points of view enabled her to construct a sharper thesis statement and a more persuasive approach to the photographs she was discussing.

Writing Multiple Sides of an Argument

Angela Rastegar's project opens up some interesting possibilities for developing your own persuasive arguments. Sometimes when we write from our own points of view, we get so locked into our individual perspectives that we fail to take into account the diverse or multiple sides of our topics. Such limited vision can weaken our persuasiveness; if we fail to consider or acknowledge alternative positions on our topics, we produce one-sided arguments that lack complexity or credibility with our readers. Recall our earlier discussion of photographs: each photograph suggests a different angle, a unique "version" of an event, and the perspective of a particular persona. When we bring these different sides to light, we find that suddenly an incident or issue that seems polarized—or "black and white"—is actually much more complex. The same holds true for the issues we confront every day as writers and rhetoricians: it is only through exploring the multiple sides of our argument that we can engage it persuasively and effectively.

Begin experimenting with inventing diverse perspectives to achieve a thorough understanding of a complex situation. Although you may be tempted to think of these various perspectives in oppositional terms—as the "pro" or "con" of an issue—such a point of view closes off the richer complexity of the issue. Try to think of arguments not in terms of right or wrong but rather as a spectrum of differing perspectives. As you turn to write your own arguments, consider how you can explore different viewpoints by trying out personas; by inventing diverse responses to your own point of view; and by exploring various writing strategies through experimentation with diction, syntax, style, image selection, arrangement of argument, and voice.

When writing arguments, you might choose to explore more than one *persona* or *rhetorical stance* to see different sides of an issue. Student Aisha Ali, for instance, developed her project on the conflict in the Middle East by creating three articles, or sides, around a single photograph (see Figure 3.13). Using the image as the foundation for each discussion, she assumed the personas of an African photojournalist, an Israeli soldier, and a Palestinian boy. Aisha's contrasting personas offered a series of riveting snapshots of the Palestinian conflict. To create this effect, she took extra care with word choice, sentence structure, and the development of her arguments. In her first side, she opens the piece by exploring the context of the Middle Eastern situation and then moves with fluid and articulate language to the central narrative: the freeing of the doves in front of an oncoming tank. Her second side adopts a different approach: using direct, informal speech, and biased language suitable to a soldier hardened by armed conflict, this persona launches immediately into the narrative itself. The last side also presents the story of the doves' release; however, as the excerpt from her work shows, the voice is clearly that of a child. Using simple sentence structures and word choices to build a narrative with an underlying pathos appeal, Aisha has brought to life the perspective of the young boy forced to free his doves in the shadow of military occupation.

Together, the variety of perspectives in Aisha's writing enabled her to avoid producing a simplistic argument about the violence in the Middle East, and instead to demonstrate its complexity. Although the photograph Aisha used in her series of articles constitutes a powerful visual argument in itself through its striking juxtaposition of fluttering doves

Student Writing
Read Aisha Ali's complete project and other student multiple sides projects.
www.pearsonhighered.com/envision/89

FIGURE 3.13. The powerful image of doves in front of a tank in the Middle East offers multiple interpretations.

(a symbol of peace) and military tanks (a symbol of war), she was able to convey the meaning of the image for diverse viewers through powerful writing. You can try this strategy of writing multiple sides of an argument in your own compositions.

Writing a Synthesis Paper

Although experimenting with writing in different styles from the perspectives of different personas, incorporating diverse strategies of arrangement for each piece, and inventing opposing arguments allow you to develop a deeper understanding of the complexity of an issue, in many academic contexts you will be asked to **synthesize** these perspectives into a single, thesis-driven text. The task then is to incorporate discussion of multiple perspectives (including positions you might find through research) in a way that reveals the complexity of the issue but ultimately advances your own, final rhetorical stance on the topic at hand.

We find an outstanding example of successfully balancing multiple perspectives with a clear, authorial thesis in Nora Ephron's article "The Boston Photographs," published in *Scribble, Scribble: Notes on the Media* (1978). This essay offers a useful model of the canons of rhetoric we've been discussing so far—invention, arrangement, and style.

Ephron offers us insight into the constant struggles that newspaper editors face in selecting photographs for publication—in this case, deciding whether or not to print the "sensationalist" images of a woman and child falling from a fire escape during a 1976 apartment fire (Figure 3.14). Ephron brings into her article at least three perspectives,

FIGURE 3.14. The *Boston Herald American* chose to print this disturbing photograph on its front page.

each embodying a unique rhetorical stance: from her own perspective to those of Stanley Forman, photographer, and Charles Seib, the *Washington Post* ombudsman (the editor who monitors the content of the paper to ensure that it is not offensive to readers). She also represents in miniature other points of view through a series of brief quotations from letters to the editor that appeared shortly after the publication of the controversial photographs. The writers of these letters each get a turn to argue their unique points from the basis of their own rhetorical stance. However, the argument that ultimately is most persuasive is Ephron's own; in this way, she *synthesizes* the arguments to arrive at her own, persuasive conclusion.

THE BOSTON PHOTOGRAPHS
Nora Ephron

"I made all kinds of pictures because I thought it would be a good rescue shot over the ladder . . . never dreamed it would be anything else. . . . I kept having to move around because of the light set. The sky was bright and they were in deep shadow. I was making pictures with a motor drive and he, the firefighter, was reaching up and, I don't know, everything started falling. I followed the girl down taking pictures. . . . I made three or four frames. I realized what was going on and I completely turned around, because I didn't want to see her hit."

You probably saw the photographs. In most newspapers, there were three of them. The first showed some people on a fire escape—a fireman, a woman, and a child. The fireman had a nice strong jaw and looked very brave. The woman was holding the child. Smoke was pouring from the building behind them. A rescue ladder was approaching, just a few feet away, and the fireman had one arm around the woman and one arm reaching out toward the ladder. The second picture showed the fire escape slipping off the building. The child had fallen on the escape and seemed about to slide off the edge. The woman was grasping desperately at the legs of the fireman, who had managed to grab the ladder. The

Ephron begins with the voice of the photographer, Stanley Forman, using a direct quote to present his perspective.

Her next two paragraphs provide background for Forman's recollections.

Notice Ephron's use of the second person to establish a rapport with her reader built on a sense of shared cultural experience.

Although this section is ostensibly description, look closely at her stylistic choices—especially word choice—to see the way she is setting up her stance on the topic.

third picture showed the woman and child in midair, falling to the ground. Their arms and legs were outstretched, horribly distended. A potted plant was falling too. The caption said that the woman, Diana Bryant, nineteen, died in the fall. The child landed on the woman's body and lived.

The pictures were taken by Stanley Forman, thirty, of the *Boston Herald American*. He used a motor-driven Nikon F set at 1/250, f5.6-S. Because of the motor, the camera can click off three frames a second. More than four hundred newspapers in the United States alone carried the photographs: The tear sheets from overseas are still coming in. The *New York Times* ran them on the first page of its second section; a paper in south Georgia gave them nineteen columns; the *Chicago Tribune,* the *Washington Post* and the *Washington Star* filled almost half their front pages, the *Star* under a somewhat redundant headline that read: Sensational Photos of Rescue Attempt That Failed.

The photographs are indeed sensational. They are pictures of death in action, of that split second when luck runs out, and it is impossible to look at them without feeling their extraordinary impact and remembering, in an almost subconscious way, the morbid fantasy of falling, falling off a building, falling to one's death. Beyond that, the pictures are classics, old-fashioned but perfect examples of photojournalism at its most spectacular. They're throwbacks, really, fire pictures, 1930s tabloid shots; at the same time they're technically superb and thoroughly modern—the sequence could not have been taken at all until the development of the motor-driven camera some sixteen years ago.

Most newspaper editors anticipate some reader reaction to photographs like Forman's; even so, the response around the country was enormous, and almost all of it was negative. I have read hundreds of the letters that were printed in letters-to-the-editor sections, and they repeat the same points."Invading the privacy of death." "Cheap sensationalism." "I thought I was reading the *National Enquirer*." "Assigning the agony of a human being in terror of imminent death to the status of a side-show act." "A tawdry way to sell newspapers." The *Seattle Times* received sixty

She establishes her ethos in the beginning of this paragraph by demonstrating her knowledge of photography.

While here Ephron finally gives her own assessment of the images (that they "are indeed sensational"), she refrains from a definitive thesis statement at this point.

Word choice once again hints at her argument: Notice how the term "sensational" (with slight negative connotations) has become "spectacular," which suggests awe and appreciation.

She focuses here on audience reaction to the photographs. The accumulation of quotations increases her ethos as a researcher and also gives weight to their outrage, even though it is a reaction that Ephron does not share.

letters and calls; its managing editor even got a couple of them at home. A reader wrote the *Philadelphia Inquirer*: "*Jaws* and *Towering Inferno* are playing downtown; don't take business away from people who pay good money to advertise in your own paper." Another reader wrote the *Chicago Sun-Times*: "I shall try to hide my disappointment that Miss Bryant wasn't wearing a skirt when she fell to her death. You could have had some award-winning photographs of her underpants as her skirt billowed over her head, you voyeurs." Several newspaper editors wrote columns defending the pictures: Thomas Keevil of the *Costa Mesa* (California) *Daily Pilot* printed a ballot for readers to vote on whether they would have printed the pictures; Marshall L. Stone of Maine's *Bangor Daily News,* which refused to print the famous assassination picture of the Vietcong prisoner in Saigon, claimed that the Boston pictures showed the dangers of fire escapes and raised questions about slumlords. (The burning building was a five-story brick apartment house on Marlborough Street in the Back Bay section of Boston.)

For the last five years, the *Washington Post* has employed various journalists as ombudsmen, whose job is to monitor the paper on behalf of the public. The *Post*'s current ombudsman is Charles Seib, former managing editor of the *Washington Star;* the day the Boston photographs appeared, the paper received over seventy calls in protest. As Seib later wrote in a column about the pictures, it was "the largest reaction to a published item that I have experienced in eight months as the *Post*'s ombudsman. . . .

"In the *Post*'s newsroom, on the other hand, I found no doubts, no second thoughts . . . the question was not whether they should be printed but how they should be displayed. When I talked to editors . . . they used words like 'interesting' and 'riveting' and 'gripping' to describe them. The pictures told of something about life in the ghetto, they said (although the neighborhood where the tragedy occurred is not a ghetto, I am told). They dramatized the need to check on the safety of fire escapes. They dramatically conveyed something that had happened, and that is the business we're in. They were news. . . .

Consider the order in which she arranges the quotes: the last two are the most colorful and memorable.

Her final parenthetical aside slightly undermines the power of this perspective by pointing out an inaccuracy.

At this point in the essay, she features the *Washington Post* editor who decided to run the photographs in that newspaper. The fact that she follows the reader-response with Seib's reaction is clearly strategic because her own stance most closely resembles his.

"Was publication of that [third] picture a bow to the same taste for the morbidly sensational that makes gold mines of disaster movies? Most papers will not print the picture of a dead body except in the most unusual circumstances. Does the fact that the final picture was taken a millisecond before the young woman died make a difference? Most papers will not print a picture of a bare female breast. Is that a more inappropriate subject for display than the picture of a human being's last agonized instant of life?" Seib offered no answers to the questions he raised, but he went on to say that although as an editor he would probably have run the pictures, as a reader he was revolted by them.

In conclusion, Seib wrote: "Any editor who decided to print those pictures without giving at least a moment's thought to what purpose they served and what their effect was likely to be on the reader should ask another question: Have I become so preoccupied with manufacturing a product according to professional traditions and standards that I have forgotten about the consumer, the reader?"

It should be clear that the phone calls and letters and Seib's own reaction were occasioned by one factor alone: the death of the woman. Obviously, had she survived the fall, no one would have protested; the pictures would have had a completely different impact. Equally obviously, had the child died as well—or instead—Seib would undoubtedly have received ten times the phone calls he did. In each case, the pictures would have been exactly the same—only the captions, and thus the responses, would have been different.

But the questions Seib raises are worth discussing—though not exactly for the reasons he mentions. For it may be that the real lesson of the Boston photographs is not the danger that editors will be forgetful of reader reaction, but that they will continue to censor pictures of death precisely because of that reaction. The protests Seib fielded were really a variation on an old theme—and we saw plenty of it during the Nixon-Agnew years—the "Why doesn't the press print the good news?" argument. In this case, of course, the objections were all dressed up and cleverly disguised

---

She gently qualifies Seib's argument, asserting the side or perspective while at the same time suggesting her own interpretation of the issue.

It is only now, after showcasing these many voices on the issue, that Ephron moves to her own argument.

By using the phrases "all dressed up and cleverly disguised," Ephron exposes her own impatience with some of the reactions elicited by the publication of the photos.

as righteous indignation about the privacy of death. This is a form of puritanism that is often justifiable; just as often it is merely puritanical.

Her clever play on words (puritanism/ puritanical) further clarifies her stance.

Seib takes it for granted that the widespread though fairly recent newspaper policy against printing pictures of dead bodies is a sound one; I don't know that it makes any sense at all. I recognize that printing pictures of corpses raises all sorts of problems about taste and titillation and sensationalism; the fact is, however, that people die. Death happens to be one of life's main events. And it is irresponsible—and more than that, inaccurate—for newspapers to fail to show it, or to show it only when an astonishing set of photos comes in over the Associated Press wire. Most papers covering fatal automobile accidents will print pictures of mangled cars. But the significance of fatal automobile accidents is not that a great deal of steel is twisted but that people die. Why not show it? That's what accidents are about. Throughout the Vietnam war, editors were reluctant to print atrocity pictures. Why *not* print them? That's what that was about. Murder victims are almost never photographed; they are granted their privacy. But their relatives are relentlessly pictured on their way in and out of hospitals and morgues and funerals.

Look at her use of rhetorical questions to make her point and to throw the issue back at her readers.

I'm not advocating that newspapers print these things in order to teach their readers a lesson. The *Post* editors justified their printing of the Boston pictures with several arguments in that direction; every one of them is irrelevant. The pictures don't show anything about slum life; the incident could have happened anywhere, and it did. It is extremely unlikely that anyone who saw them rushed out and had his fire escape strengthened. And the pictures were not news—at least they were not national news. It is not news in Washington, or New York, or Los Angeles that a woman was killed in a Boston fire. The only newsworthy thing about the pictures is that they were taken. They deserve to be printed because they are great pictures, breathtaking pictures of something that happened. That they disturb readers is exactly as it should be: that's why photojournalism is often more powerful than written journalism.

The use of the first person here marks a moment where Ephron begins to clearly assert her own opinion, rather than reporting on the perspectives of others.

In her conclusion, Ephron ends with a concession to those who were offended and then a strong articulation of her position on the topic that links to larger issues in photojournalism.

How does Ephron present her own argument despite allowing so many voices in her piece? How does she achieve the synthesis of multiple sides while developing her own argument through invention, arrangement, and style?

Let's first determine her main idea, the *invention* in her thesis statement. Where is her thesis? What new perspective on the issue of representing death in photographs has she invented in this essay in order to share it with her reading audience? Look at the final paragraph for the answer.

Now let's analyze the *arrangement* of her essay. As we read through the essay, we see that Ephron strategically allows the multiple viewpoints on the issue to play themselves out in the early part of her article, providing the reader with a firm grounding in the debate, before concluding with her own very strong point of view. By arranging her essay in this way, Ephron focuses the audience reaction to the images and to the editor's decisions to run them through the lens of her own argument. However, Ephron's strategy is just one of many patterns of arrangement that take into account incorporating counterarguments while producing a persuasive text. You have multiple options available to you when dealing with opposing viewpoints. You can follow the classical method of arrangement (see table) or select a modified version, depending on your purpose.

AT A GLANCE

The Arrangement of Ephron's Argument

1. Quotation from photographer (1 paragraph)
2. Background (2 paragraphs)
3. Ephron's general assessment of images (1 paragraph)
4. Reader reaction to photos (1 paragraph)
5. Editor's point of view (4 paragraphs)
6. Qualification of Seib's point of view (1 paragraph)
7. Her own argument (final 3 paragraphs)

Strategies of Arrangement

A Classical Speech or Oration

1. Introduction
2. Statement of facts
3. Division
4. Proof
5. Refutation
6. Conclusion

Option A

Use when you want to ground the reader in your argument before bringing up opposing perspectives.

1. Introduction, identification of rhetorical stance
2. Thesis
3. Statement of background, definition, or context
4. Evidence and development of argument
5. Opposing opinion, concession, qualification, refutation
6. Conclusion

Option B

Establish opposing opinion up front so that the entire piece functions as an extended rebuttal or refutation of that line of argument.

1. Introduction and opposing viewpoint
2. Thesis and identification of rhetorical stance
3. Evidence and development of argument
4. Conclusion

Option C

Treat diverse viewpoints as appropriate during the development of your argument and presentation of your evidence.

1. Introduction, identification of rhetorical stance
2. Thesis
3. Statement of background, definition, or context
4. Evidence, opposing opinion, concession, qualification, refutation
5. Conclusion

Attending to Arrangement in Argument

The models of arrangement in the table are not designed to be rigid parameters. Instead, they should suggest possibilities and potentially productive strategies of arrangement; in your own writing, you will have to select the most productive way to lay out your topic and the diverse opinions that surround it.

You'll need to consider first the strength of the other perspectives on the issue. Do they corroborate your argument? Then you could include them as supporting evidence. Do they offer points of view that you can disprove? Then you might present the opinion and provide a *rebuttal,* or refutation of the points, demonstrating why they are not valid. Do they offer points of view that you can't

AT A GLANCE

Dealing with Multiple Perspectives in Your Arguments

When incorporating other viewpoints into your writing, you can use them in one of three ways:

- *Evidence:* you can use the diverse viewpoints to support your own thesis statement.
- *Concession/Qualification:* you can admit that the person has a strong point but then explain why it doesn't diminish the persuasiveness or validity of your argument.
- *Rebuttal:* you can present an opposing opinion, fairly and respectfully, and then demonstrate why it is not a valid argument in this case.

disprove? Then you might *concede* the validity of their argument but go on to *qualify* their points by showing why your own argument is nonetheless persuasive. The key is to treat these other voices with respect; always represent their points of view fairly and without bias, even if you disagree with them. In a sense, when you are dealing with multiple perspectives, some of which may run counter to your own argument, you face a question of ethics quite similar to that the editors faced with the Boston photographs: How do you present possibly volatile material in a way that is both fair and yet advances your persuasive purpose?

We can see how Ephron herself answered that question by assessing her use of the canon of *style,* specifically in the persona and rhetorical stance she developed in her essay. As a careful analysis of her essay demonstrates, Ephron presents the background on the issue as if through an objective lens; however, her word choice, her selections of quotations, and even the sentence structures themselves collaborate to produce a rhetorical stance that seems all the more persuasive for its earlier objectivity when she moves to the strong statement at the end of her essay. For this reason, when her voice becomes more clearly argumentative in her conclusion, the reader does not automatically resist her argument. Instead, because of Ephron's stylistic choices, readers are more likely to be persuaded by her thesis, "That they [the photographs] disturb readers is exactly as it should be," and to welcome Ephron's fundamental redefinition of the purpose and characteristics of good photojournalism.

The Writer's Process

In this chapter, you've learned to harness the canons of rhetoric—invention, arrangement, and style—to compose effective arguments of your own. You've developed strategies for crafting titles, introductions, and conclusions; you've explored the importance of persona and rhetorical stance in argument. You've experimented with developing a position paper, crafting multiple sides of an argument, and then integrating diverse perspectives through a synthesis paper. Now it's time to implement these skills. Practice inventing a position on an issue, arranging claims and evidence for your argument (including working with images as evidence for your points), developing a rhetorical stance, and working on persona through style by crafting your prose with care. You might, for instance, try to rewrite the Nora Ephron piece from the perspective of one of the personas that she mentions in her text: the editor, the photographer, or a disgruntled reader. As you do, incorporate the other perspectives into your argument, experimenting with arrangement and style to produce a piece that synthesizes diverse viewpoints while still making its own strong argument.

PREWRITING CHECKLIST
Analyzing Photographs

❏ **Content:** What, literally, does the photograph depict? Who or what is the subject of the photo? What is the setting?

❏ **Cultural context:** What is the historical context of the photograph? If it "documents" a particular event, person, or historical moment, how prominently does this photograph factor into our understanding of this event, person, or place? (For instance, is it the only known photograph of an event, or is it one of a series of pictures taken of the same subject?)

❏ **Material context:** Where was this photograph reproduced or displayed (an art gallery, the cover of a magazine, the front page of a newspaper)? If it was published elsewhere originally, does this source credit the original?

❏ **Argument:** What, thematically, does the photograph depict? What is its message to the audience? For instance, while the photo might show a group of people standing together, its argument might be about love, family unity across generations, or a promise for the future.

❏ **Photographer:** Who took this photograph? What was the person's purpose?

❏ **Audience:** Who was the photographer's intended audience?

❏ **Purpose:** What is the photograph's purpose? Is it intended to be overtly argumentative and to move its audience to action? Or is the argument more subtle, even to the point of seeming objective or representational?

(continued)

❏ **Rhetorical stance:** How does the composition of the photo convey a sense of the rhetorical stance or point of view of the photographer? Pay attention to issues of focus (what is "in focus"? This may differ from the ostensible "focus" of the picture); cropping (what is "in" the picture, and what has been left "out"?); color (is the picture in black and white? color? sepia?); setting (what backdrop has the photographer chosen?); and perspective (are we looking down? up?).

❏ **Representation versus reality:** Does this photograph aspire to represent reality, or is it an overtly abstract piece? Is there any indication of photo manipulation, editing, or other alteration? If so, what rhetorical purpose does this serve—what argument does this alteration make?

❏ **Word and image:** Does the photo have a caption? Does the image accompany an article, essay, or other lengthy text? How does the image function in dialogue with this verbal text? Does it offer visual evidence? Does it argue an independent point? Does it provide a counterargument to the print text?

PREWRITING WITH THE *ENVISION* WEBSITE

1. In order to get started with your writing project, download two to three images from MSNBC.com's "Week in Pictures," accessible through the Chapter 3 resources on the *Envision* Website. As a group, select photos that convey different sides of a situation or event. Come up with three personas—the voice of the person in the photo, the voice of the photographer, and the voice of an observer. Now develop a thesis for each side and write a brief description of your imagined persona. Allow each person in the group to contribute a new perspective. Write up each of these sides; format them into a feature article or cover story for a newspaper or magazine, and, when you are done, present your work as a group to the class. www.pearsonhighered.com/envision/100

2. When we discuss arrangement in reference to photographs like Dorothea Lange's and Jane Gottesman's, we usually refer to the way the photographer stages a shot or orders a series of images. However, in the age of digital photo editing, the canon of arrangement is often used in producing striking arguments in the form of photo illustrations, some of which are even arranged to produce a visual joke, such as the image of a gigantic, great white shark rising from the water to attack helicopter in the San Francisco Bay, which was virally circulated around the internet. To start pre-writing about visual arguments, break into small groups and visit the following sites, linked through the *Envision* Website.

❏ The Hoax Photo Gallery: a collection of doctored photographs from the online Museum of Hoaxes.

❏ Frank Van Riper's "Manipulating Truth, Losing Credibility": an article from the *Washington Post* about the Brian Walski photo scandal.

❏ Floyd's Website: before-and-after images that demonstrate the dramatic effects of photo editing.

❏ "The Case of the Missing Limb": an article from *The Digital Journalist* about how newspaper editors altered a photograph to make it less offensive to readers.

Look through these sites and consider how the canon of arrangement functions in these cases in relation to the ethics of argument. Which altered images are the most convincing? the most disturbing? Why? How do you distinguish between creativity and manipulation? Are there times when photographic manipulation is justified? How can we apply these observations about ethics and arrangement to our consideration of written texts? Use the pre-writing checklist below to help focus your analysis of the images.

www.pearsonhighered.com/envision/101

WRITING PROJECTS

1. **Written Argument:** Write an argument about an issue that moves you; base your argument on your analysis of a powerful image; and include your interpretation of the image as part of your writing. Invent a strong thesis, pick your persona, decide on your strategy of arrangement, and write with particular attention to style. You might choose to write a popular article, such as a letter to the editor of the campus newspaper, a Weblog entry, or a newspaper column such as *Newsweek*'s "My Turn."

2. **Three Position Papers:** Write three position papers or articles, with each one commenting on the previous one so that the project forms a coherent whole. Give each persona a name, an occupation, a geographic location, and a strong perspective to argue in words. Each position can offer a new point of view on one image or can develop complexity about an issue by bringing in a new image as visual evidence. You might choose to format your project as a feature article for a specific magazine or reading audience. To do so, first conduct a rhetorical analysis on the features of

a chosen publication (*The New Yorker, The Economist,* a national newspaper, or a campus journal) and then format your three arguments as part of that publication. Include a cover page with an introduction by the editor and a closing assessment page, perhaps by a staff writer. You could also format your project as a Website or multimedia text (a flash montage or photo essay).

3. **Multiple Sides Collaboration:** Collaborate on composing multiple position papers by assigning the writing of each argument to a different member of your group. You might, for instance, write about the conflict between your college campus and the surrounding town: have someone interview locals, the sheriff, administrators, and students. Provide a series of arguments from each perspective and images to function as argumentative texts for each side. Be sure to include concession and refutation. Collaborate in the writing of the introduction and the conclusion as well as in the design, arrangement, and style of the project as a whole. The last writer in the group should compose a synthesis paper, incorporating the positions of everyone and providing a closing argument.

 Visit www.pearsonhighered.com/envision for expanded assignment guidelines and student projects. Visit www.mycomplab.com for additional general writing and research resources.

Part II

RESEARCH ARGUMENTS

CHAPTER 4
Planning and Proposing Research Arguments

CHAPTER 5
Finding and Evaluating Research Sources

CHAPTER 6
Organizing and Writing Research Arguments

CHAPTER 7
Avoiding Plagiarism and Documenting Sources

Research is never completed. . . . Around the corner lurks another possibility of interview, another book to read, a courthouse to explore, a document to verify.

—Catherine Drinker Bowen

CHAPTER 4

Planning and Proposing Research Arguments

Chapter Preview Questions

- How do I generate a productive topic and research questions?
- What prewriting techniques can I use to narrow my topic?
- What are best research practices?
- How do I keep a research log?
- What are the steps in a strong research plan?
- How do I write a formal research proposal?

What's going on in the poster shown in Figure 4.1? Why the juxtaposition of a menacing Soviet officer with a contemporary college student listening to downloaded music? Why the deep red background color and the placement of characters with the officer looking over the student's shoulder? Why is *Communism* so large and visually echoed by the hammer and sickle? At some point, you begin to realize that this poster is intended as a parody and that it pokes fun at recent publicity campaigns by the Recording Industry Association of America (RIAA) to combat file sharing and unauthorized music downloading. These observations will help you begin to make an argument about the poster, but in order to back up or substantiate your claims about its meaning, you would need to do some research. That is, you would need to place the rhetorical elements of the poster in their historical and critical contexts, including the anti-Communist propaganda posters of the cold war 1950s and the current debate about music downloading and copyright law. As you try to grasp the significance of representing the RIAA's position through a parody of anti-Soviet

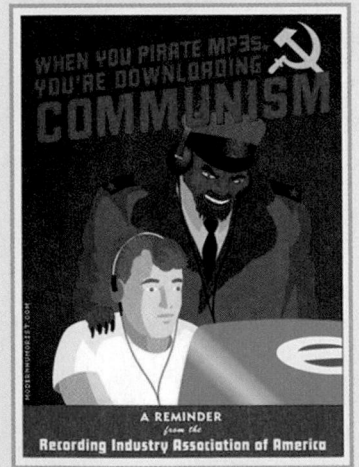

FIGURE 4.1. How does this parody propaganda poster use visual elements to undermine the RIAA's stance on file sharing?

propaganda, you would need to investigate the political and legal controversies surrounding file sharing.

Research can be conducted in any number of ways, including interviews, fieldwork, and the exploration of sources both online and in print. But the starting point of any research effort is to determine what questions to ask, what inquiries to pursue. In this chapter, you will learn the first steps of becoming an active participant in a research community and begin to develop the skills for defining a research question and creating an effective research plan and a solid research proposal.

Asking Research Questions

The discussion in this chapter focuses on a specific subset of persuasive images—propaganda posters—because such texts make very powerful public statements and because, for many of us, to understand the motivations behind a propaganda poster, we have to perform a certain amount of research. Often this research involves pursuing answers to questions we have formulated about the poster. In fact, most research begins with the act of asking questions.

One way you can get started on your research is to pick a text that moves you and start brainstorming questions about it. Let's say that you came across the 1917 American enlistment poster shown in Figure 4.2 in an exhibit on campus or as part of a class discussion about World War I posters. Approaching it for the first time, you and your peers probably will start to analyze the visual rhetoric, much as we did in the earlier chapters of *Envision*.

What are your eyes drawn to first, the words or the image? Maybe you look first at the simian figure in the middle, roaring

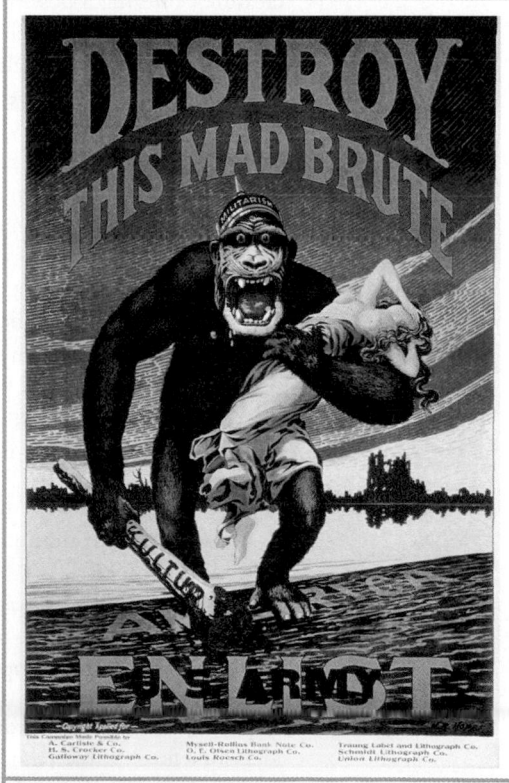

FIGURE 4.2. This World War I propaganda poster offers a wealth of detail for historical analysis.

menacingly at you, and then at the swooning, seminaked woman in his arms. In contrast, maybe the person next to you is attracted first to the bold yellow text at the top and then to the bottom, where the words "U.S. Army" in black are superimposed on the imperative "Enlist." In synthesizing various responses to the text, you most likely would find yourself with more questions than answers—a good thing, for those questions can be the beginning of your research inquiry.

You might ask, Is that gorilla King Kong? Your research would allow you to confidently answer, No, since you would discover that the poster was made decades before the movie was released. That same research might produce several books that discuss the wartime practice of casting enemies as subhuman creatures, offering a possible explanation for why the enemy nation is portrayed as a menacing gorilla in this poster. Adding to that your observation that "*culture*" is spelled "Kultur" (on the club the gorilla is holding), you probably would realize that the enemy symbolized here is in fact Germany.

Then you might ask: What is the significance of that bloody club? Why is the woman unconscious and partly naked? More research might provide insight on how bestiality emerged as a wartime theme in World War I enlistment posters. If a nation's women were threatened with potential attack by such "monsters," these posters implied, then the men would surely step up to save and protect their wives, daughters, sisters, and mothers.

By asking questions about your text, you can move beyond an initial response and into the realm of intellectual discovery. In fact, your first questions about a text will lead you to ask more pointed questions about the context, political environment, key players, and social trends informing your text. For the propaganda poster in Figure 4.2, such questions might include:

- What conflict was America involved in during 1917?
- What was the meaning of the word on the gorilla's hat, "Militarism," at that time?
- How would an appeal to enlist factor into that historical situation?
- Who is the audience for this poster, and how is this poster part of a series of wartime propaganda images?

If you were to work through these questions, you might begin to develop ideas for a feasible research topic—one that could yield an interesting paper on war propaganda and the relationship between America and Germany in 1917.

As you investigate your research topic, your questions will likely become more specific:

- Do other posters of the same historical period use similar imagery and rhetorical strategies?
- How do the techniques used in early twentieth-century posters differ from those used during World War II?
- How are the rhetorical strategies used in this poster similar to or different from enlistment posters you might encounter today?
- In what ways have enlistment posters changed over time?

In all cases, what these questions lead to is a focused *research topic* and, ultimately, a written project that draws on and contributes to the arguments that others have made about such texts. Generating a range of interesting and productive questions is the first step in any research project; the process of inquiry itself helps you to define a project and make it your own.

Constructing a Research Log

From the very beginning of your research process—as you move from asking questions about a text to identifying a productive topic, to gathering information and taking notes— keep track of your ideas in a research log. This log will help you organize your ideas, collect your materials, chart your progress, and assemble the different pieces of your research.

Your research log can take many forms, from a handwritten journal, to a series of word processing documents, a personal Weblog, or a collection of bookmarked pages from the Web. It can contain primarily written text, or it can include images, video, or audio files as well. The key lies not in what your research log looks like, but in the way you use it to help you develop an interesting and provocative research project that keeps careful track of the sources you encounter along the way.

AT A GLANCE

Constructing a Research Log

To start your research log, include a variety of entries related to the initial stages of the research process:

- Write freely on possible topic ideas.
- Insert and annotate clippings from newspaper or magazine sources that offer interesting potential topics.
- Paste in and respond to provocative images related to potential topics.
- Write a reaction to ideas brought up during class discussion.
- Insert and annotate printouts from emails or other collaborative work on research ideas.
- Track preliminary searches on the Internet and in your library catalog.
- Develop your research plan.
- Vent anxieties over your project.

AT A GLANCE

Screening Questions for Topics

1. *Am I interested in the topic?* We write best about ideas, events, and issues that touch us somehow—through curiosity, passion, or intellectual interest.

2. *Can I argue a position on this topic?* At this stage, you may not have developed a stand on the issue, but you should see promise for advancing a new perspective on the topic.

3. *Will I be able to find enough research material on this topic?* Brainstorm some possible sources you might use to write this paper.

4. *Does this sort of research appeal to me?* Since you will be working with this topic for an extended period of time, it is best to have a genuine interest in it and in the type of research that it will require (archival work or fieldwork).

Generating Topics and Research Questions

If you think back to our discussion of *invention* in Chapter 3, you'll understand that one of the most crucial aspects of starting a research project is selecting a viable and engaging topic. The word *topic*, in fact, comes from the ancient Greek word *topos*, translated literally as "place." The earliest students of rhetoric used the physical space of the papyrus page—given to them by their teachers—to locate their topics for writing. Similarly, your teacher may suggest certain guidelines or parameters for you to follow when it comes to your topic; for instance, you may be given a specific topic (such as representations of race in Dr. Seuss cartoons) or you may be limited to a theme (the rhetoric of political advertisements on television, radio, and the Internet).

In some cases, you may not have any restrictions at all. But regardless of the degree to which your topic has been mapped out for you, you still can—and should—make it your own. You do this partly by generating your own **research questions**, a set of questions that will guide your work and lead you to your final argument. You can generate these questions by responding to the rhetorical situation provided by your assignment and by considering what interests *you* most about the topic. Even if your whole class is writing on the same topic, each person will present a different argument or approach to the issue. Some will use a different stance or persona, some will rely on different sources, some will use different rhetorical appeals, and all will argue different positions about the topic. The way you make a research project your own is by developing powerful research questions.

To see how this works, let's look at one student's project on propaganda posters to see how he moved from a series of images to a more fully developed research topic. When asked to choose a topic for a research paper, student Tommy Tsai found he was interested in propaganda posters from

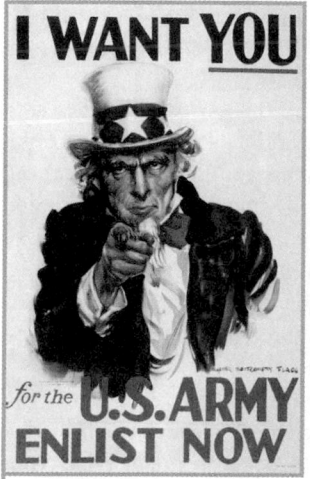

FIGURE 4.3. This Uncle Sam poster from 1917 was reissued for World War II.

FIGURE 4.4. Anti-Nazi propaganda relied on religiously charged rhetoric.

FIGURE 4.5. American war efforts employed extreme visual messages to galvanize support.

World War II. Looking at a selection of images (see Figures 4.3 through 4.5), Tommy started by asking some questions, such as the ones that follow:

- Who is depicted in these posters? Are these depictions positive or negative?
- What is the purpose of each poster?
- What strategies are these posters using to persuade their audiences?
- How do these posters reveal cultural prejudices?

Through the process of asking such questions, Tommy was able to identify his preliminary topic as "the rhetoric of World War II propaganda." He wrote in one research log entry that he wanted to analyze these posters in their historical contexts: "In particular, I plan to focus on the propaganda posters that appeared in the three most active countries in that time period: the United States, Germany, and Japan. My research paper will report my findings from the comparison of the different rhetorical strategies employed by the three nations." By generating a set of preliminary research questions, he was able

Student Writing

See Tommy Tsai's research proposal and completed research paper.
www.pearsonhighered.com/envision/109

to focus more clearly on the dialogue between those posters and his interest in them. In this way, he was able to turn an overly broad initial topic into one that was more specific and workable.

As you consider your own possible research topics, keep this key principle in mind: successful topics need to interest you, inspire you, or even anger you. Even with assigned topics, you should be able to find some aspect of the assignment that speaks to you. In general, there needs to be a *connection* between you and your topic to motivate you to follow through and transform it into a successful argument.

In addition, while selecting your topic, you might consider the type of research you'll need to do to pursue it; in fact, you might select your topic based mostly on the sorts of research it allows you to do. For instance, a student writing on propaganda of the Prohibition era will work extensively with paper sources, which might involve archival work with original letters, posters, or government documents from that time period. A student writing on visual advertising for ethnic-theme dorms on campus will be more likely to complement paper sources with interviews with the university housing staff, student surveys, and first-person observations. A student writing on sexualized rhetoric in student campaign materials might take a poll, gather concrete examples, and research the newspaper's written coverage of past and present elections. Think broadly and creatively about what kinds of research you might use and what types of research (archival work versus fieldwork involving interviews and survey taking) appeals most to you. A final important consideration is whether you can actually get your hands on the source material you need to construct a persuasive argument.

AT A GLANCE

Looking for the "Perfect" Topic

1. **Look inward.** What issues, events, or ideas interest you? Are there any hot-button topics you find yourself drawn to again and again? What topic is compelling enough that you would watch a news program, television special, film, or relevant lecture on it?

2. **Look outward.** What are the central issues of student life on campus? Do you walk by a technology-enhanced classroom and see the students busy writing on laptops or using plasma screens? Topic: technology and education. Do you see a fraternity's poster about a "dry" party? Topic: alcohol on campus. Do you see workers outside the food service building on strike? Topic: labor relations at the college.

3. **Use creative visualization.** Imagine that you are chatting casually with a friend when you overhear someone talking. Suddenly, you feel so interested—or so angry—that you go over and participate in the conversation. What would move you so strongly?

4. **Use the materials of the moment.** Perhaps the *topos* might be closer to the classical Greek model; although not a roll of papyrus, your class reading list or a single issue of a newspaper can house many topics. Scan the front page and opinion section of your school or community newspaper to see what issues people are talking about. Look at the pictures as well. What is gripping the community at large?

Bringing Your Topic into Focus

Once you have settled on a topic and generated some research questions, the next step in the research project involves exploring your knowledge—and the limitations of your knowledge—about it. A productive way to do this is through **prewriting**. Defined literally, prewriting is writing that precedes the official drafting of the paper, but, practically speaking, it can take many forms. Lists, scribbled notes, informal outlines, drawings—all different types of prewriting serve the same goal: to help you focus and narrow your topic.

Brainstorming Topics Visually

The practice of **graphic brainstorming** provides writers with a great way to develop topics. This technique transforms traditional **brainstorming**—jotting down a series of related words and phrases on a topic—into a more visible process. Also called *webbing*, *clustering*, or *mapping*, the goal of *graphic brainstorming* is to help you develop your topic by exploring relationships among ideas. You can brainstorm by hand or on a computer; in either mode, begin by writing a topic in a circle (or square or rectangle, if you prefer). Figure 4.6 shows the first step you might take in brainstorming for a paper generated from various World War I posters.

Next, brainstorm ideas and questions about that topic, and then arrange them in groups around your main circle to indicate the relationships among them. As you answer each question and pose more developed ones in response, you begin to bring your topic into focus. You'll notice that Figure 4.7 shows how we might start to do this by writing questions that differentiate between

FIGURE 4.6.

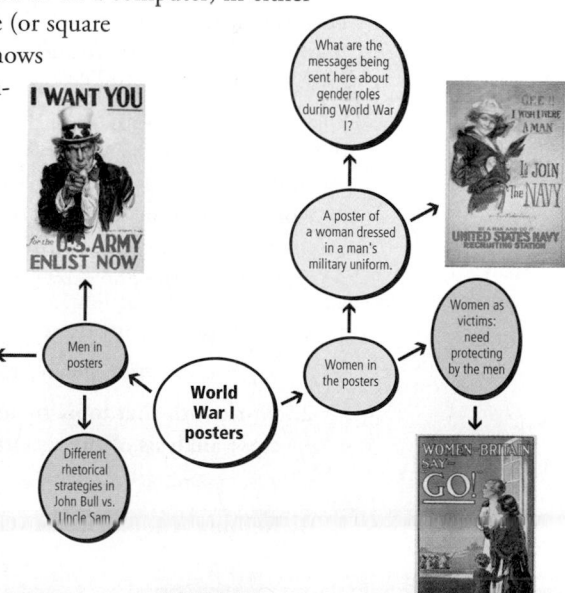

FIGURE 4.7.

various posters and by grouping them by gender issues. In addition, in our brainstorm, we use various types of notations—including words, phrases, and questions—and insert lines and arrows to indicate the relationship between the concepts. We even use images and color to further emphasize these associations. These techniques help us develop the argument and eventually can lead to a more narrowed topic and perhaps even a preliminary thesis.

As we continue to brainstorm—whether for an hour or over several sessions—it becomes clear why some people call this tech-nique **webbing**. As Figure 4.8 shows, our graphic turns into a web of ideas. By using this technique, we have done more than simply develop our topic: we have made it visually apparent that our topic is too broad for a standard research paper assignment. Our web now offers enough ideas for an entire book on the subject. But our diagram also provides us with clues about the direction in which to take our project. We can pick a *subsection* of ideas to focus on in our writing. When you try this technique, pick the subsection that interests *you* most.

Narrowing Your Topic

Let's zoom in on one part of our diagram—the part, color-coded yellow, that asks key questions about representations of women in military posters. Working with this part of the web, we could write a focused paper that examines the implications of the way women are depicted in these texts. We could write about how cross-dressing is used as a deliberate appeal to the audience, or about how military posters evoke the image of wife and mother to mobilize troops. However, to effectively narrow our topic, we should continue to sharpen our questions about these images, such as the one shown in Figure 4.9.

1. **Write down your topic.**

   Topic formulation: gender roles in World War I.

2. **Work with that topic by asking a pointed question based on close analysis of the text at hand.**

   First question: Is there a sexual undertone to the posters?

3. **Refine the topic by answering that question.**

   Topic narrowing: Yes, in one of the posters, the woman is standing in a provocative pose, looking at the audience in a sexual manner, but

FIGURE 4.8.

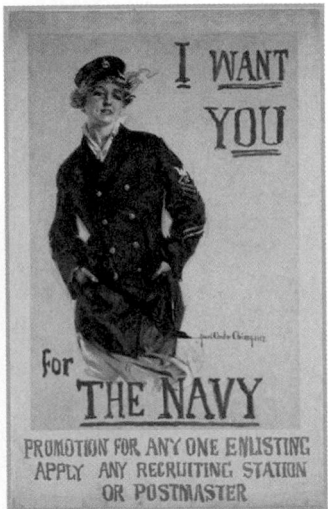

FIGURE 4.9. This 1917 U.S. poster uses a woman in uniform to present its message to enlist.

in another, the women seem more identified with family (mother, daughter) than with sexuality.

4. **Revise the narrowed topic to be more specific.**

   Revised topic formulation: the different constructions of femininity in World War I propaganda posters.

5. **Identify significant aspects of that topic to explore.**

   Second question: How so? In what way? What is the significance?

6. **Use the answers to these questions to focus the topic.**

   Final topic focus: the use of the Madonna-whore stereotype as a persuasive strategy in World War I recruitment posters.

In working with the webbing process and then asking key questions in this way, we have just completed one of the most important steps in developing a viable research topic: **narrowing** a large subject to a more manageable one. By asking such questions—and we could come up with many others along different lines of inquiry (such as race, sexuality, international representations, and nationalism)—we begin to develop a *focused* topic that will offer us the opportunity for close analysis, rigorous research, and a sharp argumentative stance. That is, we can move from a topic loosely concerned with gender roles in World War I, to one that focuses specifically on a subset of recruitment posters and how they deploy a particular sexist stereotype (the Madonna-whore trope) as a persuasive strategy. With this focused and narrowed topic, we'll be able to contribute a new opinion about war posters and add to the ongoing dialogue that we find in our secondary sources.

CREATIVE PRACTICE

Try out this practice of *narrowing a topic* with a pair of early twenty-first-century posters that protest the U.S. war with Iraq. Examine the posters shown in Figures 4.10 through 4.13, and then complete a *visual brainstorm* to develop a feasible topic for your essay. Be sure that you narrow your topic from "anti-war propaganda posters" to a more focused one that you might pursue in a research paper. You might decide during your graphic brainstorm

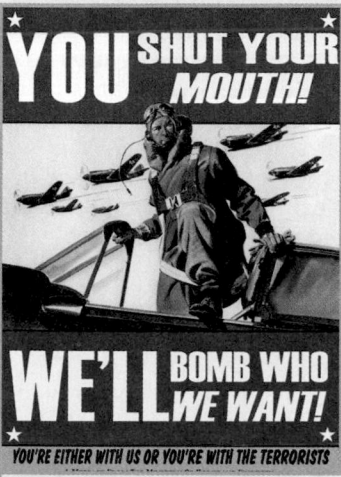

FIGURE 4.10. This recent anti-war poster uses strong language to catch the reader's attention.

FIGURE 4.11. This striking poster implies a connection between the war with Iraq and the oil trade.

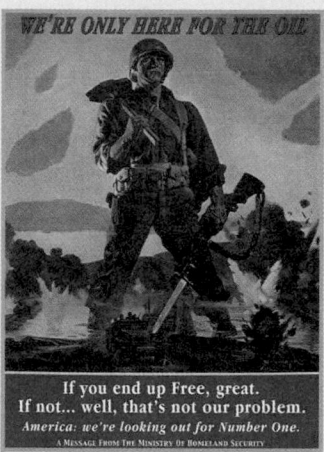

FIGURE 4.12. This poster solidifies the visual argument through a caption.

FIGURE 4.13. Originally composed to protest the Vietnam war, this poster recently re-emerged in reference to the Iraq war.

(continued)

> to focus your topic by identifying which images you'd like to write about or by generating key questions to ask about particular texts: What is the significance of the style that is used in the posters? How do the words and images work together in these posters? How do they work against each other? What is the significance of showing people who have been wounded? How does symbolism operate in these posters? The more specific the questions you ask, the more focused your topic will be.

Planning Your Research Through Writing

In completing the "Creative Practice" you most likely constructed a set of web diagrams that, like those in Figures 4.7 and 4.8, alternated between asking and answering questions. This process will narrow your focus and provide you with a direction for your research inquiry. But did you find yourself concerned that you don't have the knowledge necessary to write this essay? Are you worried that the gaps in your own knowledge will prevent you from answering those questions in a satisfactory way? If so, then you are in good company. All researchers and scholars fear the limitations of their knowledge. The key is to use that lack of knowledge as a motivation to develop a **concrete plan** for your research. We'll discuss three ways of planning your research: freewriting about your topic, developing a research hypothesis, and drafting a formal research proposal.

Freewriting About Your Research Topic

One way to start planning your research process is to freewrite about your ideas in your research log. Testing out your research plan in this way will move you from the work you did in narrowing your topic to the work you need to do in gathering sources and developing a research outline. This method also will provide an informal structure for your research, giving it shape and sharper focus as you move deeper into the research process.

Student Writing
See examples of research freewrites.
www.pearsonhighered.com/envision/116

In completing your freewrite, you may find it helpful to follow a **three-paragraph model**: in the *first paragraph*, announce your topic and state a preliminary thesis so that you can begin the project with a critical and focused perspective; in the *second paragraph*, identify the sources you plan to use to investigate this topic; in the *third paragraph*, speculate on obstacles or problems you might encounter in your research and how you might avoid or solve these problems. Let's look at a freewrite from student Bries Deerrose, who shaped his research inquiry around questions concerning a piece of contemporary propaganda: a leaflet dropped in Afghanistan by the U.S. military in the 2002–2003 campaign there.

AT A GLANCE

The Research Freewrite

- Write your ideas in full sentences.
- Use a three-paragraph model to focus your answers:
  - Paragraph 1: Announce the topic and state your hypothesis.
  - Paragraph 2: Identify key sources.
  - Paragraph 3: Anticipate problems.

Research Freewrite

Over the past decade, as America's image fell increasingly under the scrutiny of our allies and enemies alike, President George W. Bush established the Office of Global Communications, the stated purpose of which was "to advise . . . on utilization of the most effective means for the United States Government to ensure consistency in messages that will promote the interests of the United States abroad, prevent misunderstanding, build support for and among coalition partners of the United States, and inform international audiences." In this paper, I will examine how this office fulfilled its mission, especially through visual rhetoric. I will examine how the world, especially the Middle East, responded to such propaganda, and I will examine what image the office

This first paragraph introduces the research topic and describes what Bries thinks the main focus of his paper might be. At the end of the paragraph, he includes a tentative thesis to help him focus his interest and argument as he begins researching this topic.

portrayed, whether this was an accurate image of America or an example of political rhetoric. Finally, I will discuss whether such marketing was beneficial or detrimental, from both a foreign and American perspective. *Hypothesis:* America has been actively projecting an image of itself using various forms of visual rhetoric; this image responds to the *kairos* of negative scrutiny abroad and uses rhetorieal tactics to try to bring about meaningful, peaceful dialogue between America and the world.

To research this topic, I hope to examine firsthand government-generated materials: flyers, commercials, radio broadcasts, publications, etc. I will also attempt to find any commentaries on this effort as well as on domestic conceptions of what America is and what its image should be. I will compare this with foreign opinions regarding America's image and reactions to the American marketing techniques. To do this, I will need to find foreign commentaries, including visual rhetoric responding to our own visual rhetoric. I will need secondhand sources concerning foreign opinions.

The most difficult part of this assignment will be determining foreign opinion, since I am not fluent in other languages. I will also need to form my own opinion about the effectiveness, morality, and accuracy of these rhetorical tactics. Such issues are always sticky, and will require much thought and a wide array of perspectives.

In the second paragraph, Bries discusses the sources he intends to use. Notice the broad range of possibilities he considers: flyers, television commercials, radio broadcasts, and both American and international sources.

In the third paragraph, Bries anticipates the difficulties he might face and how he can solve them.

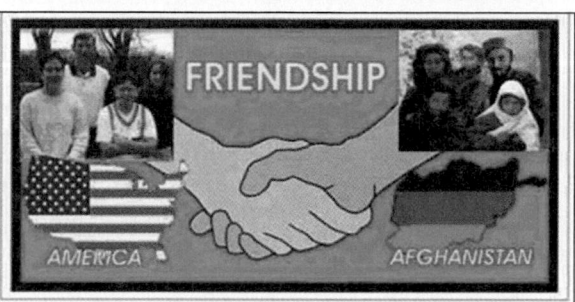

Office of Global Communications leaflet air-dropped in Afghanistan.
http://www.psywarrior.com/afghanleaf08.html.

Bries concludes with
a concrete example of
the visual rhetoric
he will use in his
research paper, a
leaflet dropped in
Afghanistan by
the United States
in the 2002–2003 cam-
paign.

Drafting the Research Hypothesis

In reading Bries's freewrite, you might have noticed that as he developed his topic, he was simultaneously trying his hand at formulating his argument. For instance, in Bries's first paragraph, he moves from the open-ended language of a proposal ("I will examine," "I will discuss") to a restatement of his subject in terms of a tentative thesis statement at the end of the paragraph. Many times as you draft your research plan, you will find that you enter into your project relying on broad questions ("What do the leaflets that Americans dropped on Afghanistan in 2003 say about our country and our international policy?") or on statements of intention (i.e., "I hope to examine. . ."). However, as we see in the example from Bries, it is also useful to use your research as an opportunity to try freewriting to define your rhetorical stance in relation to that topic.

So how do you make a claim about a topic that you have not yet researched completely? This is a key question, and it is often a frustrating one for many writers. Realize, however, that you've already taken the first step just by asking pointed questions about your topic. From these questions, you can develop a **hypothesis**, or a working thesis that makes an argumentative

 Student Writing

See Tommy Tsai's brainstorm about his hypothesis.
www.pearsonhighered.com/envision/119

claim that you'll attempt to prove. It is crucial for you to try to formulate a tentative *hypothesis* for your research as a way of looking at your project with an analytical eye. Of course, you may revise your hypothesis—and maybe your entire approach to the subject—several times over the course of your research. Indeed, most writers do modify their thesis statements, and this revision process is a natural part of what happens when you actually begin to read your sources and take notes about them in the research log. Nevertheless, trying to state your hypothesis is an important first step in focusing your argument and making the most out of the timeline available to you for research.

One way to develop your detailed hypothesis is to rewrite one of your more narrowed questions from the research proposal as a polished declarative statement that you intend to prove. For example, if you, like Tommy Tsai, asked yourself, "How were representations of race used in World War II propaganda?" then you might turn that question into a potential thesis: "Representations of race deployed in World War II propaganda functioned as a way to justify the internment of innocent civilians." As you continue your research, you may come to disagree with that statement, but at least beginning with a tentative hypothesis gives you somewhere to start your research.

This is the process that Tommy himself followed for his paper about World War II propaganda posters. His initial hypothesis, shown to the right, provided a starting point that allowed him to engage with his texts through the lens of his own argumentative claim. As he continued drafting, his hypothesis narrowed, shifting from a general focus on race in World War II propaganda posters to a compelling criticism of America's use of race in its portrayal of its German and Japanese enemies. Tommy's process underscores that a hypothesis is only the beginning of making a strong, focused research argument.

Drafting a Research Proposal

In many academic contexts, you will be asked to formalize your research plan through composing a full-length **research proposal**. This type of text is common in many disciplines and professions and is used by writers to develop agendas for research communities, secure funding for a study, publicize plans for inquiry and field research, and test the interest of potential

Working Hypothesis

I conjecture that German propaganda made use of the *ethos* appeal of its fascist leader Adolf Hitler; that Japanese propaganda utilized the *logos* appeal by continually portraying images of a victorious Japanese army; and that American propaganda for the most part employed the *pathos* appeal by evoking nationalistic feelings and associating war with glory and patriotism (see Figure 1).

Figure 1. Uncle Sam poster.

These conjectures inform my argument that the government of each nation is able to bring its political messages across effectively by employing the appropriate rhetorical appeal in its propaganda posters.

audiences for a given project. In the writing classroom, the research proposal provides a similar formal structure for developing a project, but it also serves another purpose: it is a more structured means of organizing your thoughts to help you solidify your topic and move into the next stages of the research process. For these reasons, the *genre, organization,* and *content* of the research proposal differ in important ways from other kinds of popular and academic writing that you might do. In drafting out your proposal, include the following elements:

Student Writing
See many examples of research proposals on a variety of topics.
www.pearsonhighered.com/envision/121

- *Background:* What do I already know about my topic? What do I need to find out more about?

AT A GLANCE

Key Functions of the Research Proposal

- It introduces the narrowed *topic*.
- It presents the *rhetorical stance* or *thesis* that the writer will develop.
- It explains the *significance* of the research project.
- It lists possible *sources* for investigation.
- It outlines your research *methods* or planned approach to the research.
- It delineates a detailed *timeline* for investigating the topic.
- It often anticipates any *difficulties* that might arise in pursuing this topic.
- It often includes a brief *biography* of the researcher (usually a one-paragraph description of the writer's credentials, interests, and motivations).
- It includes, if appropriate, a carefully chosen and analyzed visual rhetoric text as a case study or concrete example of the topic.

Student Writing

Examine Anastasia Nevin's research proposal on the historical mystery of the Romanov assassination, a study of archival photographs and artifacts.

www.pearsonhighered.com/envision/122

- *Methods:* How am I going to research this topic? What research questions are driving my inquiry?
- *Sources:* What specific texts will I analyze? What additional scholarly or popular sources can I reseach to help build my knowledge and my argument?
- *Timeline:* What are my goals for the different stages of research, and how can I schedule my work to most effectively meet these milestones?
- *Significance:* What do I hope to accomplish in my research? What are the broader issues or implications of my research? Why do these matter to me and to my readers?

As this list suggests, your proposal should explain your interest in your chosen subject and establish a set of questions to guide your inquiry. The proposal should delineate the timeline for your research and writing process—a crucial time management strategy.

You should also incorporate an appropriate visual text—a sample propaganda poster to be analyzed or an editorial cartoon that introduces the issue—into your proposal to show readers an example of the materials about which you'll be conducting your research.

Your proposal serves to clarify your research intentions, but it should also *persuade* an audience of the feasibility and significance of your project. In fact, perhaps the most important step in launching your research inquiry is to address the issue of your project's significance or, as some writing instructors call it, the "So What?" part of the project. It is the "So What?"—an awareness of the *significance* of the topic you're addressing and the questions you're asking—that moves the proposal from being a routine academic exercise to a powerful piece of persuasive writing. When addressing the "So What?" question, consider why anyone else would care enough to read a paper on your topic. Ask yourself:

- What is at stake in your topic?
- Why does it matter?
- What contribution will your project make to a wider community?

Let's look at an example: a research proposal Susan Zhang developed on digital manipulation.

Susan Zhang

Little Photoshop of Horrors?: Digital Manipulation
of Media Images

When O. J. Simpson was arrested in the summer of 1994, Newsweek and Time magazines featured his mugshot on their covers. But while Newsweek's photo was unaltered, Time had darkened the color of his skin and reduced the size of his prisoner ID number. To anyone who saw the two magazines on the news rack, the difference was obvious. To some it was even unethical: minority groups protested that the digital manipulation made O. J. look darker and more menacing, thereby presuming his guilt. The Time illustrator who altered the image later claimed that he only "wanted to make it more artful, more compelling." The impartiality of the photography was widely contested.

You can't always believe what you read in the news, but a photograph doesn't lie, right? Because the photographer and

> Susan begins with a specific example to hook the audience and to set up the context for her proposal.

> In the proposal she turned in for class, Susan also embedded images from the *Newsweek* and *Time* covers in her introduction as visual evidence for her claims. She uses questions to identify common assumptions that her audience might hold about her topic.

the camera are perceived to be mere vehicles for converting reality into image, people are more apt to trust a photo, believing it to be the product of a machine rather than a human, and consequently free of bias. But with the advent of digital imaging, that credibility has been compromised. Image-editing programs such as Photoshop make it possible to perform cosmetic touch-ups, graft parts of pictures onto others, even construct a picture entirely from scratch. In many ways, digital imaging has redefined the field of photography. With words like "composograph" and "photoillustration" being coined to describe altered images indistinguishable from the real thing, people have grown wary of deeming the photograph a purveyor of truth.

She then clearly states her research goals. She suggests some key research questions and then ends with a declarative sentence that underscores her intentions as a researcher. Notice how she mentions the significance—or importance—of the project early on in the proposal.

For my research project, I want to explore how the capacity of image manipulation has affected the way we perceive photos in the news and media. Has it led to a permanent loss of faith? Or, on the flip side, to the establishment of stricter standards for allowable alterations? By examining past incidences of digital manipulation and current guidelines for photographs in the media, and the contexts in which they apply, I hope to gain a better understanding of the credibility of news and media imagery in the digital age.

Methods

First, I want to approach my topic through its historical context. I will start with the pre-digital era and look at whether photo manipulation existed then. Surely there were tricked, staged, and doctored photos also? To what extent were photos altered using darkroom techniques? What kind of ethical considerations governed the editing of media images then? By comparing past precedents with the types of digital manipulations commonly used today, I can determine whether digital imaging really has made photo manipulation a bigger and more prevalent problem.

Next, I will look at digital manipulation from the public's point of view. In the past when a digital image was altered, how did the public respond? For example, if a photograph is altered in an obvious or humorous manner, it could be perceived as satire or social commentary, but if it is altered subtly and the change not announced, it could be perceived as deception. How easily can people recognize an altered photo? And when a magazine or newspaper is exposed for digitally manipulating a photo, does this automatically discredit it in the public eye?

I will also consider the photographer's point of view. Do photographers consider photo manipulation a recent development stemming from digital imaging? What are the moral and ethical justifications for manipulated photographs? What kinds of standards exist in the field of photojournalism and media photography? How do these standards regulate the integrity of digital photojournalism?

Sources

To begin my research, I will look at books on the ethics of photojournalism. So far I have checked out Paul Lester's

Susan uses her research questions to structure her "Methods" section: the historical perspective, the audience's perspective, and the photographer's perspective. She carefully thinks through each line of inquiry.

Although this was written before she began serious research, Susan increased her proposal's persuasiveness (and her own ethos as a researcher) by including the titles of specific texts she located through a computer search of her library's holdings. She carefully groups her intended sources and also explains briefly why these types of sources would be useful for her research.

Photojournalism: An Ethical Approach and Julianne Newton's *The Burden of Visual Truth: The Role of Photojournalism in Mediating Reality.* These books will help me understand the history of ethical photojournalism, the ways in which a photograph conveys a message, and the public's response to photographs.

Then, moving toward the digital side of media images, I will turn to books such as Thomas Wheeler's *Phototruth or Photofiction?: Ethics and Media Imagery in the Digital Age* and Larry Gross's *Image Ethics in the Digital Age.* The first book examines specific examples of photo manipulation and later provides an ethical framework for considering image manipulation in photojournalism. The second book is a collection of articles on aspects of digital image ethics.

By including search terms and specific database names, Susan shows that she is ready to move to actual research.

I will also search online databases such as EBSCO and LexisNexis for articles on digital manipulation and recent controversies over digital manipulation. Search terms I might use include "photo manipulation," "digital photojournalism," and "digital image ethics." Through these databases I hope to find authoritative opinions from photojournalists as well as public reactions to altered images in magazines and the news.

Susan finishes her discussion of sources with attention to primary sources—the actual photographs themselves—that she intends to find to use in her paper.

As a primary source, I will look at photojournalism Websites. I will visit large news and magazine sites and smaller photojournalism communities, browsing their photographs to see if they use digital manipulation, and if so, how it is addressed. Also, there are many web resources that explain the guidelines that have been development by photojournalists. For example, the National Press Photographers Association's Website features a digital code of ethics. These sites will clarify the guidelines of digital photojournalism and how closely they are being followed.

Timeline

1/20 Research proposal due

1/20–1/22 Search for articles on photojournalism and digital manipulation using online databases

1/22–1/27 In-depth research using books

Primary research using photojournalism sites

1/27–1/31 Review notes and write a thesis

Talk with classmates and instructor for advice on my thesis

Evaluate which sources to use

2/1–2/5 Outline paper: decide on the major arguments, draft topic sentences, and choose support for each argument

2/5–2/12 Write first draft of paper

2/12 Research paper draft due

2/15–2/28 Obtain and reflect on feedback

Additional research and revision as necessary

3/3–3/6 Review second draft for polish, errors

3/6 Revision of research paper due

Significance

With advancements in technology, photography has moved from the darkroom to the computer lab, making it possible to alter

In her timeline, Susan lists not only deadlines imposed by her instructor but also key steps in the research process: finding books, evaluating sources, taking notes, constructing a thesis, peer review, a second round of research, drafting, and revising.

With this detailed timeline, Susan shows her careful time management and builds her ethos by demonstrating her understanding of the research process; she even uses colored font for due dates to highlight their importance.

In her conclusion, Susan reasserts the importance of her project, broadening to address the "So What?" that she needs to answer as she enters into her research.

photographs beyond what is considered ethical. The abuse of this technology has resulted in manipulated photos being passed off as real in the media, and a resulting public skepticism over the reliability of all media images. A closer look at the occurrences of digital manipulation today, as regulated by the evolving guidelines of photojournalism, could reveal to what extent such skepticism is warranted.

The Writer's Process

Now that you've learned about the process of generating research questions narrowing your topic, developing a hypothesis, and then writing up your plans for research in a structured freewrite or a formal proposal, what can you argue about the first propaganda poster of this chapter (Figure 4.1)?

In answering this prompt, you might start to work through the writing projects related to the research process. You might develop a research focus that begins with questions and ends with a "So What?" statement of significance. You might try to incorporate visual images into a proposal that will conclude with a clear statement of your future authority on this topic as a researcher. Try the strategies for keeping track of your ideas and work in progress in a research log, a key tool that you'll be using in the next chapter as we turn to gathering and evaluating sources for your topic. It's time to get started on the research process for writing a persuasive argument about an issue that matters to you.

PREWRITING CHECKLIST

Analyzing Propaganda Posters

❑ What is the underlying message of this poster?

❑ What are the specifics of the rhetorical situation informing this piece of propaganda? Who produced the poster? Who was its intended audience?

❏ What is the historical context for this poster? What country was it produced in, and what was the social and political situation of the time? How does an understanding of its context affect our understanding of its message?

❏ What type of rhetorical appeal does the poster feature? Does it rely primarily on logos, pathos, or ethos to make its point? How does attention to this appeal manifest itself visually in the poster?

❏ Recalling the discussion of exaggerated use of appeals from Chapter 2, does the poster rely on any logical fallacies? any exaggerated use of pathos? If so, how do these work to persuade the audience?

❏ What is the relationship between word and image in the poster? How do design elements such as color, font, layout, and image selection (photograph or illustration) work as persuasive elements in this text?

❏ Does the poster use stereotypes to convey its message? How do stereotypes figure as rhetorical devices in this situation? How does the stereotype place the poster in the context of a larger cultural discussion?

❏ What research questions can you develop about this poster?

❏ What kinds of sources might you look at to understand better what's going on with this propaganda poster?

PREWRITING WITH THE *ENVISION* WEBSITE

One way to begin approaching your research project is to explore the poster collection available through the *Envision* Website. Come up with a list of three research questions that you might explore based on two to four of the posters. Share your list with classmates and discuss the differences in your questions. Based on your discussions, create three or four concrete research topics that you might want to pursue. Then, you can apply this process to the visual rhetoric of your choice. But while you are online, check out the many student models of research available as proposals, plans, and research logs.

www.pearsonhighered.com/envision/129

WRITING PROJECTS

1. **Research Freewrite:** Freewrite about your research ideas by first writing out answers to the questions provided in the "Prewriting Checklist" and then developing them into a three-paragraph *freewrite*. In the first paragraph, introduce your research paper topic and describe what you think the main focus of the paper

might be. Include a tentative thesis in this paragraph. In the second paragraph, discuss the sources that you intend to use. In the third paragraph, speculate on what obstacles you foresee in this project and/or what you anticipate to be the most difficult part of the assignment. If appropriate, use an image to complement your written text. Show your answers to your instructor or your peers for feedback.

2. **Research Proposal:** Write a detailed research *proposal* that discusses your topic, planned method, and purpose in depth. Be sure to cover your topic, your hypothesis, your potential sources and problems, your method, timeline, and, most importantly, the significance of the proposed project. For more specific instruction consult the Writing Guidelines on the *Envision* Website. When you are done with the writing, present your proposal at a roundtable of research with other members of your class. Answer questions from your classmates to help you fine-tune your topic and troubleshoot your future research.
www.pearsonhighed.com/envision/130a

3. **Peer Review:** Collaboratively peer review your research proposals. Assume that you are on the review board granting approval and funding to the best two proposals of each group. Complete research proposal review letters for each member of your group. When you are done, discuss your letters and what changes you can recommend. Then revise your proposals to make them stronger, better written, and more persuasive. For more specific instructions and for peer review forms for the research proposal, consult the *Envision* Website.
www.pearsonhighed.com/envision/130b

 Visit www.pearsonhighered.com/envision for expanded assignment guidelines and student projects. Visit www.mycomplab.com for additional general writing and research resources.

CHAPTER 5

Finding and Evaluating Research Sources

Chapter Preview Questions

- What is the best way to locate research sources?
- What is the difference between a primary and a secondary source?
- How do I critically evaluate both print and electronic sources?
- How do I pursue field research for my project?
- What is an annotated bibliography, and how can it help me?
- How should I take notes while researching?

As you move from planning to conducting research, you'll need to investigate resources and evaluate them for your project. You can use your analytical skills to make important distinctions when locating, evaluating, and using sources for your research project. Look, for instance, at the covers in Figures 5.1 and 5.2. Although they focus on the

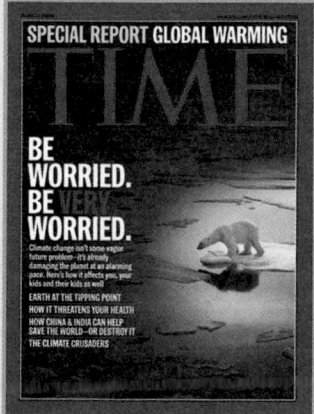

FIGURE 5.1. Cover of *Time*, April 3, 2006.

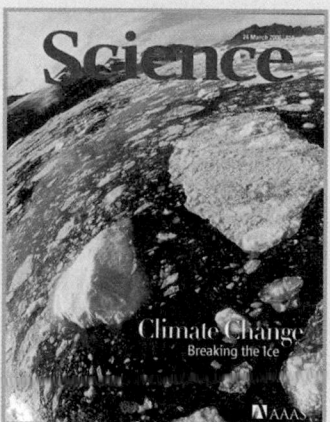

FIGURE 5.2. Cover of *Science*, March 24, 2006.

same topic—climate change—the visual rhetoric suggests that the content of each journal will be quite different. The audience for *Time* magazine differs from that of *Science*, and, consequently, the writing styles within the articles will be different as well. The cover of each magazine previews the distinct content inside. Studying the covers can help you look back in history to understand how climate change has been understood in the past. In this way, you are finding and evaluating research sources for your project.

Specifically, the cover of *Time* in Figure 5.1 conveys how the editors chose to represent global warming to their audience in 2006. Ask yourself: What is the argument conveyed by the visual rhetoric of the cover? What is the significance of the choice to use a polar bear as the main character in their image? How is color used strategically? How does the "spotlighting" of the polar bear and the positioning of the image in relation to the words contribute to the rhetorical effect? What kind of stance toward the dangers of global warming does the cover suggest?

In contrast, the *Science* cover (see Figure 5.2) features a photograph of an ice-covered lake. The photo appears to have been taken with a "fish-eye" lens, bringing several ice fragments into prominence in the foreground. How do such different rhetorical strategies appeal to the journal's very scientifically informed audience?

Clearly, the editors deliberately located, evaluated, and used materials for the covers that would reflect their magazine's contents. As a researcher, you can use your skills in rhetorical analysis to help you evaluate sources for your own research project, looking to the different elements of a text— from the cover design, to the table of contents, to the index—to better understand the text's perspective on your topic and its usefulness for your project.

CREATIVE PRACTICE

Working in small groups, compare Figures 5.1 and 5.2 with the cover of the August 26, 2002, issue of *Time* (see Figure 5.3). What contrasts emerge in the use of visual and verbal rhetoric? What stance does the cover suggest that *Time* will take on the topic? How is that stance represented in the cover design? What do these differences suggest to you in terms of how the *conversation* around global warming has changed over the years?

Now go to the *Envision* Website to find other *Time* covers that have addressed the issue of climate change. What different approaches do these covers take to this issue? How does context seem to inform this approach? Look in the table of contents for each issue; do the article titles seem to support the position suggested by the covers? Finally, as a group, develop your own stance on this issue. Together, sketch a design for a new cover for an upcoming issue of *Science,*

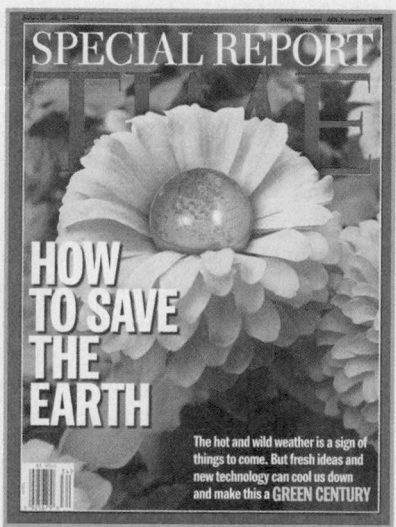

FIGURE 5.3. Cover of *Time*, August 26, 2002.

The Economist, or *Time.* Use the cover to suggest an argument for a specific perspective on global warming and to provide a visual preview for the contents inside. Share your design and argument with the class.

www.pearsonhighered.com/envision/133

Your task as a researcher is quite similar to that of the editors of *Time* and *Science.* As you begin gathering and evaluating sources for your own research argument, keep in mind that you will need to shape the argument into a paper addressed to a particular audience: your writing class, a group of scientists, a lobbying organization, an advertising firm, or browsers on the Web. To take part in any of these conversations, a researcher needs to learn

- what is being talked about (the *topic*),
- how it is being discussed (the *conversation*), and
- what the different positions are (*research context*).

Visualizing Research

To grasp the specifics of the topic, the conversation, and the research context, it is helpful to take a moment to visualize the research process. When you think of the act of research, what comes to mind? Surfing the Web? Looking through a library? Interviewing experts in the field? All these images represent different research scenarios. The material you gather in each situation will compose the foundation for your research; it will inform your essay, but not all of it will find its way into your final paper. Nevertheless, you need to research widely and thoroughly to be fully informed about your topic and write a compelling research-based argument. One helpful way of visualizing the relationship between the *process* and the *product* of research is through the metaphor of the **iceberg of research** (see Figure 5.4). In essence, your topic or final paper will be only one small part of your research; beneath the surface lie the many different sources you will explore: books, journal articles, Websites, field surveys, historical materials, interviews, multimedia and more. All these constitute the research material. Your task as a researcher is to move beyond a surface knowledge of your topic; you need to gather, assess, keep, throw out, and ultimately use a variety of sources. By exploring such a wide range of material, you will encounter a rich array of scholarly and popular perspectives on your topic. In many ways, your research argument will be, in fact, a discussion with those research sources themselves. You add your voice to theirs. But your final paper may appear as only the "tip of the iceberg" or a result of your careful study of the work of others.

Sometimes, this process of building on others can be intimidating; we fear that we will have nothing new to add to the conversation. Yet if we think of research sources as texts written by people who were once, like us, struggling to figure out what we are trying to say, then we can see the process of gathering and assessing

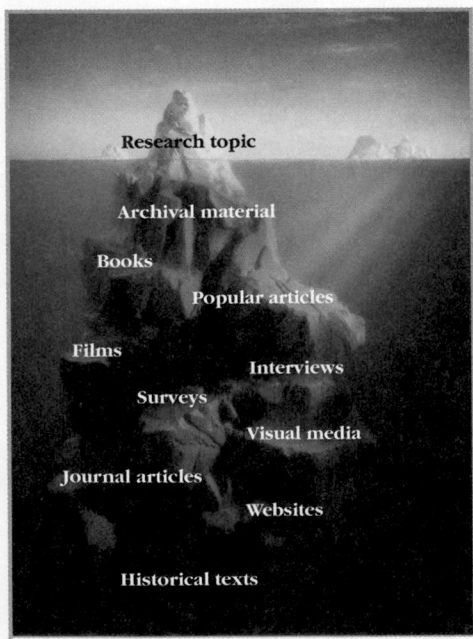

FIGURE 5.4. The iceberg of research.

sources as a very social one, a process in which you *respect* and *acknowledge* the ideas of others and then seek to add your own voice to an ongoing conversation. One way to begin that conversation is to discover what others before you have said, thought, written, and published—and to keep track of that process in your research log, as explained in Chapter 4.

In this chapter, we'll use the metaphor of the *conversation* to accentuate the point that the research process is an act of *composing a response to an ongoing dialogue about a topic.* By gathering, synthesizing, and sorting the perspectives of others, you begin to shape your own stance on a research topic. By adding your voice as a writer, you are responding to others. Research is a *relationship* that you develop with the source material and the writers you encounter along the way.

Developing Search Terms

The first step in the research process lies in locating relevant and interesting sources to draw into your conversation. This involves finding the best **search terms** to use in looking for sources on your topic. Your search terms will change depending on whether you are searching the Web, an academic database, or a library catalog. You will need to identify the most productive keywords for searching in each of these situations.

Let's take as our example a project about Internet advertising. In a preliminary Web search, specific terms such as "pop-up ads," "Facebook ads," and "ethics & advertising online" probably yield more results than generic terms like "Internet advertising" and "Internet advertisements." If you search a database such as LexisNexis (a resource for news articles as well as legal, medical, and business articles), your keywords might be closer to your preliminary topic. Using the term "Internet advertising" in a database search would provide you with more than 90 citations in popular magazines and journals, while "pop-up ads" might yield fewer than 20 hits—the opposite of your results with a basic Internet search. Finally, you would likely find that a successful search of your library catalog requires still *different terms*—typically more academic terminology, such as "electronic commerce," "social media marketing," or "Internet marketing," because those phrases appear in scholarly book titles.

AT A GLANCE

Tips for Using Search Terms

- *Web:* Use popular or colloquial terminology in your Internet searches because search engines pick up actual terms from pages as they crawl across the Web.
- *Library:* The Library of Congress has created a set of terms, called Library of Congress Subject Headings (LCSHs) used by librarians to catalog information. These headings may not always be obvious to you. (For example, the Library of Congress calls the Vietnam War the "Vietnamese Conflict, 1961–1975." A search under "Vietnam War" will produce no results.) You can find the LCSH terms in two ways: by looking at a library record online, or by consulting the print index. By plugging the terms into your library catalog, you can access information for your project more efficiently.
- *Databases:* Since databases can house a wide range of materials, from academic publications to popular articles, you will have to customize your language based on the database you have selected. Match your search terms in diction and formality to suit the type of resource you are exploring.

Narrowing Your Search

In many initial searches, the list of potential sources returned to you will be much larger than you can efficiently process. Your main task, then, will be to find ways to narrow your search. Experimenting with a range of terms—particularly more limited ones—can help you with this task by finding materials specific to your topic. For instance, you might use the narrower term "Internet advertising & law" to eliminate irrelevant sources and focus on the legal aspect of the issue, if that interests you. Through such experimentation you will find the search term that yields the most productive results.

Primary and Secondary Sources

Your initial searches will yield a range of sources—from magazine articles to books, video recordings, and perhaps even manuscripts or a photograph collection. Each of these sources can play a vital role in your research. Scholars divide research into primary and secondary research, and sources, likewise, into **primary sources** (original texts you analyze in your research paper) and **secondary sources** (sources that provide commentary on your primary material or on your topic in general).

Consider, for instance, Tommy Tsai's project, examined in detail in Chapter 4. Propaganda posters were Tommy's *primary sources,* and the articles, books, and transcribed interviews providing analysis of those posters were his *secondary sources.* His paper is now *another* secondary source, one that contributes to an ongoing intellectual discussion about the meaning and power of the posters.

But as you search for your research materials, keep in mind that no sources are *inherently* primary or secondary; those terms refer to *how you use them* in your paper. For instance, if you were working with the topic of Internet advertising, you might use actual Facebook ads and Flash animations as your primary sources, as well as press releases and advertising Websites. For secondary sources you might turn to articles that discuss innovations in social media marketing, a Website on the history of digital advertising, and perhaps even a book by a famous economist about the impact of technology on corporate marketing strategies. However, imagine that you shift your topic

> ## AT A GLANCE
>
> ### Primary and Secondary Sources
>
> - *Primary sources:* materials that you will analyze for your paper, including speech scripts, advertisements, photographs, historical documents, film, artwork, audio files, and writing on Websites. Primary sources can also include testimonies by people with firsthand knowledge or direct quotations you will analyze. Whatever is under the lens of your analysis constitutes a *primary source.*
>
> - *Secondary sources:* the additional materials that help you analyze your primary sources by providing a perspective on those primary materials; these include scholarly articles, popular commentaries, background materials (in print, video, or interview format), and survey data reinforcing your analysis. Whatever sources you can use as a lens to look at or understand the subject of your analysis constitutes a *secondary source.*

slightly, making your new focus the economist's theories about the corruption of traditional advertising by multimedia technology. Now, that same book you looked at before as a *secondary* source becomes a *primary* source for this new topic.

As you can see, your inquiry will determine which sources will be primary and which will be secondary for your argument. In most cases, you will need to use a combination of primary and secondary materials to make a persuasive argument. The primary sources allow you to perform your own analysis, whereas the secondary sources offer you critical viewpoints that you need to take into account in your analysis and integrate into your argument to build up your ethos. How you respond to and combine your primary and secondary sources is a matter of choice, careful design, and rhetorical strategy.

Finding Primary Sources

Searching for **primary sources**—original texts you analyze in your research paper—can be challenging, but they can be found in many places: in your library (whether in the general stacks, archives, or multimedia collections); at community centers such as library exhibits, museums, and city hall; or even in online digital archives such as the one maintained by the Library of Congress. These materials can be some of the most exciting sources to work with in your research process and might include:

- Original documents (a handwritten letter by Mahatma Gandhi or Charles Lindbergh's journals)
- Rare books and manuscripts (Roger Manvell's manuscripts on the history of the Third Reich)
- Portfolios of photographs (photos of Japanese-American internment camps or of Black Panther demonstrations from the 1960s)
- Government documents (U.S. censuses and surveys, reports from the Department of Agriculture, or congressional papers)
- Other one-of-a-kind texts (AIDS prevention posters from South Africa, a noted artist's sketchbook, or a series of leaflets produced by the U.S. Psychological Warfare Department)

Student Writing

See James Caputo's annotated bibliography for his research project.
www.pearsonhighered.com/envision/138

In many cases, you can work directly with these materials so you can perform your own firsthand analysis of that piece of cultural history.

Consider the sources that student James Caputo used in his project on media representations of the early years of the NASA space program. James had many fascinating primary resources to work with: John F. Kennedy's inspirational speeches about the formation of the space program; front pages of both American and Russian newspapers detailing the successful completion of the first Apollo mission; publicity shots of the astronauts; the first images—both still and moving—from the moon's surface; and advertisements published after the first moon landing that showed the space program's attempts to win public support through publicity. He chose to focus on multiple magazine covers and images from magazine articles for his primary source materials (see Figures 5.5 and 5.6).

FIGURE 5.5. James used this illustration, "The Rocket Blitz from the Moon," which originally accompanied a 1948 *Collier's* magazine article, as a powerful primary source for his research paper.

FIGURE 5.6. James also analyzed other primary sources, including magazine covers like this one from a 1969 issue of *Time*.

The image in Figure 5.5 originally appeared in an article published in *Collier's* magazine on October 23, 1948, concerning the military applications of space travel. James analyzed it and found that it was intended to warn American readers of the consequences of falling behind in the "space race" with the Russians. Similarly, Figure 5.6, a cover shot from *Time*'s July 25, 1969, issue, relied on pathos to persuade the American readers to view the U.S. space program in a certain light. James found that the image, with its strong nationalistic overtones, cast the successful Apollo 11 mission once again in terms of the Cold War and the American-Soviet space race. He placed these primary sources at the center of his research argument, and then he turned to secondary sources to substantiate his own claims about them.

Searching for Secondary Sources

Just as important as your primary materials are your **secondary sources**—texts that provide commentary on your topic and often analyze the texts you have chosen as primary sources. The writers of these texts offer the

AT A GLANCE

Finding Secondary Sources

- **Dictionaries, guides, and encyclopedias** provide helpful background information for your topic.
- **Library catalogs** allow you to search the library holdings for relevant books or documentaries.
- **CD-Rom indexes and bibliographies** contain vast amounts of bibliographic information.
- **Electronic databases and indexes** are available on the Internet through subscription only; many provide access to full-text versions of articles from a range of sources.
- **Electronic journals and ebooks** offer access to the full digital versions of books and academic journals from a wide range of disciplines.
- **Google scholar and Google Books** can be helpful resources, but should be used in conjunction with academic databases and library catalogues.

voices with which you will engage in scholarly conversation as you develop the substance of your argument.

Although your instinct may send you directly to the Internet, your first stop in your search for secondary sources should actually be your library's reference area, the home of reference librarians—people trained to help you find what you need—as well as a treasure trove of encyclopedias, bibliographies, and other resource materials. These storehouses of information can be invaluable in providing you with the *foundational sources* for your project, including basic definitions, historical background, and bibliographies. Yet, while such "background" materials are necessary to help you construct a framework for your research argument, they represent only one part of your iceberg of research. For more rigorous analysis, you should turn to books and articles that provide critical analysis and arguments

AT A GLANCE

Using One Source to Locate Additional Sources

Here's the process for finding sources:

1. Locate one relevant source through the library catalog.
2. Retrieve it from the library stacks.
3. Spend some time looking over books in the same area to discover additional books on the same topic.
4. Assess briefly the applicability of each text to your project, and check out the ones most valuable to you.
5. Look at the bibliographies in the backs of your most useful books to locate sources that were helpful to the authors and may be of use to you.
6. Repeat the process often to build your iceberg of research.

about your specific research subject. To locate these more specific secondary sources, you might search your library catalog for relevant books and films and other published materials.

You can also consult databases and indexes, indispensable research guides that will provide you with bibliographic citations for academic articles on your topic. Databases can come in many forms: collections of electronic journals, Internet resources, or CD-ROMs. Although some databases provide bibliographic citations that you can use to locate the source in your library catalog, many include a detailed abstract summarizing a source's argument, and others link you to full-text electronic copies of the articles you are searching for.

Finally, although databases, catalogs, and search engines provide indispensable tools for conducting your research, remember also that your classmates can serve as secondary sources

Student Writing

See Vivian Chang's record of her searches in her research log.

www.pearsonhighered.com/envision/141

AT A GLANCE

Recording Searches in Your Research Log

Use your research log to keep careful track of the dates, details, key terms of your searches and to organize your sources and your notes.

- Date each entry in your log to keep track of your progress and show the evolution of your ideas.
- Keep a running list of your sources by call number and title.
- Write down complete identifying information for any source you consult, including images on the Web, articles online, journals or magazines in the library, articles from library databases, and chapters in books.
- Double-check transcribed quotations for accuracy while you still have the source before you, and include page numbers (or paragraph numbers for Website articles).
- Include printouts (or digital copies, if your log is electronic) of relevant articles or database entries, and especially of Web-based articles or Websites that might disappear when their site is updated.
- Annotate the entry by including an evaluation of the source and an indication of how you might use it as part of your final paper.
- If you are using Web sources, be aware that Websites tend to be updated often and sometimes simply disappear. To avoid losing important source material, print out significant Webpages and insert them into your log or download them to your hard drive and include them on a CD-ROM with your research log.

you might consult or even interview. Ask others who are working on similar topics to share resources, and help each other along the route of your research. This is particularly true for the stage in your research when you produce a **preliminary bibliography**—a working list of the sources for your iceberg of research.

Evaluating Your Sources

Implementing these research strategies to locate primary and secondary materials will provide you with access to many interesting sources, but how do you discriminate among them to find those that are credible, reliable, and authoritative? How do you know which ones will be the most useful for your argument? The key rests in understanding the argumentative perspective, or *rhetorical stance*, of each source. At times, the source's stance may be self-evident: you may automatically gravitate toward experts in the field, well known for their opinions and affiliations. It is just as likely, however, that you may not be familiar with the names or ideas of your sources. Therefore, it is essential to develop a method for evaluating the sources you encounter.

Evaluating Websites

For many of us, when we hear the words "research paper," our first impulse is to log onto the Internet and plug our topic into a search engine such as Google (http://www.google.com) or Bing (http://www.bing.com). That will certainly provide a start, but how do you assess the credibility of the hundreds of sites that may turn up? How do you evaluate the reliability and usefulness of these sites?

To understand how best to evaluate Websites, let's take the example of a research paper on the stem cell debate. An initial Google search on "stem cell research" brings up a list of over 5 million sites. On the one hand, such a plentiful search gives you ample means to "eavesdrop" on the ongoing conversation about your topic; on the other hand, the sheer magnitude of hits can be overwhelming. Even after refining your search terms to get a smaller result, how do you sort through them to identify those most helpful to your research?

AT A GLANCE

Evaluating Websites

- Who is the author of the Website? Is it a personal Website or is it institutionally affiliated? What sort of authority does it draw on?
- Does the author take responsibility for the page by offering a place for comments or an email link for feedback?
- Who is the audience?
- What is the purpose?
- What is the rhetorical stance of this Website? Does it deal with both sides of the issue or only one side?
- Does it offer links to other sites on the Web?
- How timely is the page? Does it have a date? Does someone maintain the Website? Are there broken links?
- Is it an archive of primary material? If so, does it cite the original sources in a correct and complete manner?
- Is it easy to navigate? Does it have a search engine?

First evaluate the author, source, or publisher. For our search, the first hit is quite credible: NIH Stem Cell Information, hosted by the National Institutes of Health of the U.S. government (Figure 5.7).

Second, consider the arrangement, or organization, of material. As you study this Website, you probably notice first the title, Stem Cell Information, at the top of the page, which suggests that this page is intended to be informational—to get the basic facts out. You may also note the small NIH logo next to it. Does the fact that this is a government-sponsored site suggest that it is authoritative? Objective?

Clicking on the first topic listed—U.S. Policy on Stem Cell Research—brings you to a page about executive orders. You may notice that it emphasizes President Barack Obama's executive order, which is titled "Removing Barriers . . ." and, the site notes, revokes an earlier one signed by President George W. Bush. Do you see any rhetorical strategies at work here? Is there any persuasive message embedded in the site?

The next site listed on your Google search, Wikipedia, may provide a good starting point for your search. It contains background information,

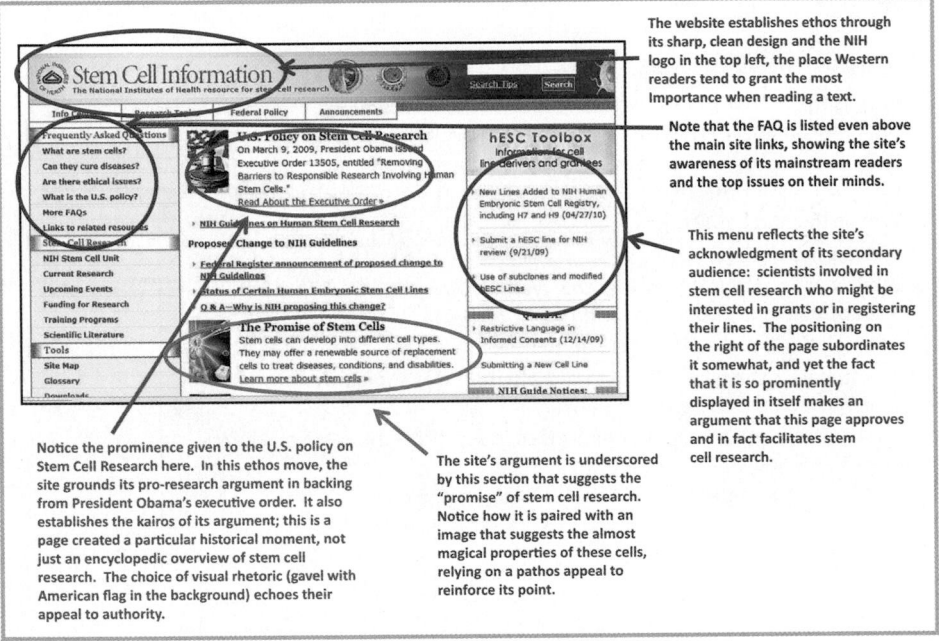

FIGURE 5.7. A screenshot of the NIH Stem Cell Information page.

and the references at the end of the article provide a useful starting point for research. However, Wikipedia itself is often considered a questionable source (since each entry can be edited by anyone), so it is best to substantiate what your learn there by continuing on with your search.

Lower down on your Google results list is another site—Do No Harm: The Coalition of Americans for Research Ethics. The site's title, unlike that of the National Institutes of Health, suggests a point of view: The sponsors of this site believe in ethical research. But how is that defined? Does "ethical research" include or reject research based on embryonic stem cells?

Finding the answer to this requires some careful analysis of the site, shown in Figure 5.8. Looking at the homepage, you may first notice the appeal to authority: the quote from Hippocrates at the top of the page that includes the familiar admonition to the medical profession to do no harm.

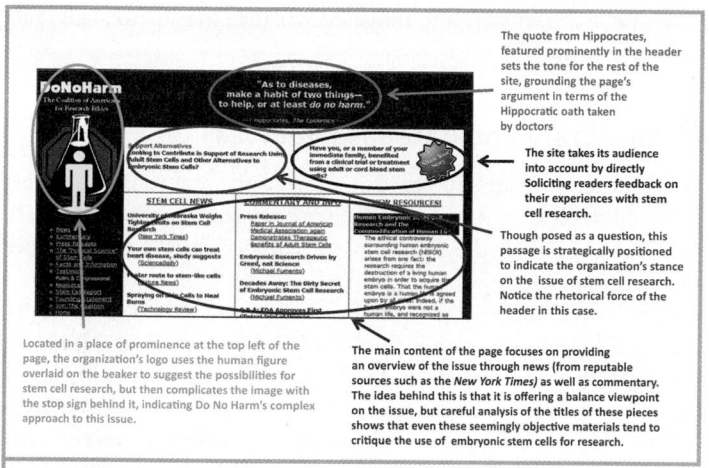

The quote from Hippocrates, featured prominently in the header sets the tone for the rest of the site, grounding the page's argument in terms of the Hippocratic oath taken by doctors

The site takes its audience into account by directly Soliciting readers feedback on their experiences with stem cell research.

Though posed as a question, this passage is strategically positioned to indicate the organization's stance on the issue of stem cell research. Notice the rhetorical force of the header in this case.

Located in a place of prominence at the top left of the page, the organization's logo uses the human figure overlaid on the beaker to suggest the possibilities for stem cell research, but then complicates the image with the stop sign behind it, indicating Do No Harm's complex approach to this issue.

The main content of the page focuses on providing an overview of the issue through news (from reputable sources such as the *New York Times*) as well as commentary. The idea behind this is that it is offering a balance viewpoint on the issue, but careful analysis of the titles of these pieces shows that even these seemingly objective materials tend to critique the use of embryonic stem cells for research.

FIGURE 5.8. Homepage for the Do No Harm site.

But initially we don't know how that quote is being interpreted or applied. A quick glance at the page shows that the center frame is given over to news, commentary, and resources, suggesting that it is providing an overview of the topic for its audience. However, as we look closer, the stance becomes more clear. The titles of the links show a clear tendency toward critiquing the use of embryonic stem cells for research. In fact, we can find the organization's position in the upper left quadrant of the page, submerged in the question under the suggestive header "Support Alternatives." As their "Founding Statement" confirms, this group is opposed to embryonic stem cell research as morally unacceptable, but its position is more nuanced than some groups because it endorses what it sees as morally acceptable alternatives—using adult stem cells.

Having identified the stance, your task as a researcher is not only to take this position into account while reading but also to broaden your research to include many different perspectives on the issue. Identifying the stance or bias of a Website's sponsor or author is critical to evaluating the credibility and usefulness of that site.

As you can see, attention to the visual and verbal rhetoric of a site's homepage—its "cover"—is essential to understanding its argument and therefore its suitability as a research source. After assessing the "cover" pages of each Website, the next step is to move deeper into the site to analyze its content and argument.

Evaluating Library and Database Sources

While Websites can provide sources for a project on stem cells, for almost all college research papers you will need to seek out sources through library shelves and databases since they host scholarly materials that will be more useful for your project.

How might you evaluate library and database sources for a research paper on stem cells? Your first stop is the library's reference area, where you look up foundational information in the *Encyclopedia of Bioethics*. Then you search the library catalog for books, and finally, you might locate journal articles that, you reason, will provide balance to your iceberg of research because they often represent the most current discussions on a topic. To find relevant articles, you begin searching the electronic databases that most closely suit the specific focus of your project: SciSearch, MEDLINE, LegalPeriodical, BIOSIS. You produce an impressive list of citations and even retrieve a few full-text articles. You also search some sources that are more news related, including LexisNexis and ProQuest, to find a selection of references to popular newspaper and magazine articles that will balance the scholarly sources.

Your first search complete, you can now retreat to a quiet space and assess the significance and value of your findings. You can be relatively confident in the quality of the texts you've accumulated because library holdings and scholarly databases tend to contain materials that have been more rigorously screened than those found through an Internet search engine. However, keep in mind that you'll still need to apply the same evaluation criteria to these texts as you would to Websites.

Start by assessing the visual rhetoric of the journal covers, assessing topic, stance, and reliability. You might have come across the two covers found in Figures 5.9 and 5.10. A rhetorical analysis reveals differences in purpose, audience, and focus. *Stem Cells*, by using an actual image of embryonic cells, signals its focus on cellular biology and scientific applications; in addition, by listing its table of contents—complete with authors and article titles—on the front cover, it privileges ethos as an appeal. *Yale Scientific* chooses a different approach, using a powerful visual metaphor

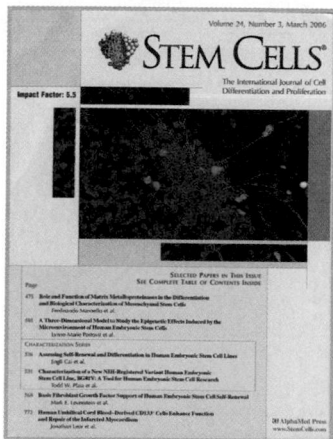

FIGURE 5.9. The cover of *Stem Cells* emphasizes its scientific approach in choices of cover image and text.

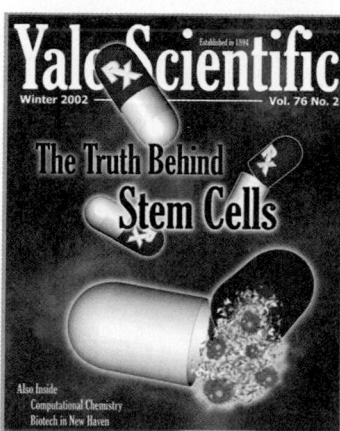

FIGURE 5.10. The cover of *Yale Scientific* zooms in on the debate rather than on the science of stem cells.

coupled with the term "Truth" to suggest its engagement with the debate surrounding stem cell research.

However, in many cases you may not be able to use a cover image as a guide to evaluation; many scholarly journals and books have been re-covered in plain library bindings. In that case, the steps you should take to select and evaluate the best sources are outlined in the "At a Glance" box on page 148.

As with evaluating Websites, rhetorical attention to the writing of journal articles and books will help you make good choices as a researcher. You can assess the language, tone, date, context, and stance of the author.

Realize that the most important assessment question is how *useful* a source will be for your project and your potential argument. Then you are on your way to knowing *how* you will use that text from your iceberg of research to craft your own research-based argument on the issue.

Using Field Research

Consider the resources available to you right on your campus. For instance, you might interview faculty members from your university who have written or lectured on subjects related to your topic. This is a great way to

AT A GLANCE

Evaluating Academic Sources

- Assess the **author**. Perhaps your teacher recommended the author to you or you notice that the author has written many books and articles on the topic. You can look this person up in a bibliography index or on the Web to assess the ethos of the writer. If the author turns out to be disreputable or affiliated with an extremist organization, would the source still be an important one to consider? Would the exaggerated stance help you examine extremist positions on your topic?

- Check out the **place of publication**. Is it a university press (suggesting peer-reviewed scholarship) or a trade press (suggesting a commercial venture)? Is it published by a foundation or organization (suggesting a political agenda) or self-published (suggesting the author's struggle to have his or her views accepted for publication)?

- Look at the **date**. Is it a recent contribution or an older study? An older source can provide historical context, but sometimes it can be too outdated to be useful. Usually, you should pick the more recent sources to engage the most timely perspectives on your topic.

- Go beneath the cover of the book or journal. Open it and turn to the **table of contents** and the **index** to see exactly what the book contains. Is it a collection of articles by different authors, or does it reflect the viewpoint of a single author? Now flip through the pages, looking for interesting arguments and judging the quality or complexity of the writing. You may note its **voice** or **tone**: Is it written for specialists in the field or for a popular audience? Does it focus on issues relevant to your research?

make contacts and develop your iceberg of research. In addition to interviewing the faculty member as a secondary source, ask the professor to recommend two or three key books in the field that you might consult as you continue on your research journey.

Or let's look at a more ambitious approach to fieldwork. Student Vincent Chen used field research quite prominently in his research project about the rhetoric of climate change. Specifically, he included photographs he took while attending the Copenhagen Conference on Climate Change in December of 2009. Included in this conference was a special session on the "15th Conference of the Parties to the UNFCCC (United Nations Framework Convention on Climate Change)," commonly known as "COP15." At the COP15, Vincent conducted impressive field research, such as taking photographs of people milling through the halls, attending talks, and listening to speakers present position statements about the environment. But Vincent's most powerful field research was a single photo, showing the crowds of attendees stopping mid-motion to hear the speech of Mohamed Nasheed, president of the Republic of Maldives. The photo became central to making his argument that Nasheed strongly differentiated himself from other climate leaders at the conference through his inflammatory rhetoric about the danger of rising seas as well as the logos argument of his country's small size and limited economic power. To argue this position, Vincent used a photo he took as visual evidence documenting the power of President Nasheed's conference-stopping speech (see Figure 5.11). He also included additional field research in the form of interviews with other students who attended at the conference and an interview with Professor Stephen Schneider of the Interdisciplinary Environmental Studies Program at his university.

This field research added depth and power to Vincent's argument by allowing him to include his own evidence as strategic argumentative support for his argument. With regard to the photo in Figure 5.11, rather than just asserting his claim to be true, Vincent could allow his readers to *see* the evidence that would support his point that President Nasheed, out of all

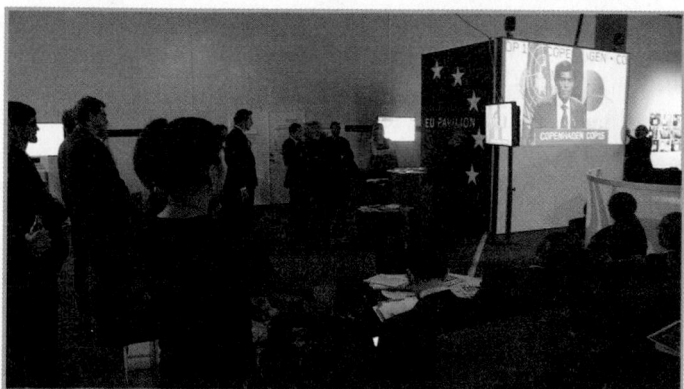

FIGURE 5.11. Vincent Chen's field research includes this powerful photo of Mohamed Nasheed, president of the Republic of Maldives, speaking to a riveted audience at the 2009 Copenhagen Climate conference. © Vincent Chen 2009.

leaders at the climate conference, made people stop and listen to an argument for action.

Of course, not all fieldwork involves trips around the world. Sometimes you can gather your own evidence for your research project by using resources available within your local community. Consider these possibilities: if you were studying the layout and impact of a new park in your community, you might meet with a city planner or the landscape architect responsible for the project; if you were writing about a city water reservoir, you might visit the site, take photographs, and meet with the site manager; and, if you were writing on the marketing strategies of a local baseball team, you might even write a letter to that team's marketing coordinator. Fieldwork such as this allows you to take your research to the next level and make a truly original contribution of your own.

Student Writing

Look at Sean Bruich's letter he wrote to the marketing coordinator of the Oakland Athletic's baseball team as part of his fieldwork.

www.pearsonhighered.com/envision/150

Evaluating Field Research Sources

When you conduct interviews and surveys, you are looking for materials to use in your paper as secondary sources. But keep in mind the need to evaluate your field research sources as carefully as you assess your Web and print sources. If you interview a professor, a marketing executive, a witness, or a roommate, consider the rhetorical stance of that person. What kind of bias does the person have concerning the topic of your project? If you conduct a survey of your peers in your dorm, assess the value and credibility of your results as rigorously as you would evaluate the data of a published study. Don't fall into the trap of misusing statistics when making claims if you haven't taken into account the need for **statistical significance**, or to paraphrase the social psychologist Philip Zimbardo, the measure by which a number obtains meaning in scientific fields. To reach this number, you need to design the survey carefully, conduct what's called a *random sample*, interview a *large enough* number of people, and ask a *range of different people*. These are complex parameters to follow, but you will need to learn about them to conduct survey research that has reliable and credible results.

"Statistics are the backbone of research. They are used to understand observations and to determine whether findings are, in fact, correct and significant. . . . But, statistics can also be used poorly or deceptively, misleading those who do not understand them."

—Philip Zimbardo (595)

As Professor Zimbardo points out, statistics—though we often think of them as Truth—actually function rhetorically. Like words and images,

AT A GLANCE

Conducting Interviews and Surveys

1. *Target your population:* Is the best source for your field research a professor at your college who is expert in this area? a professional from the community? peers in your class, dorm, athletic team, or town?

2. *Develop questions:* Review your list of question with a peer or your instructor. Avoid general questions. Design interview questions to elicit usable quotations; design surveys that balance short, multiple choice questions, which yield primarily statistical data, with short answer question that will produce more nuanced responses. Keep your survey short; the longer your form, the fewer completed surveys will probably be returned to you.

3. *Prepare:* Know your interviewee: read an online biography, read something he or she has written, have some sense of the interviewee's position on the issue. Research the best delivery method for your survey, given your target population.

4. *Make contact:* For interviews, explain your purpose, your identity, and your goal for the field research clearly. Offer two or three times. Follow up unanswered requests with polite emails or phone calls. Don't hesitate to persist, but do so respectfully. For surveys, state your deadline clearly, and make sure the respondent knows where and how to return the form.

5. *Record and document:* Get written permission from interviewees and survey subjects to use their words in your paper. If you record an interview with a tape recorder or cell phone device, be sure to ask permission first and to create a transcript as soon as possible after the interview. Document all uses of the interview with quotation marks in your paper.

6. *Follow-up:* Send a thank-you note to any interviewees and offer a copy of your completed paper. Consider sharing your findings with survey participants, if possible, through a local newsletter or college newspaper article.

numbers are a mode of persuasion that can mislead readers. You need to be especially vigilant when using a survey or statistics as a supposedly "objective" part of your iceberg of research, particularly if you plan to depend on such materials in your argument.

Take as much care with how you convey information visually as you do with how you convey it in writing. Consider David Pinner's writing project about grade inflation. David accumulated enough quantitative information through fieldwork and primary research to compose his own charts. He discovered a wealth of information in archived faculty senate minutes, which he sorted through during his research. From that work, he came across important statistical data that reflected the change in grade distribution at Stanford over the course of 25 years. In addition to

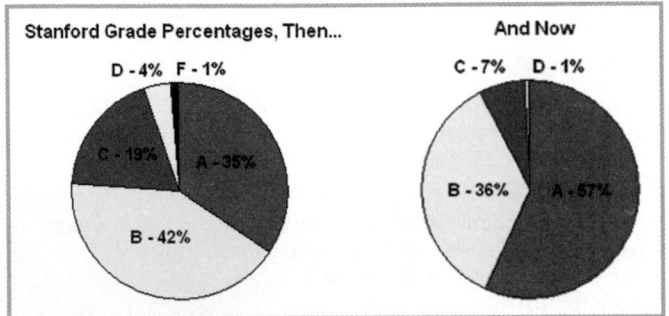

FIGURE 5.12. Student David Pinner created these information graphics from his research data to suggest the difference in grade distribution between 1968 and 1992.

including the numbers in his written text, he created two pie charts (see Figure 5.12), using a visual comparison of statistics to underscore his point. His argument was more powerful not just because of his impressive field research but also because of how he represented it graphically through responsible use of statistics.

Creating a Dialogue with Your Sources

Throughout this chapter we have emphasized that research is social, a conversation with the people whose ideas and writing came before yours. As you gather, assess, and use sources, you are contributing to this conversation, building on the work of others, and adding a new perspective. Indeed, this notion of writing as communal is the reason why you need to use the author's name when citing a quotation or an idea; remember that all your sources are authored sources; each source mentioned in this chapter was composed by a person or a group of people. If you think of these texts as written *by people like you*, you will have an easier time remembering to acknowledge their ideas and integrate their quotations into your essay. In the process, you will go a long way toward avoiding unintentional plagiarism. You can begin this process through an exercise we call a **dialogue of sources**—a fictional conversation among the primary and secondary sources of your research paper designed to help you identify each one's central argument and main idea.

To prepare for her research paper on tobacco advertisements, Amanda Johnson (AJ) wrote this dialogue between several sources she had found: RJ Reynolds Tobacco Co. (RJRT); Larry C. White (LW), author of *Merchants of Death*; and Hugh High (HH), a professor of economics, finance, and law who published a collection of tobacco studies titled *Does Advertising Increase Smoking?* among others, which she presents in a literal dialogue with herself acting as scholarly moderator.

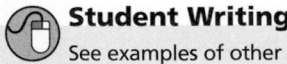

Student Writing
See examples of other source dialogues.
www.pearsonhighered.com/envision/152

AT A GLANCE

Creating a Dialogue of Sources

- *Identify the key players* from your research log and your notes. Which ones have the most influential or important arguments?
- *Create a cast of characters list* with a short "bio" for each speaker, including yourself. Describe each person's credentials and rhetorical stance—his or her ethos and argument. (You may even want to create identifying icons or pictures to give "faces" to the participants.)
- *Draft the script.* Write the key questions you want to ask your sources about your topic. Use quotes from your sources to respond where possible, and include page numbers.
- *Consider what your sources would say to each other.* Write their fictional conversation by using quotes from your sources.
- *Don't just play the "objective" moderator.* Respond to the sources and, in the process, start to develop your own argument.

Dialogue of Sources

AJ: I would like to thank the panel for joining us this afternoon. We have quite a diverse group of writers, researchers, spokespeople, and a professor here to discuss the focus and objectives of current tobacco advertising. Since I know your comments on this subject vary widely, I suppose I will start off by asking you to talk about what you believe to be the focus of tobacco advertising as it exists today.

RJRT: RJ Reynolds tobacco products are among the best advertised in the industry, and we take pride in our commitment to maintaining honest advertising to the public. We do not intend for our advertising to manipulate nonsmokers into trying our products, nor do we choose to target these audiences.

Amanda's complete dialogue begins with a list of speakers and their bios. Then she introduces the topic of her research project. She reproduces the argument of each source, both print and interview, through paraphrase.

By allowing debate to evolve, Amanda begins to see how she might use quotations from these sources in her paper.

Advertising is simply a method by which we are able to maintain our share of the market and compete with other tobacco manufacturers.

LW: How can you possibly claim to avoid targeting specific audiences and replenishing your older dwindling population with new younger smokers!?! The whole point of advertising is to get more people to buy your product, and, since market shares don't change all that much for large companies like yours, the best way to get more people to buy your product is to increase the number of overall smokers. Youth are your best option because if you can get them hooked now, you will have a steady flow of income for several decades to come.

HH: Mr. White, you make a good point about general economic objectives. However, studies show that advertising does very little to change the number of new smokers. Countries that have banned advertising for tobacco-related products have seen very little decline in the number of consumers that buy their product. As RJRT stated previously, advertising is only successful at making adjustments within the market concerning the relative amounts each company is able to sell.

AJ: I recently reviewed a chart concerning the prevalence of smoking among U.S. adults and found that over the past 40 years since the surgeon general first warned about cigarettes' cancerous effects, the steady decline in smokers has slowed

Most importantly, she begins to develop her own argument for her research paper in the context of these other perspectives.

She does this by questioning the responses, adding facts from her research, and moving the argument forward as she will need to do in her paper.

> to rest around 25 percent of the population over the age of 18. With the number of people dying each day, it is surprising that this number does not continue to go down. How would you account for the slowed change?

Notice how Amanda's work here allows her to write out the process of research *as a conversation* and will help her avoid unintentional plagiarism since she is giving credit to her sources.

Writing an Annotated Bibliography

As you move further into your research, you might want to synthesize your notes in what researchers call an **annotated bibliography**—a list of research sources that provides informational notes about each source and how you might use it as you turn to drafting your paper.

Realize that composing entries in the annotated bibliography involves much more than merely recording information: it is a way for you to synthesize arguments and add your response to what the source has to say about your research topic. Be sure to include quotation marks and page numbers if you quote directly from sources to distinguish between direct quotes and your own paraphrases or commentary; in this way, you can avoid potentially misquoting or plagiarizing sources.

As you compose your annotated bibliography, consider including images that you might use as primary or secondary sources as well. In this way, you are crafting a **visual annotated bibliography**—a working list of potential sources in which you include images. This is very helpful if you plan to analyze images in your paper or if your rhetorical analysis covers visual and multimedia texts, such as James Caputo's project on the government's space program.

Student Writing
See samples of annotated bibliographies on a variety of topics.
www.pearsonhighered.com/envision/155

Consider the excerpt from Carly Geehr's visual annotated bibliography for her research project on the representations of swimming as a gendered sport in the American media throughout history (see Figure 5.13). Both the image of a swimmer from the early 1920s in the secondary source by Douglas Booth and Colin Tatz and the advertising from *U.S.A. Swimming* were key images that Carly analyzed in her paper to make an argument about the feminization of swimming in American sports culture. From this annotated bibliography, it was a short step to generating a full research paper complete with responsible integration of research sources. In this way, you too can make your contribution to the conversation of research.

AT A GLANCE

Composing an Annotated Bibliography

1. Put your sources into alphabetical order; you can also categorize them by primary and secondary sources.

2. For a visual annotated bibliography, include images of your primary and secondary sources (covers, screenshots, photographs, drawings, charts, cartoons, posters) to show each source's stance through visual rhetoric.

3. Provide complete identifying information for each source, including author's name, title, publication, date, page numbers, URLs for Websites, and database information for online sources.

4. Compose a three- to five-sentence annotation for each source:

   • First, summarize the main argument or point of the source; use concrete language. Include quotations if you wish.

   • Next, indicate the writer's stance. How credible or biased is this source?

   • Finally, and most importantly, describe the relevance of this source to your research argument. Will the source be used as background for the opening part of your paper? Does it offer a key counterargument? Will it provide the main authority to back up your claims?

The Writer's Process

As you begin to articulate your contribution to the research conversation about your topic, use the strategies that you've learned in this chapter. These include visualizing research as a conversation that you are joining and understanding

Carly Geehr
Visually Annotated Bibliography

Dr. Alyssa O'Brien
May 13, 2003

The American Media and Swimming: Investigating the "Uphill Battle"

Booth, Douglas and Colin Tatz. *One Eyed: a View of Australian Sport*. Allen and Unwin 2000.

In order to make my argument that swimming could be a more popular sport in the United States, I will need to present strong evidence: this book provides it to me. Booth and Tatz chronicle the history of Australian sports in both society and in the media. From their descriptions of media coverage and the role of gender in sports, I can find out why, culturally and historically, swimming has been able to achieve such a high level of popularity in Australia. Of particular interest to me so far has been their focus on the traditional, accepted role of women in sports-it is drastically different in US history. By comparison to my sources about American sports culture, I will find out the key differences between the two countries and hopefully draw some concrete conclusions as to why swimming is not as popular in the United States as it is in Australia. This photo is the image of a female Australian swimmer whose look and demeanor demand respect, unlike her beautified American counterparts (212). I will be able to compare the Australian images of swimmers with the American images of swimmers, hopefully noting some key differences in visual rhetoric techniques employed—preliminarily, I suspect that the American images will focus much more on aesthetics while Australian images will focus on intensity and ruggedness (more pertinent to the sport itself).

"Duel in the Pool Advertisement." 3 Apr 2003. http://www.usaswimming.org/Duel.

[A little background: USA Swimming recently staged its first "made-for-TV" dual meet versus the Australian national team. The goal was to attract network attention and draw the people who would normally be watching sports on weekend afternoons into watching swimming for a change. According to Mary Wagner, the ratings were good but not exceptional.] This image is one of the advertisements put out by USA Swimming before the event to attract its target audience of teenagers and others (particularly males) who would be watching television on Saturday and Sunday afternoons. It appeals mostly to ethos, citing Michael Phelps as a world record holder, but also appeals more subtly to pathos in using the national colors and the national flag to create a sense of nationalism and passion for the event. However, this image helps me support my claim that USA Swimming's promotions have fallen short of successful in that it is not an exciting image—if the intent was to attract teenagers and adults who typically watch traditional, exciting American sports, then this image fails to create sufficient energy to generate interest or a desire to deviate from watching normal weekend sports on TV.

FIGURE 5.13. Well-chosen images and detailed annotations show Carly Geehr's progress on her research project.

the process of researching your argument as a movement from surface to depth. As you learn to search and locate both primary and secondary sources, you can engage in critical evaluation of these texts in your research log. You can also engage in innovative fieldwork of your own to generate original resource material to use in your argument. In writing your own annotated bibliography, remember that effective annotations and note-taking practices can help you develop the strategies of an academic writer and that these practices will move you toward finalizing your own argument about the topic. By moving from covers to contents, you will

AT A GLANCE

Note-Taking Strategies

As you read through your sources, take notes on materials that you could use in your paper:

• Particularly memorable quotations

• Background information

• A well-written passage providing context or a perspective useful to your argument

Be sure to double-check your notes for accuracy, use quotation marks for direct quotes, and include complete source details and page numbers.

watch your iceberg take shape, and you will begin to let your own voice be heard.

Along the way, be sure to take careful notes. This is a crucial step in your writer's process. You can use the dialogue of sources as a note-taking strategy while you work through your research sources. Indeed, many students find this approach to note taking to be the best way to create thorough research logs for their projects, one that keeps their own thesis evident. But honor your own learned techniques, such as taking notes in a software program such as Endnote, on note cards, in a binder, or on your laptop.

PREWRITING CHECKLIST

Focus on Evaluating Covers and Contents

❑ What images are featured on the cover? Do the images lend themselves to an appeal to logic? to an appeal to emotion? to an appeal to authority?

❑ Do the words included as headings and subheads on the cover contribute to any of these appeals?

❑ What do the cover images suggest about the contents of the larger text? Do they suggest a specific rhetorical stance or point of view? What is the effect of each visual choice?

❑ How do the words on the cover or homepage work in conjunction with the image to suggest the entire text's rhetorical stance? Do the words complement the image? Do they offer a contrast to the image?

PREWRITING WITH THE *ENVISION* WEBSITE

Visit the Websites listed for "stem cell research" at the *Envision* Website. What rhetorical decisions are apparent from each site's homepage design? How do the images suggest different approaches to the stem cell issue? How does the organization of information, the menu, and the written text contribute to this impression? Follow the site links to explore how the rhetorical stance suggested by the "cover" is reflected in the site's contents. Develop a list of criteria for evaluating Websites.

www.pearsonhighered.com/envision/158

You might include in this list a focus on issues of authority, accessibility, and suitability. You might look at the URL to establish the author or host of a Website, or you might examine the selection of images or the word choice for indications of bias or sensationalism. Look also at the "last updated" note to check the currency of the site or for the "contact" link to evaluate the author's sense of accountability for his or her work. Follow the links to see if the site is self-contained, linking only to its own materials, or whether it contains external links, connecting it to the broader conversation on the topic. Finally, assess the type of material the site contains: primary documents or secondary commentary.

WRITING PROJECTS

1. **Research Log Entries:** Keep a running commentary/assessment of potential research sources for your project. Realize that careful research notes are a crucial part of the process and will help you avoid unintentional plagiarism of material. Include a combination of typed notes, highlighted photocopies, emails, sources from databases, note cards, scanned images, and other means of processing all the information you encounter.

2. **Working with Your Preliminary Bibliography:** Create a *dialogue of sources* or an *annotated bibliography* to showcase the primary and secondary sources you'll employ in the major paper. Be sure that your writing provides a range of primary and secondary sources. Include both print and electronic sources and, if appropriate, include images to demonstrate the kinds of materials you'll be analyzing in the project.

3. **Collaborative Peer Review:** Present your annotated bibliographies to one another in groups. Pull the "greatest hits" from your research log, and tell the class about how your research is going. In other words, *present a discussion of your work in progress.* Identify obstacles and successes so far. You'll get feedback from the class about your developing research project.

 Visit www.pearsonhighered.com/envision for expanded assignment guidelines and student projects. Visit www.mycomplab.com for additional general writing and research resources.

CHAPTER 6

Organizing and Writing Research Arguments

Chapter Preview Questions

- What strategies of organization work best for my paper?
- What are the best ways to get started writing a full draft?
- How do I integrate research sources responsibly and rhetorically?
- How will I know when to quote, paraphrase, or summarize?
- How can collaboration and peer review help me revise?

Constructing a research argument is a complex and ongoing process. From selecting a topic to locating and evaluating sources and taking notes, it involves a series of interrelated steps. This is true of the *drafting* stage as well. In fact, organizing, drafting, and revising information is a prominent part of the process of creating any text—an academic essay, a television commercial, a radio essay, or even a film. Figure 6.1, for instance, lets us glimpse the drafting process behind a film called *Serenity* (2005). In this scene, one of the main characters, River, fights a roomful of Reavers— the cannibalistic bad guys of the film—to protect her brother and friends. What you see in Figure 6.1 are the storyboards for this scene—an artist's draft that lays out the action in chronological increments, mapping out not only the movement of the characters but also the camera angles and thus the audience's experience of the events depicted. Notice the way it captures a sense of motion by rapidly changing perspectives and how it creates a narrative tension in the last panel with the close-up of the Reavers grabbing River to

FIGURE 6.1. This storyboard for Joss Whedon's film *Serenity* shows an initial draft for one of the film's climactic action scenes.

drag her back during her attempted escape. Storyboards like this clearly operate as visual outlines, an organizational strategy that underlies almost all films. The polished final version seen in the theater is actually made possible by drafting steps like this one.

In many ways, the process of writing is like film production:

- Both have many small steps that support a grounding vision or main idea
- Both have a carefully planned structure
- Both involve rigorous editing

Because producing a film and producing a research argument share such rich similarities, we'll use the medium of film throughout this chapter to understand the process of writing a research paper: from constructing a visual map and formal outline to integrating sources, key quotations, and evidence. We'll talk about incorporating sources responsibly in a way that sustains the conversation you began in the previous chapter, and we'll walk through the drafting and revision process. Just as filmmakers leave many scenes on the cutting room floor, you too will write, edit, cut, and rearrange much of the first draft of your research paper before it reaches its final form. You'll find that the process of completing your research argument is as collaborative as film production. Additionally, both film and writing involve parameters of length, cost, and time that you need to contend with to produce the best possible text. No matter what your topic, you can think of the way in which film works to help you visualize the final product and move from notes to writing the completed paper.

Organizing Your Draft in Visual Form

It can be quite challenging to turn on the computer and try to crank out a complete draft without first arranging materials into some kind of order. Storyboards like those shown in Figure 6.1, or the bubble webs or graphic flowcharts described in this section, can be productive ways to prewrite through visual means. In fact, filmmakers often begin the production process by visually mapping out movie ideas, key scenes, and plot progressions. You too can use various forms of graphically organizing your research notes and argumentative points in order to sort, arrange, and make connections between ideas.

The most basic way to get organized is physically to stack your research books and materials and then write labels for each pile. This organizational strategy functions as a concrete way of categorizing the resources you have and figuring out, visually, how they relate to one another. Next, you can produce a visual map of these sources by using colored pens and paper or by cutting out shapes and constructing a three-dimensional model for your paper's organization.

Using a computer, you can turn your handwritten visual map into a **bubble web**, in which you arrange your ideas into categories using shapes and colors. You could also try more hierarchical or linear graphic flowcharts as a means of organizing your materials. In **graphic flowcharts**, you list one idea and then draw an arrow to suggest cause and effect and to show relationships among items. Figure 6.2, for example, presents Ye Yuan's graphic flowchart of his ideas about war photography, arranged in a tree structure. This

Student Writing

See examples of visual maps generated by students for their research projects.
www.pearsonhighered.com/envision/162

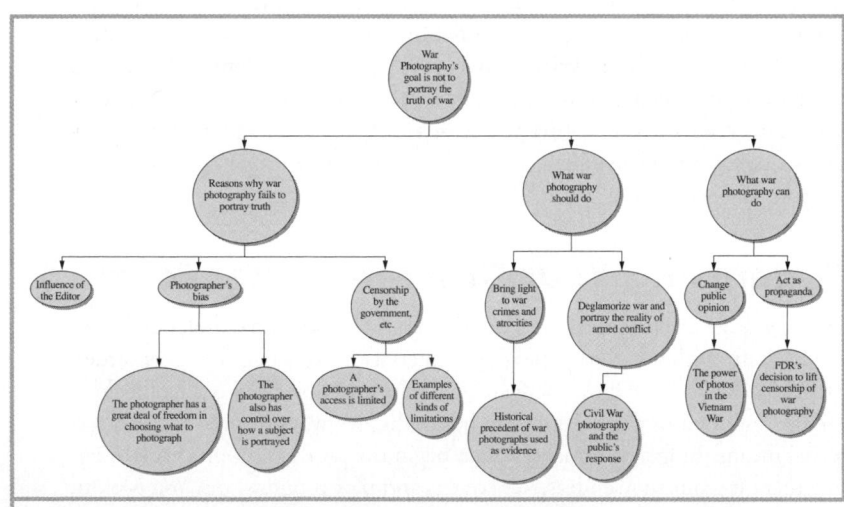

FIGURE 6.2. This graphic flowchart by Ye Yuan, created with the software program Inspiration, allowed him to visualize the sections of his written paper.

visual hierarchy helped him assess his project by asking questions and checking to see if he had enough research or points to make:

- Is each point developed thoroughly?
- Do I have a balance among the sections?
- Is there a coherent whole?

Learning Outline Strategies

Visual maps can help you sort out your materials and prepare you for the next step: the detailed, written **outline**. For a longer, more complex paper, such as a research-based argument, an *outline* is an extremely useful method of arranging ideas and expediting the drafting process. Outlines offer a plan for your paper and should show the relationships among the various sections in your argument. If your outline simply consists of a list of topics, you won't be able to see the argument of the whole paper, nor will you be able to check for a strong progression between your individual points. In other words, the secret to producing a successful outline—and by extension a successful paper—is to pay special attention to the flow or development of ideas.

It's often hard to know for certain the best way to put together points in an outline. We can learn a lot from films about the ways in which various texts are organized. Consider how a film's **trailer**, or short prerelease video, provides a brief *outline* of the key scenes, the main conflict, the crucial characters, and the message of the movie. Figure 6.3 shows still shots from one of the several theatrical trailers for *Avatar*.

Structured loosely as a narrative, this trailer suggests an outline of the film, moving from an introduction of the human characters, to scenes showing the main avatar (Jake) and his Na'vi girlfriend, to scenes of the final physical conflict between the two civilizations. In doing so, the trailer reproduces one of the central themes of *Avatar*: the identification of both good and evil in the human civilization, and the conflict between the corporate part of that civilization and the spiritual Na'vi civilization. There are many ways in which these elements might have been arranged, each suggesting a different argument for the film—and indeed, different *Avatar* trailers made different arguments. The power of the trailer as an organizational tool or outline is that it allows filmmakers to experiment with order and, ultimately, meaning.

FIGURE 6.3. These still shots from one of several trailers for the film *Avatar* transition the viewer from the the human perspective into the world of Pandora, and then into the climactic conflict between the worlds.

Keeping the idea of the trailer in mind, take your ideas from the visual map you have created and craft them into a **formal outline**, a detailed list that uses numbers and letters to indicate subsections of your argument. Rather than list three sections only—such as Introduction, Body, and Conclusion—create several points within the body to show the development of your argument.

As you organize your ideas, remember that formal outlines can help you work step by step through the process of arguing your position. That is, they can save you a lot of time as you approach writing the essay itself. Consider using full sentences to most clearly articulate your thoughts or inserting sources right into the outline; these techniques can help you troubleshoot areas where you might need to do supplemental research or expand your argument.

Student Writing
See several examples of research outlines on a variety of topics.
www.pearsonhighered.com/envision/165

Another benefit of outlining is that it allows you to work with the rhetorical canon of **arrangement** (discussed in Chapter 3), experimenting with different organizational structures. Depending on your topic, you might try several approaches, just as filmmakers rearrange a film to create a variety of trailers. You might start your paper with a question, move through evidence, and then arrive at a declarative thesis statement toward the end of the essay. Alternatively, begin with a firm thesis statement up front, followed by an accumulation of supporting evidence that broadens out to a larger issue. Or, try moving thematically through your research offering a progressive argument. See the "At a Glance" box for additional ways to organize your material in an outline.

Outlines with Argumentative Subheads

Outlines can also help you develop the complexity of your research argument if you incorporate subheads and transitions into your writing. **Subheads**, or labeled headings for each subsection of your outline, are a terrific way to structure your ideas into discrete units to show the progression of your argument and help your

AT A GLANCE

Useful Organization Strategies for Writing

- *Chronological:* relevant for historical discussions
- *Thematic:* helps with diverse case studies
- *Cause and effect:* focuses on consequences
- *Problem-solution:* useful for social issues papers
- *Illustrative:* emphasizes examples of a pattern
- *Macro to micro:* moves from the general to the specific
- *Micro to macro:* moves from the specific to the general
- *Narrative:* employs the personal experience

AT A GLANCE

Assessing Outlines

- **Thesis:** Is it complex, contentious, and interesting?
- **Argument:** Is there a fluid progression of ideas? Does each one relate back to the thesis? Is there extraneous information that you can cut? Do more points need to be developed?
- **Sources:** Are primary sources identified for analysis in the paper? Are secondary sources listed to provide support and authority for the argument? Are there sufficient sources listed for each point? Are visual texts included as argumentative evidence?
- **Format:** Are there argumentative subheads? Do they move the argument of the essay along?

readers make sense of a complex argument. Subheads work particularly well for longer, research-based essays. You can transform the key parts of your outline into a short list of **argumentative subheads**, or subheads that indicate the progression of your argument at each point.

If you were writing a detailed outline, you might insert into the body of your paper subheads that indicate specific parts of your argument. You can feel free to get creative by connecting your subheads thematically or by using a single metaphor to add a rich layer of vivid words to your essay. For a film-marketing paper, for instance, instead of using subheads like "Background", "Movies Online," and "Advertising Movies," you might experiment with "Movies Online Are a Big Splash," "Surfing for Movies," and "The Next Wave in Viral Marketing." After you write a list of working subheads, exchange them with a partner. Suggest modifications and new ideas to each other; keep focused on using subheads to advance the argument of the essay. Look at how Dexian Cai met this challenge by incorporating argumentative subheads into his outline.

Notice how Dex includes the opening line for his paper, the hook, right in the outline, setting the tone for the paper.

Dexian Cai
PWR1 H-1
Dr. Alyssa O'Brien

Research Paper—Outline

I.   Introduction

1. Hook: A brief description of a current McDonald's video advertisement. While ostensibly American and Western, the interesting aspect is that this video is in fact an ad targeting an Asian market.

2. Thesis: McDonald's video advertising in East Asia has evolved over time, adapting to trends and changes in Asian societal values. The paper will argue that McDonald's both shapes and is shaped by these evolving trends, creating a dynamic relationship between the restaurant and consumers.

His thesis comprises two sentences since this argument is complex, although he could develop the "how so" part of the thesis more.

3. Implications: What are the effects of McDonald's influence on Asian values and societal evolution? Is this a healthy trend or merely a restaurant moving with the times? Are accusations of cultural imperialism or degradation of morals justified?

He ends the intro with questions to engage the reader.

II. The Background Behind the Arches

- A brief history of McDonald's entry into the various East Asian markets. In particular, research will center on Japan, Hong Kong, Korea, Taiwan, China, and Singapore.
- A summary of McDonald's image and *ethos* in the United States.

After a brief background section, Dex moves on to the heart of his argument. The subhead "From Homely to Hip" reflects in words the point Dex will make in this section, namely, that McDonald's has changed its brand image from conservative to trendy. The play on words in the subhead helps keep Dex on track and to interest the reader.

III. McDonald's: From Homely to Hip

Then

- Rhetorical analysis of ads from the 1970s and 1980s, when McDonald's first broke into the Asian markets.
- Argument that McDonald's was using *pathos*, attempting to portray itself as a family restaurant that made children feel special. Highlight the fact that the campaigns differed across the various countries because McDonald's tailored each campaign to the specific market's characteristics and perceived needs.
- Compare and contrast with contemporary American campaigns. Family vs. fast food.
- Source: McDonald's Corporation. (Pending the approval of a request sent via e-mail.)

Note that he includes his sources right in his outline so he'll be sure to weave them into his paper.

- Secondary Source: Watson, James L. *Golden Arches East: McDonald's in East Asia*. Palo Alto, CA: Stanford UP, 1997.

Since his paper focuses on the visual rhetoric of McDonald's advertising in Asia, it is appropriate for Dex to include images in his outline. These images will serve as evidence for his argument. [Images were removed for copyright purposes but appeared in Dex's original outline.]

Now

- Rhetorical analysis of most recent video ads.
- Argument that McDonald's marketing strategy has evolved to embrace East Asia as an "assimilated market," as the campaign and slogan are standardized the world over. There is no longer a uniquely Asian campaign; instead it is replaced by the homogeneous American set of ads.
- Image of fun and relaxation is interspersed with images of McDonald's products. Using youth to drive the campaign is a clear signal of the target audience and the aim of creating a "cool" and "hip" image for the franchise. This contrasts the familial tone of ads from the "early days." A switch from *pathos* to *ethos*.
- Sources: McDonald's Country Websites

IV. Getting Behind the Arches

He includes a key research question as a transition into this section. His next subhead again uses language to convey this point in the progression of his argument; with such argumentative subheads, he can be certain that his argument is building in significance.

- Key Question: What has brought about this evolution in advertising strategies in East Asia? Why the shift in image?
- Argument: The dynamics of influence are mutual and interactive. Although McDonald's largely responds to perceived societal trends, it also seeks to influence attitudes and sell its version of "hip" or "cool," especially to Asian youth.
- Analyze how the Asian case is reflective of McDonald's marketing strategy internationally. Discuss the moral/ethical implications of such strategies.

He is still working on points of the argument, even in the outline, as shown in his question whether to bring in Joe Kincheloe's argument as a secondary source here.

- Consider the McDonald's "Culture of Power" argument in Kincheloe's book. Are the claims leveled against the franchise valid?
- Source: Kincheloe, Joe L. *The Sign of the Burger: McDonald's and the Culture of Power*. Philadelphia: Temple UP, 2002.

V. Amer-Asia? A Peek at the Future of Asia
*   Summarize/recap the arguments of the paper.
Larger Questions
*   Given the trend of increasing global integration, is homogenization under American leadership an inevitable end of modern civilization?
*   Discuss ways in which this is not so ("dissenting opinion"). Asia's cultures continue to greatly influence McDonald's, causing wide variations between McDonald's image in Asia and in America.
*   Answer these bigger concerns: What are the implications of changing societal trends for Asian youth? How does McDonald's advertising affect and influence these trends? Do the ads exacerbate/speed up the "Americanization" of Asian youth? or do they merely reflect what is already present?

The final section is not titled "Conclusion" but instead uses an argumentative subhead to transition into the closing argument of the paper, namely that the presence of McDonald's is potentially changing distinctions between nations, blurring cultures into a combined identity Dex calls "Amer-Asia."

As you can see from Dex's example, using an appropriate metaphor in a subhead provides consistency in language that in turn can help the flow of your essay.

Transitions

You can also enhance the flow of your writing with careful attention to **transitions**—phrases that provide the connections between the paragraphs or sections in your paper. When creating transitions, even during your outlining phase, think about how you can signal the next idea, build on the previous idea, or reiterate the key terms of your thesis as you advance your argument. Many students like to think of the game of dominoes when composing transitions: each domino can only touch another domino with a matching number; two connects with two, three with three. Using this notion of progressive, connecting terms, you can incorporate transitions within sections of your outline to give it overall structure and flow. Then, when you turn to writing the paper, you will avoid big jumps in logic. Instead, by incorporating the transitions from your outline, you will produce a polished piece of written work.

Spotlight on Your Argument

As you turn now from writing an outline to fleshing out the full draft, consider the decision before you concerning what kind of voice or rhetorical stance to take in the language of your prose. Again, we can learn a lot from filmmakers as they face similar decisions.

In his 2007 documentary, *Sicko*, Michael Moore is careful to introduce and acknowledge his sources, but even while he includes many other voices in his film, he ultimately emphasizes his own argument. Of course, the film relies on research as background material, offering the narrator's comments as interview segments, in which a primary or secondary authority speaks directly to the audience, and as quoted material spoken directly by the narrator or through voiceover. But as the poster in Figure 6.4 suggests, Moore's opinion provides the foundation for everything disclosed in the film, making his rhetorical stance a prominent part of the text.

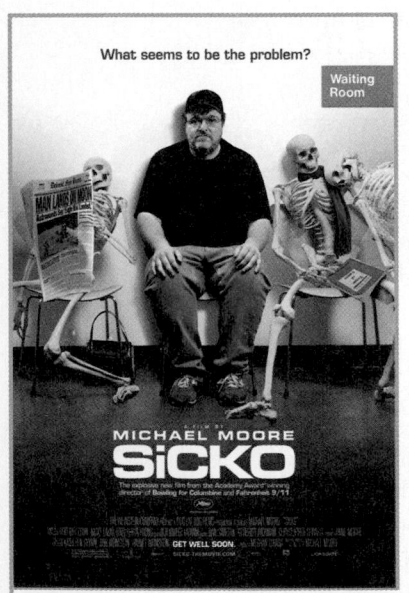

You should also consider diverse ways to present your argument. Think of the power of a casting director on a film set. In a film such as Franco Zeffirelli's version of *Hamlet* (1990), for instance, the entire sexual politics of the narrative was influenced by the decision to cast Glenn Close (age 43 at the time) as Queen Gertrude, mother to Mel Gibson's Hamlet (Gibson was 34). Their close proximity in age set in relief an incest plot at which Shakespeare himself had only hinted. In essence, what audiences watched in the movie theater was less Shakespeare's *Hamlet* and more Zeffirelli's interpretation of it. In your own writing, you have a comparable power; the way you "cast" your sources can influence your reader's understanding of your argument.

FIGURE 6.4. The promotional poster for *Sicko* reveals the way Michael Moore emphasizes his own argument in the film.

In fact, your treatment of your sources will define your approach to your topic. Consider the "objectivity" of a celebrity biography shown on TV: although the text purports to offer no explicit argument, the selection of quotations used, the identities of people interviewed, and the emphasis given to certain stages of the artist's career collaborate to produce not some objective *truth* but a single *version* of that artist's life. Or think about Oliver Stone's *W* (2008) and the controversy it stirred. The film was in fact an argument: Stone used primary and secondary evidence to create his own interpretation of the events surrounding George W. Bush's life and presidency.

Sometimes you want to put your sources center stage and direct from behind the scenes, and sometimes you will want to step out of the shadows and articulate your argument more explicitly to the audience. Whichever way you go, you should decide what role you, the writer, will play in your paper. The key is to choose the role that will produce the most effective argument on your topic, one that fits the needs of your rhetorical situation. Your voice is your spotlight on your argument; it should have rhetorical purpose and complement the content of your project.

Analyzing a Published Argument

As you outline your research paper and consider ways to bring your sources into your argument, you should study carefully the writing found in articles that you encounter throughout your research project. You can learn a lot about how to organize and spotlight your own argument from a *rhetorical analysis* of the formal properties of your secondary sources. Examine the article by Bret Schulte posted in both the print and online editions of *U.S. News & World Report*. The article provides an excellent snapshot back in time of the rhetorical situation from 2006—when *An Inconvenient Truth* first appeared in cinemas and people were beginning to learn about global warming. Schulte's piece demonstrates many of the writing techniques we've been learning in this chapter, including arranging his points into a progression of ideas and making his own voice quite strong as a spotlight on his argument. Specifically, you'll see that the piece uses interview research and reformats it into an argument that reflects the writer's own perspective on the film. The piece structures itself with subheads that are argumentative, cites interview with quotations, integrates statistics as research, and ends with a memorable conclusion.

SAYING IT IN CINEMA
By Bret Schulte
Posted 5/28/06 *U.S. News & World Report*

Notice how Schulte's voice emerges immediately when he calls *An Inconvenient Truth* a "docu-horror film"

President Bush doubts he'll see it, but millions of other people undoubtedly will. Former Vice President Al Gore's docu-horror film about the frightening future promised by global warming— an apocalyptic world of deadly hurricanes, rising oceans, disease, drought, and famine—is pushing the debate to a new level. While tracking Gore's political ascent and contentious loss of the presidency in 2000, the film zeroes in on Gore's newest campaign: to educate the public about the perils of global warming one PowerPoint presentation at a time. Although Gore insists he has no plans to run for national office, the film has thrust him back into the national limelight and sparked an industry of "Al Gore for president" speculation. His well-publicized movie has also provoked critics to run campaign-style ads challenging climate change science. Gore spoke with *U.S. News* about the film, *An Inconvenient Truth,* already playing in select cities and slated for 125 markets by July 4. Excerpts:

The alliteration (public–perils– PowerPoint presentation) and exaggerated *pathos* further develop Schulte's rhetorical stance

Rather than enclosing direct quotations from Gore's interview in quotation marks, Schulte opts for an innovative structure. He pairs a rhetorical subhead of his own (his argument) with an excerpt from interview (his source). The merger of Schulte's and Gore's voice provides a unique rhetorical effect on the reader.

Public indifference. We are dumping tens of millions of tons [of carbon dioxide] into the atmosphere every day, and it has literally changed the relationship between the Earth and the sun. It's a challenge to our moral imagination to understand we are now like a bull in the china shop. [And] there has been a very well-organized and lavishly funded effort by a few irresponsible polluters to intentionally confuse the American people by spending millions of dollars a year on pseudo-science reports—the same way the tobacco industry used that technique to stave off action to save the lives of smokers.

Saving the Earth vs. saving the economy. The companies that are doing well . . . are the ones that have become more efficient. Reducing pollution actually creates jobs and strengthens the economy. Pollution is waste, and the modern approach to pollution reduction dovetails with successful business making higher profits.

Gore's stiff personality. I benefit from low expectations.

Losing the presidency. I don't cry over spilled milk. It's very difficult in a national campaign for any candidate to be seen and heard without the distortions his or her opponent makes on an hourly basis. I think I've been through a lot since the 2000 campaign, and that old cliche, "What doesn't kill you makes you stronger," is sometimes true.

Global warming and the media. The debate over global warming is over. The slide [in my presentation] people most ask me about is the one that contrasts the massive study of 10 years of peer-reviewed scientific articles on global warming, zero percentage of which disagreed with the consensus, and the study of 14 years of newspaper articles, 53 percent of which expressed doubt about whether the problem is real or not. That is really a striking contrast.

The Competitive Enterprise Institute's TV campaign. I'm not surprised. They're funded by Exxon Mobil, and they put a lot of money into trying to confuse people. Unfortunately, they have succeeded. I'm hopeful they will soon be recognized for what they are and put in the same category as people who still believe the moon landing was staged in a movie lot.

Looking back on the Senate's turndown of the Kyoto Protocol. I did push as hard as I knew how to. The truth is that Congress was not willing to ratify it. It was already controlled by the Republicans, but if it had been controlled by the Democrats, I dare say at that point, the result would have been nearly the same. I think that is changing.

Lobbying the people, not the politicians. Nothing is going to change in Washington until the sense of urgency felt and

At this point, the sarcasm in the subhead "Gore's stiff personality" indicates that you should not take the article as a literal transcription of an interview. Instead, the writer crafts an argument *about Gore* through strong references to history, in this case the 2000 election.

Here, the writer refers to research incorporated by Gore in his film, primarily *logos*.

The references to the TV campaign—and to people not believing the truth of other events—builds the argument.

The subtle allusions to steps Gore recommends we take to save the environment serve to build the writer's ethos, as they show his strong familiarity with the content. At the same time, these references mock Gore's film. By ending with humor, the writer packs a memorable punch.

expressed by the American people changes. I'm concentrating on that task.

Practicing what you preach. We have a hybrid car and all the new light bulbs. My family is completely carbon neutral. That means reducing as much carbon dioxide as we possibly can and then buying offsets to cancel out the rest.

If Gore were president. One difference is that you might see George W. Bush doing a cold opener on *Saturday Night Live* from an alternate universe.

CREATIVE PRACTICE

Visit the *Envision* Website and follow the link for The Age of Stupid (2009). How does this recent film about global warming and climate change make a different argument than Gore's *Inconvenient Truth*? What rhetorical strategies does the filmmaker use to convey his opinion? Notice the voice over, the images, the narrative, the logical and pathos appeals. How does the interplay between image and word construct the argument of the film? How would you characterize the "voice" of the film?

www.pearsonhighered.com/envision/174

Integrating Research Sources

After you decide on your approach to working with sources—as a strong explicit narrator or as the synthesizer of information—you need to start turning your outline into a rough draft. But how will you introduce and weave these other voices (your sources) into your written prose? Specifically, you will need to include your sources not only appropriately (to avoid plagiarism) and rhetorically (to decide on how much of a presence you will have in the paper) but also strategically (to provide a range of quotations and supporting evidence for your paper). We call this process **integrating sources**, and it's a complex process that occurs in three basic ways:

- **Summary:** synthesizing a great deal of information from a source
- **Paraphrase:** putting a source quotation into your own words
- **Direct quotation:** excerpting a specific passage from a source, enclosing it in quotation marks

You'll want to alternate among these methods while incorporating your sources with stylistic variety. This means knowing your options as a writer and selecting the best method for each rhetorical situation within your research essay. Realize that you have many "choices" for how to integrate research sources, and your decisions should be determined by the specific need of each part of your argument as well as the value of the research to build your *ethos*, provide background, offer an alternative perspective, or convey foundational knowledge.

Selecting Summary

A **summary** is a brief version—in your own words—of the overall content of a text. You might want to summarize the plot of a film or a book in a review, or you might want to summarize the basic argument presented by one of your sources in order to respond to it. Summaries are not analyses; you are not exploring your own ideas when you summarize but merely laying out the ideas explored by another writer in another text. You need to make sure that you tell your readers exactly what you are summarizing and provide complete bibliographical information at the end of your paper. For example, a research paper about the Italian films produced after WWII might include a summary that begins:

> In their influential study *Italian Neorealism and Global Cinema*, cultural critics Laura Ruberto and Kristi Wilson provide a concise history of film innovations at the turn of the twentieth century and argue that Italian documentaries allowed international conflicts to seem real to viewers. . .

Your summary would follow, and your list of works cited at the end of your paper would include the following reference:

Ruberto, Laura E. and Wilson, Kristi M. *Italian Neorealism and Global Cinema.* Detroit: Wayne State UP, 2007. Print.

If you wanted to include a brief quote within the body of your summary, then you would use quotation marks and a page number, as follows:

> In their influential study *Italian Neorealism and Global Cinema,* cultural critics Laura Ruberto and Kristi Wilson provide a concise history of film innovations at the turn of the twentieth century and argue that Italian documentaries "had a way of making the global seem local" (2).

Note that in this case, you are still writing a summary, but you include a direct quotation because it is rhetorically concise and powerful (with *pathos*-laden language), but also because citing the text gives you more *ethos* or authority as a writer.

Picking Paraphrase

Unlike a summary, a **paraphrase** focuses in and restates one part of a text. While a summary is often shorter than the text it summarizes, a paraphrase may be longer or shorter than the text it paraphrases. You might want to paraphrase a text to help your readers understand it, particularly if the original text is dense or difficult. Or you might simply want to paraphrase to make sure that you understand the source yourself—to offer yourself an opportunity to think clearly about the words you are reading. For instance, you might select the following lines to paraphrase:

> "Film had a way of making the global seem local, and the effect of movement, and, later, sound created an immediacy that still photos and written narratives could not approach" (Ruberto and Wilson 2).

Your paraphrase might read as follows:

> Italian film brought world events home to viewers, especially through moving images and audio (Ruberto and Wilson 2).

Note that you replace all the words, not just some of them, for a paraphrase. When in doubt, put quotes around the words from the original source. This not only allows your reader to see what words come from the text, but it also enables your reader to discern how you are having a conversation with your research sources. You need to be careful that you are using your own words to create a new text, not simply cutting and pasting the words of your source together in a different order. If you follow both the structure and the language of the original source closely, substituting only an occasional synonym to avoid directly quoting, then you are actually plagiarizing—even if you do so accidentally and even if you provide an appropriate citation. You are plagiarizing because you are not informing your reader that the structure, ideas, and much of the language used in your paper were created by someone else.

How to avoid this problem? Provide your reader with the appropriate bibliographical information about your source by offering a lead-in phrase ("As Ruberto and Wilson argue in their book *Italian Neorealism and Global Cinema. . .*") and then make sure that you list the complete reference for this source at the end of your paper. Or you can provide a parenthetical citation after the summary or paraphrase including the author's name and, for a paraphrase, the page number where the passage you are paraphrasing appears in the original text (see *Envision* Chapter 7 for guidelines on documentation).

Using Direct Quotations

Quoting directly from a source may seem much simpler than paraphrasing or summarizing, but quotations should be included to accomplish a specific rhetorical purpose, and they must be integrated responsibly so that you give the writer credit. Consider how you might feel if someone took your writing and recycled it without giving you credit. More importantly, realize that naming the author and background of a great passage can build your authority and *ethos* as a writer, so it is a wise move to name your sources in your paper. However, be careful not to swing to the opposite extreme and fill your paper with quotations from others. If a quotation does not fit into any of the categories listed in the "At a Glance" box, consider paraphrasing or summarizing it. What you want to avoid is a paper dominated by unnecessary quotations; in such a case, your argument—what readers expect most in your paper—gets buried. It's similar to what happens in film when the filmmaker splices together too many different scenes—the audience becomes lost in the montage and can no longer follow the narrative.

AT A GLANCE

Reasons to Use Direct Quotations

- *Evidence:* the quotation provides tangible evidence for part of your argument.
- *Ethos:* the original author is a primary source or an expert on the subject, and including a direct quotation would increase the *ethos* of your argument.
- *Language:* the original author used memorable phrasing or has a particular voice that would be lost in paraphrase.

Integrating, Not Inserting, Quotations

But how, practically, do you go about *integrating* sources appropriately and effectively rather than simply *inserting* them? To work successfully with quotations, try out various strategies of introducing the quotation listed below.

These examples are from a paper on Al Gore's 2006 film, *An Inconvenient Truth*. Note that these examples do not include page numbers because they refer to an online source without numbered pages, as is true of many of the sources we use today. However, if you are quoting from a print source, your citation should also include the page number where the original material appeared.

- **Use an introductory clause/phrase** that refers to the original author or title of the source:

   Reacting strongly to the environmentalist message, online columnist Joseph Blast argues, "*An Inconvenient Truth* contains very little truth, and a big helping of propaganda."

- **Use an incorporated structure** that seamlessly melds the quotation into your sentence so that it flows smoothly as part of your essay:

   Joseph Blast articulated one of the most common critiques of Al Gore's global warming film in a June 2006 online editorial when he claimed that "*An Inconvenient Truth* contains very little truth, and a big helping of propaganda."

- **Use an interrupted structure,** breaking the quote into two halves and embedding information regarding the author and/or the original text in the middle of the quotation itself:

   "In the style of a previous generation of propaganda films," Joseph Blast argues in his June 2006 editorial, "Gore substitutes vivid images of the alleged effects of global warming for an accurate account of the scientific debate."

- **Use an end comment,** inserting the quotation and then providing an interpretation, or closing comment, that importantly advances the argument:

   Joseph Blast's claim that "*An Inconvenient Truth* contains very little truth, and a big helping of propaganda" exemplifies the critical tendency to undermine the legitimacy of an opposing point of view by categorizing it as "propaganda."

AT A GLANCE

Integrating Sources Appropriately and Effectively

- *Read.* Read the source actively and carefully, underlining passages that move you or suggest moments of deep meaning, or passages that might contribute to your argument. If you are working with online texts, cut and paste the citation into a document and note the paragraph number (for Websites) or page number. Always note the page number if you transcribe quotations as you read.

  You'll need this part in order to provide the citation in your own writing.

- *Record.* Keep a notebook or an annotated file of citations in which you record your reactions to a particular passage you've read. Does this passage move you? Does it reveal the theme of the text, the climax of a scene, the point of the argument, the purpose of the passage?

  You'll need this part in order to provide your interpretation of the citation.

- *Relate.* Place the citation and your interpretation in an appropriate place in your own essay. Think about where in the essay, and in which particular paragraph, the citation should appear. Think about the context—what comes before and after the citation? How is the citation related to the text around it? Never just insert a quotation because it feels like one should be there; use citations (quotations, paraphrases, summaries) strategically to help support your own argument.

  You'll need this part in order to integrate your citations effectively.

Experiment with these strategies in your own writing to determine which best serves your rhetorical purpose. For instance, if you want to draw attention to the *author* of a quotation to add ethos to your argument, you might opt to integrate using an introductory clause; however, if you want to emphasize *information* rather than authorship, an incorporated structure might be more effective. One key to remember is to avoid overusing any one type of integration strategy; in that case, your writing style might become monotonous, like a film that relies too heavily on the same types of shots.

Additional strategies for integrating quotations include the following techniques:

- To quote a source within a source, use (quoted in ___) to indicate where *you* found the quotation, for instance:

  > Film critic Millicent Marcus argues that "neorealism is first and foremost a moral statement" (quoted in Ruberto and Wilson 7).

- To edit part of a quote, use square brackets as such [ ]. You might do this to get concisely to the heart of the issue in your chosen quotation. For instance, you might edit the Blast quote above:

  > Joseph Blast argues in his June 2006 editorial, "Gore substitutes vivid images [. . .] for an accurate account of the scientific debate."

Remember that the purpose of integrating sources is to demonstrate your work as a researcher and to show that you are building your argument on the work of others. Therefore, choose what types of integration strategies work best for each source and for each part of your paper. If you're worried that you have integrated too many sources (and lost your own voice), spend some time reviewing the draft and ask yourself:

- Am I still the moderator of this conversation?
- Is my voice clear, compelling, and original?
- Do I allow my own argument to emerge as foremost in this piece?

In your efforts to integrate sources effectively, keep in mind that source material should *support* your argument, not supplant it.

AT A GLANCE

Check for Integrating Sources

- Did you *introduce the quote* in various ways?
- Did you *link the reference* to your argument to show the relevance?
- Did you *comment* on it afterward to advance your argument?
- Did you *cite* it properly using the appropriate documentation style for your subject area?

Documentation During Integration

As you incorporate sources into your draft, be sure to include citations for each quotation or paraphrase. This would also be a good time to begin drafting your works-cited list or bibliography, to save time later. The purpose of this is not only to provide a "list of credits" for your references but also to supply interested readers with the resources to continue learning about your topic. Just as you undoubtedly found certain articles inspiring while investigating your topic and used them as springboards for more focused research, so too might your paper serve as a means of leading your readers to intriguing ideas and articles. You can go back over the correct format for citations in your final edit, following the guidelines in Chapter 7 for documentation to do so.

Drafting Your Research Argument

As you continue to forge ahead with your research argument, turning it from an outline to a full draft or composing sections of your argument in separate time blocks, remember that there are many strategies for getting it done. For each of these ways of working, the key is to start and then just keep writing. Try out one of the many methods described in the "At a Glance" box.

Also realize that to write is to struggle with the process, as noted by Stanford University psychologist David Rasch: "Almost all writers are familiar with the experience of feeling stuck, blocked, overwhelmed, or behind schedule in their writing." What can help? Staying motivated and relying on others.

AT A GLANCE

Strategies for Drafting

- *Following the linear path:* Start at the beginning, write the introduction, and then move sequentially through each point of argument.
- *Fleshing out the outline:* Gradually transform the outline into a full draft, moving from a keyword outline to a prose outline by systematically expanding each of the sections; as you add more detail, the keywords fall away, leaving behind drafted paragraphs.
- *Writing from the middle:* Start writing from a point of greatest strength or start with a section you can complete easily; then write around it and fill out sections as you go.
- *Freewrite and then reverse outline:* First, freewrite a few pages; then compose a **reverse outline** in which you record the point of each paragraph to assess the argument's flow and structure, and finally, reorder and rewrite the paper until it begins to take the proper form for the argument.

Keeping Your Passion

As you move deeper into the writing process, integrating quotations and working out the flow of your argument, don't lose sight of your enthusiasm for your subject. Reread your earliest freewrites and your entries in your research log. What goals, what motivations prompted you to begin the project? What aspects of your topic excited you, angered you, or inspired you? What contribution did you imagine yourself making to this discussion? As you begin synthesizing your information and creating a unified argument, you are in effect realizing that initial vision. Remember, your audience will be reading your paper to learn *your* particular point of view on the subject. Your drafts are your shooting scripts, if you will—the versions of your paper that ultimately you will transform, through careful review, editing, and revision, into your "release" of the text into final form.

You should also allow yourself well-needed energy breaks. Brief periods away from the writing process can often recharge and reinvigorate your approach to the paper and help you think through difficult points in the argument. Ironically, a pause in drafting can also help you avoid writer's block by allowing you to remember what interested you about this project in the first place.

Finally, if you are having trouble getting through the draft process, allow yourself to write what Anne Lamott, author of *Bird by Bird,* famously calls the "shitty first draft." In the words of Lamott, "All good writers write them. This is how they end up with good second drafts and terrific third drafts." That is, you should realize that the first version by no means has to be perfect or even close to what the final paper will look like. It is instead simply your first attempt at getting your ideas on paper. Freeing yourself to write something—anything— can help you escape from the weight of perfectionism or the fear of failure that often paralyzes writers. You will have plenty of opportunities to rework the material, show your draft to others, and move forward with the writing process.

Collaboration Through Peer Review

Take advantage of the community of writers in your class to talk through your ideas and share work in progress. You might find your organizational plan confirmed by your peers, or you might be pleasantly surprised by their suggestions for alternative structures, ways of integrating sources, or images to include in the paper. Such discussions can help you get back your fire for your project as well as give you extremely useful advice to implement in the writing of the draft. Moreover, your peers' responses to your work in progress can help you determine if your writing is persuasive or not.

Consider how collaboration works in the film industry. Even though a film is generally recognized as a unified expression of a single idea, in reality it is the product of the collaborative effort of dozens of individuals, from the screenwriter and actors to the key grips and camera operators. But there is another, often less recognized collaborator: the audience. Think about how novels are adapted to the large screen: whether by adding a romantic subplot or substituting a "Hollywood ending" for a less palatable one, many script-

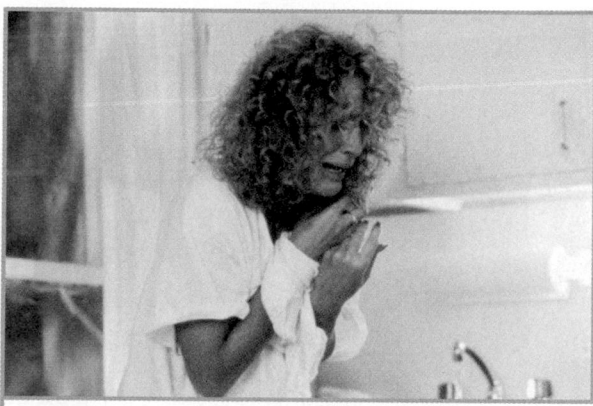

FIGURE 6.5. When preview audiences saw the original ending for the film *Fatal Attraction*, in which the villainess, Alex, survived, their reactions were so negative that the director Adrian Lyne reshot it, adding a completely new ending in which the young wife stabs her husband's tormentor to death. The film became a huge hit.

writers deliberately revise original texts to accommodate the perceived desires of a mass audience. Sometimes an entire narrative is recast to make it more marketable; the 1995 hit, *Clueless*, and the 2001 teen film *O*, are good examples of films in which literary classics (Jane Austen's *Emma* and William Shakespeare's *Othello*) were updated to appeal to a mainstream modern audience.

Sometimes the audience's intervention is more direct. It is common practice for many filmmakers to hold "advance screenings" of major releases, designed to gauge audience reaction. In 1986, a preview audience's reaction to the ending of the film *Fatal Attraction* was so negative that director Adrian Lyne reshot the final scenes (Figure 6.5). When the film was released in the following year, it featured a markedly different conclusion. Similarly, the version of *Blade Runner* released in 1982 was significantly edited in an attempt to increase its box office appeal; however, director Ridley Scott changed the ending yet again years later, premiering his *Blade Runner—The Director's Cut* 11 years after the movie first appeared. In each case, collaboration shaped the final version and made evident the rhetorical triangle between audience, writer, and text. Similarly, writing needs to take into consideration the audience's expectations; we write to show an audience our work, so we need to respond to audience needs when we write and revise our texts.

As a writer you can benefit from "advance screenings" of your argument; the collaborative work you do on the structure and content of your outlines and drafts should guide you to a revised product that satisfies both you and your audience. But to do so, you need feedback from your audience in the form of peer review; then you will need to revise your draft to accommodate the suggestions you receive.

Analyzing a Student Essay About Film

Let's examine now the draft of Stanford student Wan Jin Park, who developed a research project comparing Gore's film *An Inconvenient Truth* (2006) to Gore's more recent PowerPoint slide show during his talk at TED, a conference organized to showcase the most innovative thinking to date. Wan Jin conducted a range of academic and field research, wrote a detailed outline, and then composed his draft. After feedback from his course instructor and his classroom peers, he revised his first partial draft and outline substantially, as demonstrated later in this chapter. But throughout, Wan Jin kept his passion for his project and his respect for Gore as a leader trying to use rhetoric to persuade people of the importance of attending to the environment. We can study his first draft and conduct a *rhetorical analysis* of his writing strategies to see how you, too, can approach putting your research argument down on paper.

In particular, you'll see that the excerpt from Wan Jin's draft integrates research sources in a variety of ways, begins to showcase Wan Jin's own voice as a writer, and effectively relies on the outline as a prewriting tool.

Wan Jin's working title is strong and raises a problem—but in the revision, he will introduce his argument more forcefully.

His organizational strategy is to open with a counterargument, acknowledging that, today, our *kairos* is that even middleschoolers know about global warming.

Wan Jin Park
Working Draft + Outline

Environmental Leadership:

How Al Gore Illuminated an Overlooked Crisis

Rising levels of carbon dioxide emissions do not contribute to global warming. It has become silly and naïve to argue thus even before a group of middle school students. The awareness of the dangers of our carbon addicted lifestyle, however, would not be as widespread as it is today had it not been for the one man spearheading the global movement against climate change: Al Gore. Gore's rise to environmental influence is in large part due to Davis Guggenheim's documentary *An Inconvenient Truth*, which was then followed by a revised presentation at the TED Conference in March 2008. What strikes the audience, however, is not the revision of data and graphics in the slides, but rather, it is the change in Gore's rhetoric. In *An Inconvenient Truth*, Gore focuses on drawing the audience and persuading them to join the environmental movement through the depiction of himself as a warm, dedicated, but lonely leader in the face of a global crisis; by contrast, at the TED presentation, Gore has garnered huge support, but senses a lack of change in the United States, and thus focuses on pushing the public toward increased initiative through his urgent and passionate rhetoric.

Gripping the Flames: Gore Leading the Environmental Movement

At the forefront of the global environmental movement against climate change is Al Gore. In fact, The Nielsen Company, a leading global marketing and advertising research company, conducted a survey in conjunction with Oxford University which serves as a testament to Gore's environmental prominence. In a survey of 26,486 people across 47 countries, Gore has been voted as "the most influential spokesperson to champion the global warming debate," even "ahead of former United Nations" Secretary General Kofi Anan (Nielsen).

Then he introduces the film fully as well as his second primary source: Gore's 2008 TED talk.

Even in a draft, Wan Jin has strongly developed his thesis—this work will sustain him through the rest of the paper. He can use the key terms of the thesis to structure the remaining sections of the essay.

Wan Jin's subheads show his gift for creative language—he uses *pathos* but also indicates this new part of his argument with the subhead.

Already bringing in research, Wan Jin starts with facts and statistics (*logos*) from survey and field research.

Gore has been active with the environmental movement since the beginning of his political career; however, his lasting, and perhaps, most influential contribution did not come until the release of Davis Guggenheim's *An Inconvenient Truth* in May 2006. Although based on lectures "that Gore has been presenting in one form or another for nearly three decades," *An Inconvenient Truth* has achieved levels of popularity and influence unrivalled by those of any other medium employed in the environmental movement (Rosteck). Earning over $49 million, it currently ranks as the fifth-highest-grossing documentary in the history of the United States. Further indicative of the documentary's influence are the results of another survey conducted by The Nielsen Company in April 2007. Of the viewers who have seen *An Inconvenient Truth*, eighty-nine percent reported to have become "more aware of the problem"; sixty-six percent "changed their mind about global warming"; and most importantly, seventh-four percent changed their habits as a result (Nielsen).

Next, he provides background and cites an article from his research (Rosteck).

Considering the fact that *An Inconvenient Truth* is Gore's most influential rhetorical medium, an analysis of the documentary will thus illuminate the key characteristics that define the success of Gore's environmental leadership.

At this point, Wan Jin offers a road map for the rest of his essay, referring back to his title and his thesis in a way that offers powerful coherence for the essay.

Contrasting Images: the Beautiful and the Doomed

An Inconvenient Truth begins with a beautiful depiction of nature. The camera focuses close-up on a branch full of small green tree leaves. The green hue is accentuated by the bright sunlight that is reflected off of the leaf blades. After a few seconds, the camera shifts to the right to reveal a sparkling river. The soft piano music in the background adds to the calm and peaceful mood. Al Gore then narrates in the background, purposefully emphasizing the sibilants as if to imitate the sounds of the river and the rustling leaves:

> You look at that river gently flowing by. You notice the leaves rustling with the wind. You hear the birds. You hear the tree frogs. In the distance, you hear a cow. You feel the grass. The mud gives a little bit on the riverbank. It's quiet; it's peaceful. (Inconvenient)

The first thirty seconds of the film is beautiful. However, Gore interjects and introduces human neglect of nature by stating, "all of a sudden, it's a gearshift inside you and it's like taking a deep breath and going 'Oh yeah, I forgot about this'" (Inconvenient). By using the word "gearshift," Gore metaphorically compares the audience to machines that are equipped with a gear; in essence, Gore argues that we have become the products of our industrial production, and have thus become so separate from our nature that we have completely forgot about it.

The consequences of our neglect are horrifying. After the establishment of our neglect, Gore's presentation shows images of the damages we made to nature. We see images of factories emitting thick black smog that obscures the sun. In one of the images, the hue of the sky is grayish purple; considering how the corpses of formerly sick bodies usually show this hue, this

As Wan Jin gets into the body of his essay, he takes his evidence one piece at a time, first providing a strong rhetorical analysis of the visual and audio elements of the film, then quoting directly from Gore's voice-over.

With the word, "However," Wan Jin lets us know his view, introducing his argument.

The careful analysis of specific words such as "gearshift" make this rhetorical argument persuasive.

Just as he analyzed the words in the film, Wan Jin carefully analyzes the images, building his argument. His own voice as a writer here becomes adamant and urgent, evoking the mood of the film but also forcing us to take his argument seriously.

This section ends with a mini summary and strong statement of Wan Jin's argument. In this way, he creates an effective organization for his larger paper, and from here can go about completing it one section at a time.

The next sections of the draft show in outline form the content Wan Jin plans to cover: including his main arguments, his section of evidence, and his secondary source citations.

He provides an *ethos*-building introduction for his secondary source.

image is suggestive of the damage we have done to nature. Furthermore, as a demonstration of how global warming has aggravated natural disasters, we see footages of the aftermath of Hurricane Katrina. We see footages of crying babies without shelter and caretakers, a bloated dead body lying face down in the water, and a man stroking the forehead of his dead wife. Although Hurricane Katrina has been an American natural disaster, these footages shock even the most foreign audience.

The presentation of these images after Gore's argument that we have forgotten about our nature compels the audience to feel guilt and responsibility. In effect, Gore induces the audience to personalize the issue of climate change, thereby making us more receptive to Gore's message of change.

The Dedicated Leader

- After fear, Gore portrays himself as a dedicated leader
- autobiographical threads in the documentary
- vulnerable moments in Gore's personal history
- Source: these stories "strengthen[ed] the hero's resolve"
- Secondary source: Kathryn Olson, Director of the Rhetorical Leadership Graduate Certificate Program at University of Wisconsin-Milwaukee, claims the autobiographical threads "persuasively documents Gore's single-mindedness in pursuing his public cause, often at his own expense, through a lifetime of disappointments and sacrificing a comfortable retirement to carry the message globally."
- Gore in a Beijing taxi on way to Tsing Hua University.

Lonely Leader

- personal footages depict Gore as "emotional suffering"
- Senator James Inhofe attacks Gore's ideas
- Secondary Source: Gore "inviting impression that encourages auditors to join him or her in social action" (Olson).

TED Presentation

- More passionate; more religious; his sense of urgency is raised
- His tone of voice, joking, moral issue
- Quote: "The only two countries that didn't ratify—and now there's only one. Australia had an election. And there was a campaign in Australia that involved television and Internet and radio commercials to lift the **sense of urgency** for the people there. And we trained 250 people to give the slide show in every town and village and city in Australia"
  - There has been progress: Gore contributed to the change through his environment
- "The cities supporting Kyoto in the US are up to 780"
- Returning to religious rhetoric, passion, urgency
- Evidence; He does not begin his presentation about how far we have come since 2006, when the documentary film *An Inconvenient Film* was released. Instead, he begins by quoting Karen Armstrong (I believe she is someone prominent in religious studies) who said "religion really properly understood is not about belief, but about behavior."
- In arguing this, he essentially says that what we lack with our response to climate change is a change in behavior
  - "But, as important as it is to change the light bulbs, it is more important to change the laws. And when we change our behavior in our daily lives, we sometimes leave out the citizenship part and the democracy part."

He will comment on this secondary source with an example of his own.

By selecting and arranging quotes in his draft, Wan Jin can approach the writing with a keen sense of his argument and overall plan for persuading the reader. He has chosen his evidence and uses the draft to sort through it effectively.

As shown by Wan Jin's paper, a working draft should have a strong and well-developed thesis. This will drive the entire argument. Then, you can begin to work through the sections of an outline, providing specific evidence and secondary source support in what in Chapter 5 we called "a conversation with your sources." As you continue, fill in parts of your draft and rely on your peers for support and feedback.

Revising Your Draft

As many professional writers can attest—and Wan Jin would agree with this based on his drafting experience—a text goes through numerous drafts on its way to becoming a polished final product. Even filmmakers produce multiple drafts of their movies before they release their film, experimenting with different sequencing, camera shots, and pacing to create what they consider to be the fulfillment of their artistic vision. We've all seen the results of this process: deleted scenes or *outtakes* from popular film or television programs. What these segments represent are moments of work (writing, producing, and shooting) that, after review and editing, were removed to streamline the film.

As you might imagine, often it's difficult or even painful to reshape your work during revision; it's hard to leave some of your writing behind on the cutting room floor. However, as your project develops, its focus may change: sources or ideas that seemed important to you during the early stages of research may become less relevant, even tangential; a promising strategy of argumentation may turn out to be less suitable to your project; a key transition may be no longer necessary once you reorganize the argument. As you turn to your draft with a critical eye, what you should find is that in order to transform your paper into the best possible written product, you'll need to move beyond proofreading or editing and into the realm of macro changes, or **revision**.

Troubleshooting

Proofreading remains a critical part of the revision process. Careless grammatical and punctuation errors and spelling mistakes can damage your *ethos* as an author, and they need to be corrected. It is very probable that you've been doing such *micro-revision* throughout the drafting process—editing for style, grammar, punctuation, and spelling. However, sometimes it's difficult to do *broader revisions* until you have a substantial part of your paper written. It is only once your argument starts coming together that you can recognize the most productive ways to modify it in order to optimize its effectiveness. This is the key to successful revision: you have to be open to *both* microediting and large-scale, multiple revisions. Think of this process as **re-vision**, or seeing it again with new eyes, seeing it in a new light.

Let's look at decisions some students made during the revision process:

■ **Content Overload.** Reading over her draft about the propagandistic elements in World War II films, Jennifer realized that she had gotten so caught up in presenting background information that her paper read more like a historical report than an argument.

> **Revision:** Jennifer sharpened her focus, cut down on some of the background information, and brought her own argument to the forefront.

■ **Lack of Reliance on Sources.** Miranda had the opposite problem; in her draft she made a compelling argument about the literary status of graphic novels but did not really quote from or mention any of her sources, so she wasn't showcasing her work as a researcher.

> **Revision:** She more prominently integrated her source material into her argument, both by referring to specific authors and articles she had read and by using additional direct quotations. In doing so, she greatly increased her *ethos* and the persuasiveness of her argument.

■ **Overly Broad Thesis.** After drafting her paper on hip-hop and gender identity, Sharita realized that her thesis was too broad and that in trying to cover both male and female imagery, she wasn't able to be specific enough to craft a really persuasive argument.

> **Revision:** Realizing that her interest really lay in exploring the conflicted stereotype of powerful, sexualized women in hip-hop

---

AT A GLANCE

Questions for Assessing Your Draft

- *Argument consistency:* Are your introduction and conclusion arguing the same points, or have you changed your argument by the end? Either revise the end to be consistent with your original thinking, or embrace your new vision and rework the beginning.

- *Organization and progression:* Does your paper flow logically, developing one idea seamlessly into the next? Do you provide important theoretical foundations, definitions, or background at the beginning of the paper to guide the audience through the rest of your argument?

- *Your voice versus sources:* Do you foreground your own argument in your paper or do you focus primarily on your sources' arguments, locating your point of view primarily in the conclusion? If the latter is true, bring your voice out more in commentaries on the quotations.

- *Information:* Are there any holes in your research? Do you need to supplement your evidence with additional research, interviews, surveys, or other source materials?

- *Opposition and concession:* Do you adequately address opposing arguments? Do you integrate your opposition into your argument (i.e., deal with them as they arise), or have you constructed a single paragraph that addresses opposing opinions?

videos, Sharita cut large sections of her paper revolving around the male imagery and focused on the female. The result was a provocative argument based on concrete, persuasive examples.

■ **Overreliance on Design.** Max, a dedicated Mac user, wrote his draft on the aesthetics of design in the Apple product line. The first version of his paper was visually stunning, detailed, and eloquently written. But it was so one sided that it read more like a marketing brochure than an academic argument.

> **Revision:** His task in revision was to provide a more balanced perspective on the Apple computer phenomenon. After further research, he incorporated a greater diversity of perspectives in his paper and softened some of his language to be less biased in favor of Apple products.

AT A GLANCE

Revision Strategies

1. *Read your essay out loud or have someone read it to you.* You can hear mistakes and inconsistencies that you unknowingly skipped over when reading silently.

2. *Gain critical distance.* Put your essay away for a few hours, or even a few days, and then come back to it fresh.

3. *Answer peer review questions for your essay.*

4. *Don't be chained to your computer.* Print out your draft, making revisions by hand. We conceptualize information differently on paper versus on a screen.

5. *Look at your writing in different ways.* Take a paragraph and divide it into distinct sentences, which you line up one under another. Look for patterns (for instance, is the repetition deliberate or accidental?), style issues (is sentence structure varied?), and fluidity of transitions between sentences.

6. *Take into account feedback even if initially it doesn't seem significant.* You might not decide to act on the advice, but at least consider it before dismissing it.

7. *Revise out of order.* Choose paragraphs at random and look at them individually, or begin at the end. Sometimes our conclusions are the weakest simply because we always get to them last, when we're tired; start revision by looking at your conclusion first.

8. *Look at revision as a whole.* As you correct mistakes or prose problems, consider the impact that the revision makes on the rest of the essay. Sometimes it is possible just to add a missing comma or substitute a more precise verb, but often you need to revise more than just the isolated problem so that the sentence, paragraph, or essay as a whole continues to "fit" and flow together.

As these examples indicate, you need to enter into the research process looking not just for mistakes to "fix" but also for larger issues that might relate to your structure, your thesis, your scope, or the development of your ideas.

In addition to your own assessment of your writing, you should take into account **peer evaluations** of your drafts; consider your peer review sessions "advance screenings" with your audience. Sometimes you'll find that your peer reviewers vocalize ideas that echo your own concerns about your draft; other times you may be surprised by their reactions. Do keep in mind that their comments are informed *suggestions*, not mandates; your task, as the writer, is to assess the feedback you receive and implement those changes that seem to best address the needs of both your argument and your audience. Like the filmmaker looking to transform a creative vision into a box office hit, you want to reach your audience without sacrificing your own voice or argument in the process.

One way to facilitate a productive peer session is to use directed peer review questions for one-on-one discussions of your draft, rather than to rely exclusively on oral comments. When exchanging drafts with a peer group, you also may find it helpful to attach a cover memo that points your readers to specific questions you have about your draft so that they can customize their responses to address the particular issues that concern you as a writer.

Analyzing Student Writing

Let's return now to Wan Jin's draft paper and see how he used the peer review suggestions he received to revise his paper and develop it further.

Park 1

Wan Jin Park
Research-Based Argument–Final
March 15, 2010

Balancing the Soft and the Passionate Rhetorician:

Gore's Dynamic Rhetoric in His Environmental Leadership

At the forefront of the global environmental movement is

one man with the power to blur national boundaries, urge political

---

First, Wan Jin's revised title actually conveys part of his argument—he has traded the general claim "Illuminates" to offer several new terms: soft, passionate, and dynamic rhetoric

Next, his introduction has a new sense of urgency, shown in short and long sentence variety, strong diction, and sign-posting (the two-part rhetoric).

Moreover, Wan Jin spends a great deal of time advancing a more developed thesis, naming Gore as lonely leader with soft rhetoric and then as passionate leader with dynamic rhetoric. With this thesis, the paper will offer a more forceful argument.

Most importantly, Wan Jin ends the opening with a "So What?" significance statement.

He introduces his own term—one he made up. Wan Jin did not want to use "I" so he speaks in third person but he clearly establishes his own argument in this revision.

His microedits to style and descriptive language make his writing even more vivid and memorable.

leaders to adopt reforms, and motivate hundreds of thousands. That man is Al Gore. Gore has been a pivotal leader, attracting unprecedented levels of support for the once overlooked issue, especially through Davis Guggenheim's *An Inconvenient Truth*. The success of the documentary can be attributed to Gore's two-part rhetoric. He first induces fear and guilt in us, the audience, making us more receptive to his message. He then portrays himself as a warm, dedicated, but lonely leader, thereby arousing our desire to join him in social action. Despite the success of his soft rhetoric, Gore sets it aside two years later at the TED2008 Conference and adopts a heightened sense of passion and urgency. The shift in rhetoric mirrors a change in Gore's agenda, and it is this dynamic rhetoric that Gore molds to fit specific goals that defines the success of his leadership. An understanding of Gore's rhetoric offers us invaluable insight on how to use dynamic rhetoric to bring overlooked social issues into the light.

Before showing us a change in his rhetoric, Gore uses soft rhetoric in *An Inconvenient Truth*. Soft rhetoric, a newly coined term, refers to a rhetorical tool that draws in a guarded audience, not through impassioned words, but through the appeal to the audience's sense of guilt and the establishment of a warm and inviting *ethos*. Because the public was still guarded toward the issue of climate change before the release of the documentary, Gore shies away from passionate speech that are meant to inspire, and instead focuses on convincing his audience to join him through soft rhetoric.

Park 3

Contrasting Images: the Beautiful and the Doomed

Gore begins his soft rhetoric by inducing fear and guilt in us, the audience, through the juxtaposition of beauty and doom. He first offers us a beautiful depiction of nature. The camera focuses close-up on a branch full of green tree leaves. Bright sunlight reflects off of the leaf blades, accentuating the green hue. After a few seconds, the camera turns to the right to reveal a glistening river. The river is a mix of green and blue, both defining colors of nature. The soft piano music in the background adds to the calm and peaceful mood. Gore then narrates in the background, purposely emphasizing the sibilants as if to imitate the sounds of the river and the rustling leaves:

> You look at that river gently flowing by. You notice the leaves rustling with the wind. You hear the birds. You hear the tree frogs. In the distance, you hear a cow. You feel the grass. The mud gives a little bit on the riverbank. It's quiet; it's peaceful. (Inconvenient)

The sequence of images and narration encapsulates the beauty of nature so well that Professors Thomas Rosteck and Thomas Frentz write in "Myth and Multiple Readings in Environmental Rhetoric: The Case of An Inconvenient Truth" that "we experience, visually and through Gore's voiceover, the awe, sublime beauty, and wonder of Earth" (5).

Gore suddenly interrupts the experience and interjects that we have forgotten about nature in spite of its beauty: "all of a sudden, it's a gearshift inside you and it's like taking a deep

In the revision, Wan Jin begins with a topic sentence that conveys his *argument*, rather than just launching into the rhetorical analysis of the film's details.

He has also incorporated more research, so he is not over-relying on only one source.

Park 4

breath and going 'Oh yeah, I forgot about this'" (Inconvenient). Through the use of the word "gearshift," Gore metaphorically compares us, the audience, to machines that are equipped with a gear; in essence, he argues that we have become so addicted to the industrial age that we have transformed into its products, becoming separate from and oblivious to our nature.

* * *

The images arouse such horror that Bret Schulte, Assistant Professor of Journalism at University of Arkansas, writes that Gore shows us "the frightening future promised by global warming—an apocalyptic world of deadly hurricanes, rising oceans, disease, drought, and famine" (Schulte).

By deliberately introducing the "frightening" images only after his "gearshift" metaphor, Gore compels us to feel not only frightened, but also responsible and guilty for the damages done to nature (Schulte, Inconvenient). The arousal of guilt is crucial in shaping An Inconvenient Truth into an effective environmental medium, as it "sets up the rhetorical tension with which Gore will leverage his message" (Rosteck and Frentz). Kathryn Olson, the author of "Rhetorical Leadership And Transferable Lessons For Successful Social Advocacy In An Inconvenient Truth," agrees and elaborates on what Gore's message is: "he asks [us] . . . to share the guilt of insufficient action with him and to redeem [our]selves . . . now that [we] grasp the gravity . . . of climate change" (11). The arousal of guilt, the first part of Gore's soft rhetoric, thus draws in a once guarded and reluctant public into the environmental movement.

Here, Wan Jin cites the article analyzed earlier in this chapter. He picks a strong quotation, sets it up by building the ethos of the source, and then, most importantly, comments on it in the next paragraph, emphasizing "frightening" and the building on Schulte's reading to develop his point about guilt.

Notice here, he offers a strong conversation with many of his sources: Rosteck & Frentz, Olson, and looking back to Schulte.

Most powerfully, he ends with his own point, making sure the spotlight is on his argument.

Dedication Molded by Frustration and Failure

After rendering us more receptive through the appeal to our sense of fear and guilt, Gore portrays himself as a warm, vulnerable, and dedicated leader. Rosteck and Frentz also explore the second part of Gore's soft rhetoric and argue that Gore establishes such *ethos* through "personal images of frustration and failure" that are interspersed throughout the documentary (9). In fact, Gore expresses his frustration right from the beginning of *An Inconvenient Truth*, confessing that "I've been trying to tell this story for a long time, and I feel as if I've failed to get the message across" (Inconvenient). We then meet a naively optimistic Gore who fails to change the world through the first Congressional hearings on global warming; he almost loses his son to a car accident; he loses the presidential election in 2000; and his family, a group of tobacco farmers, loses Gore's sister, Nancy, to lung cancer (Inconvenient).

What these stories of failure and pain have in common are that they "strengthen[ed]" Gore's "resolve" and dedication to the environmental movement (Rosteck 7). His son's near-death-accident taught him how anything taken for granted, even our beautiful environment, can easily vanish. His sister's death taught him the importance of connecting the dots, of connecting our actions to future consequences. His presidential election "brought into clear focus the mission that [he] had been pursuing all these years," convincing him to "[start] giving the slideshow again" (Inconvenient).

The revised subheads show his advanced thinking and reflect the suggestions of his classmates from peer review.

Wan Jin's essay performs a strong rhetorical analysis of the strategies of the speaker as well as of the film.

He has fleshed out the points from his working draft and outline.

Park 6

Because these stories "persuasively [document] Gore's single-mindedness in pursuing his public cause, often at his own expense, through a lifetime of disappointments," Olson also agrees with Rosteck and Frentz that the stories of personal failure and frustration are essential to Gore's portrayal as a human, vulnerable, but dedicated leader (Olson 99). This portrayal places us "in a position to hear demand for action in a more sympathetic light," and when coupled with our sense of guilt, it renders Gore's message irresistible (Rosteck and Frentz 10). And Gore's message is clear. He "shows his evolution from interested observer to committed activist" with the goal of "invit[ing] our own journey of transformation" through the environmental movement (Rosteckand Frentz 5).

Gripping the Flames: The Lonely Leader

Rosteck, Frentz, and Olson's arguments have merit. Gore's transformation into a dedicated leader as a result of his frustrations and failures does create an "inviting impression that encourages [us] to join him . . . in social action" (Olson 102). However, they leave unexplored a crucial aspect of Gore's rhetoric. What is more responsible for creating the warm and inviting *ethos* is the portrayal of Gore as a lonely leader (Olson 102).

* * *

Park 7

No Longer the Soft Leader

Despite the success of his soft rhetoric in *An Inconvenient Truth,* Gore sets it aside and instead adopts a heightened level of passion and sense of urgency two years later in his follow-up presentation at the TED2008 Conference. The change reflects a change in Gore's primary agenda. Gore's primary goal is no longer attracting support for the environmental movement, as he already achieved that goal. Gore even acknowledges in his TED presentation the extent of his success. He claims that "sixty-eight percent of Americans now believe that human activity is responsible for global warming, [and] sixty-nine percent believe that the Earth is heating up in a significant way" (Gore). Furthermore. . .

* * *

Even his body language is imbued with the increased level of passion. As he delivers the line, "we need a worldwide, global mobilization for renewed energy, conservation, efficiency, and a global transition to a low carbon economy," he not only stresses each word, but also moves his hands up and down as he speaks, visually emphasizing each word (Gore). He also twists his upper body from left to right, with his arms extended, as he says, "the political will has to be mobilized," visually enacting the word "mobilized" (Gore).

After a significant amount of evidence (excerpted), Wan Jin moves to the next point in his argument. His heading refers to terms in his title, using diction to offer coherence and force in the writing.

He sets up the argument about Gore's 2008 TED talk through citing Gore's own words and leading the reader through the *logos* from his rough draft.

In this revision, Wan Jin took the suggestion of his peers: he analyzes not only the images and words, but also the embodied rhetoric or body language of Gore's persona.

Park 8

Introducing new con-
cepts such as "honor"
and "heroism," Wan
Jin increases the
power of his words
and the significance of
his argument. He
chooses then to use a
direct quote as
evidence.

The heightened passion in Gore's rhetoric becomes fully
manifested near the end of the presentation when Gore appeals
to honor and heroism, both qualities we have treasured
throughout history, as he stresses the need for a hero generation:

> What we need is another hero generation. We have to . . .
> understand that history has presented us with a choice. And
> we have to find a way to create, in the generation of those
> alive today, a sense of generational mission. (Gore)

Gore then alludes to "the hero generation that brought
democracy to the planet . . . another that ended
slavery . . . and that gave women the right to vote" in order to
illustrate the level of passion and dedication that we need to
emulate as we fight the climate crisis (Gore). The climate
crisis is no longer just a global issue, but is now the
"opportunity to rise to a challenge that is worthy of our best
efforts" (Gore). In his last efforts to move the audience toward
increased sense of urgency and initiative, Gore closes with
the line:

> We are the generation about which, a thousand years from
> now, philharmonic orchestras and poets and singers will
> celebrate by saying, they were the ones that found it within
> themselves to solve this crisis and lay the basis for a bright
> and optimistic human future. (Gore)

He carefully chooses
his lines and concludes
with a strong interpre-
tation of their
meaning.

The appeal to *pathos,* the appeal to honor, heroism, and love for
our children and the ensuing desire to promise them a better

Park 9

future illustrates how Gore sets aside his soft rhetoric and transforms into an impassioned leader, urging his audience to become heroes of our generation.

Seesaw: Balancing the Soft and the Passionate Rhetorician

Gore adopts different styles of rhetoric in *An Inconvenient Truth* and in his follow-up presentation for the TED2008 Conference. Gore uses a two-part soft rhetoric in *An Inconvenient Truth* in order to draw in a guarded audience. He first compels us to feel fear and guilt through the juxtaposition of images of the beautiful and the doomed, making us more receptive to his environmental message. He then builds his *ethos* as a warm, dedicated, but still lonely leader, creating the inviting impression that draws us in and encourages us to join him in social action. When Gore delivers his TED presentation, his primary goal changes to motivating increased initiative and political will; he thus sets aside his soft rhetoric and adopts a heightened level of passion and sense of urgency.

This dynamic rhetoric, which Gore molds to fit his specific agenda, is the key to Gore's successful environmental leadership. He can be the warm, authentic, and soft leader when he wants to disarm a guarded audience. He can be the energized leader when he needs to inspire increased initiative in those that look up to him. In light of the recent sufferings caused by earthquakes in Haiti and Chile, the understanding of Gore's rhetoric offers us invaluable insight. In order to bring the countless pertinent but overlooked issues into the light à la

Moving to his conclusion, Wan Jin explains the final term in his paper: dynamic rhetoric.

He also brings in contemporary events, appealing to *kairos* to make the reader receptive to his argument.

The impassioned tone in Wan Jin's own writing suggests that he is moving toward the end of his paper, and indeed he closes with a compelling call to action.

Gore, we need to learn how to mold our rhetoric and master the art of balancing the soft and the passionate rhetorician in us.

Park 10

Works Cited

An Inconvenient Truth. Dir. Davis Guggenheim. Perf. Al Gore. Paramount Classics, 2006. DVD.

Gore, Al. "Al Gore's New Thinking on the Climate Crisis." Lecture. *TED: Ideas Worth Spreading*. TED.com, Apr. 2008. Web. 15 Jan. 2010. http://www.ted.com/talks/lang/eng/ al_gore_s_new_thinking_on_the_climate_crisis.html.

Gore, Al. "Al Gore on Averting Climate Crisis." Lecture. *TED: Ideas Worth Spreading*. TED.com, Feb. 2006. Web. 20 Jan. 2010. http://www.ted.com/talks/lang/eng/ al_gore_on_averting_climate_crisis.html.

Olson, Kathryn M. "Rhetorical Leadership and Transferable Lessons for Succsesful Social Advocacy in Al Gore's An Inconvenient Truth." *Argumentation & Advocacy* 44.2 (2007): 90–109. *Communication & Mass Media Complete*. EBSCO. Web. 24 Feb. 2010.

Rosteck, Thomas, and Thomas S. Frentz. "Myth and Multiple Readings in Environmental Rhetoric: The Case of An Inconvenient Truth." *Quarterly Journal of Speech* 95.1 (2009): 1–19. *Communication & Mass Media Complete*. EBSCO. Web. 24 Feb. 2010.

The Works Cited, on a separate page, provides proper MLA citation for all the research Wan Jin quoted or paraphrased or summarized in the paper.

MLA suggests that writers include URLs in their Works Cited only when absolutely necessary to find the original source, but this student's professor required that they be included as part of the assignment.

He might also have included field research in the form of interviews with professors or surveys with students who had watched any of Gore's presentations.

Park 11

Schulte, Bret. "Saying It In Cinema." *U.S. News*. 28 Mar. 2006.

    Web. 17 Jan. 2010. http://www.usnews.com/usnews/

    news/articles/060605/5warming.b.htm.

The Nielsen Company. *Global Consumers Vote Al Gore, Oprah*

    Winfrey and Kofi Annan Most Influential to Champion

    Global Warming Cause: Nielsen Survey. Nielsen: Trends &

    Insights. 2 July 2007. Web. 18 Jan. 2010. http://

    nz.nielsen.com/news/GlobalWarming_Jul07.shtml.

He shows a well balanced "iceberg of research"—including scholarly journals, popular articles, videos, and surveys.

The strong, developed ending of Wan Jin's paper shows how careful revision can help you develop a compelling argument that offers a power fully from beginning to end. Be sure to save some energy for your conclusion: you want your parting words to ring memorably in your reader's ears.

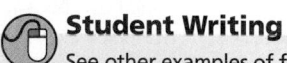 **Student Writing**

See other examples of fully developed research-based arguments.

www.pearsonhighered.com/envision/203

The Writer's Process

In this chapter, you have learned strategies for visual mapping, organizing, outlining, drafting, and revising your research paper. You have explored ways of casting your argument and acquired concrete methods for integrating both written sources and visual texts as evidence for your argument. Chances are you have written the first full draft of your paper. But don't forget revision. Revision shows us the way that all *writing is rewriting*.

Sometimes, when writing, we may continue to revise our papers even after we have "finished." Think back to the earlier *Blade Runner* example and how Ridley Scott revised the film for re-release years after its first showing. Similarly, while you may be satisfied with your final research product when you turn it in, it is possible that you have set the groundwork for a longer research project that you may return to later in your college career. Or you may decide to seek publication for your essay in a school newspaper, magazine, or a national journal. In such cases, you may need to modify or expand on your argument for this new rhetorical situation; you may produce your own "director's cut"—a paper identical in topic to the original but developed in a significantly different fashion. Keep in mind that revision is indeed "re-vision."

As you approach revision—as well as the preceding steps of outlining, drafting, and integrating sources—feel free to be creative by composing a hypertext outline or packaging your research paper electronically with links to visual material such as film clips, advertisement videos, or audio files. Your work as a writer has only just started, and the "premiere" of your project awaits.

PREWRITING CHECKLIST

Focus on Analyzing Film and Documentary

❑ Assess the genre of the film (comedy? horror? drama? documentary?) and how this affects the audience's response to its content. Does the film combine elements of different genres? What is the rhetorical effect of this combination?

❑ What is the plot of the film? What is the organizational structure?

❑ Is this plot arranged chronologically? in parallel sequences? thematically? What is the rhetorical significance of arrangement?

❑ What is the message conveyed to readers? Is it persuasive or informative? Is this message conveyed through reliance on *pathos*, *logos*, or *ethos*?

❑ How is the *ethos* of the filmmaker conveyed to the audience?

❑ What notable types of shots does the filmmaker use? Jot down one or two instances where cinematic techniques (zoom-in, cuts between scenes, fade in/fade out, montage) are used for rhetorical effect.

❑ Is there a narrator in the film? voice-over? What is the effect on the audience?

❑ Is there any framing—a way of setting the beginning and end in context?

❑ How is time handled? Does the film move in chronological order? reverse chronological order? What is the significance of such rhetorical choices on the meaning and power of the film? Are flashbacks used in the film? What effect is achieved through the use of flashbacks?

❑ How are *pathos, ethos,* and *logos* produced by the different cinematic techniques? For instance, is *pathos* created through close-ups of characters? Is *ethos* created through allusions to famous films or filmmaking techniques? Is *logos* constructed through the insertion of a narrator's viewpoint?

❑ What is the audience's point of identification in the film? Is the audience supposed to identify with a single narrator? Does the film negotiate the audience's reaction in any specific ways? How?

❑ How is setting used to construct a specific mood that affects the impact of the message of the film?

❑ Is the film an adaptation of another work—a play or a novel? To the best of your knowledge, what modifications were made to customize the narrative for a cinematic audience? Does the text as film differ in content or message from the text in its original form? Can you see traces of revision and rewriting?

PREWRITING WITH THE *ENVISION* WEBSITE

One way to get started organizing and writing your argument is to work on these tasks with peers in your class. In groups of three or four, visit the movie trailers site on Apple.com through the *Envision* Website and view two or three trailers, either for the same film or different ones. Write down the main features of each trailer. How does each one function as an outline of the film's key scenes, characters, conflict, and message? What tone or style is conveyed through the selection of imagery, the choice of music, and the emphasis on a particular plot or character? What can you apply to your own outline strategies of arrangement? Together, compose an outline for a potential essay.
www.pearsonhighered.com/envision/205

WRITING PROJECTS

1. **Visual Map or Outline:** Create a visual representation of your argument: a bubble map, flowchart, hierarchal set of bubbles, or handmade construction paper model. Write an annotation for each part of your drawing, model, or storyboard to help you move from mass of material to coherent research-based essay.

2. **Detailed Written Outline:** Working with your research materials and notes, create a written outline of your ideas, using numbers and letters to indicate

subsections of your argument. Rather than simply calling the second section "II. Body," create several points within the body to show the development of your argument. You may want to start with a topic outline, but ideally you should aim for argumentative subheadings. Include your working thesis statement at an appropriate place in your outline, and include visuals that you will analyze in the essay itself. After you draft the outline, go back and insert your primary and secondary sources in the outline. Insert actual quotations (with page numbers) from your research where possible, and don't forget to cite your sources for both paraphrase and summary. This outline might easily turn into the paper itself. Use it to check the balance of sources, the progression of ideas, and the complexity of your argument.

3. **Research-Based Argument:** Write a 12- to 15-page argumentative research paper on a topic of your choice. If you wish to analyze and research visual rhetoric, consider the images that shape a debate, tell a certain history, or persuade an audience in a certain way. In other words, address an issue through a visual rhetoric lens. You should integrate research materials that can include articles, books, interviews, field research, surveys (either published or that you conduct yourself), TV programs, Internet texts, and other primary and secondary sources, including visuals. Keep in mind that, because this is a research paper, you need to balance primary and secondary materials. Ultimately, your goal should be proving a thesis statement with apt evidence, using appropriate rhetorical and argumentative strategies.

4. **Reflection Essay:** After you have completed your essay, compose a one-page reflection letter that serves as a self-evaluation. Think back on the development of your argument through research and revision. Include comments on the strengths of the essay, the types of revisions you made throughout your writing process, and how the collaborative process of peer review improved your essay. Conclude by explaining how you might continue to write about this issue in future academic or professional situations.

 Visit www.pearsonhighered.com/envision for expanded assignment guidelines and student projects. Visit www.mycomplab.com for additional general writing and research resources.

CHAPTER 7

Avoiding Plagiarism and Documenting Sources

Chapter Preview Questions

- How can I avoid unintentional plagiarism?
- What is the difference between rhetorical imitation and stealing intellectual property?
- Why is it important to learn the conventions of a documentation style?
- What are the proper methods for in-text citations and bibliographies?

"Creativity always builds on the past." For many writers, the debt to those who have written before them is carefully acknowledged—whether through direct references, parenthetical citations, or a list of sources. Even visual artists and multimedia writers name their sources explicitly to show that they belong to a larger community of writers and that they respect the work of others.

But Justin Cone, a designer and animator based in Austin, Texas, makes this point more emphatically through the multimedia montage shown in Figure 7.1, a short film called *Building on the Past*, which recycles and modifies public-domain film footage to make an argument about the relationship between creativity and legislation. The visuals are accompanied by a musical score and a voice-over that repeats the same sentence intermittently throughout the film: "Creativity always builds on the past." In the scene shown here, which opens the film, Cone re-edited the public-domain footage to run in reverse, showing the children

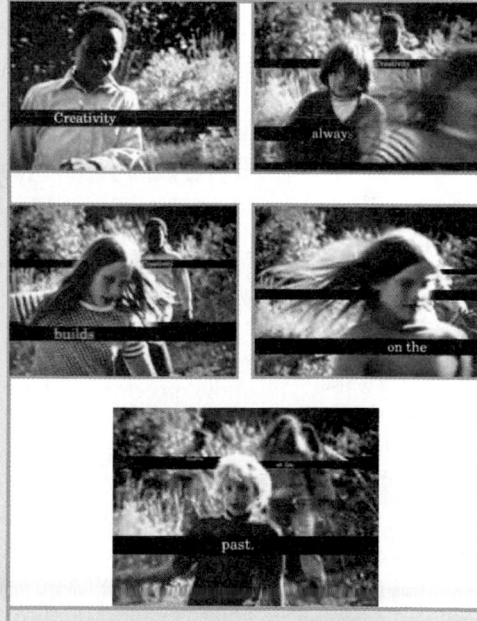

FIGURE 7.1. Justin Cone's film, *Building on the Past*, remixes visuals and sound to emphasize how all our ideas rely on the works of those before us.

running backward uphill instead of forward downhill, offering a powerful argument about how we rely on others for our own creativity. Cone expresses that idea visually, through his strategy of organization, word choice, and design.

Your research project, too, can draw its strength from previous work on the subject. It should be a merger of your argument and the already existing dialogue on the topic. So even as you "re-edit it" to suit the purpose of your paper—by selecting passages to quote, paraphrase, summarize, or even argue against—it is crucial that you let your readers know *where* the ideas originated by providing what we call complete and ethical **source attribution**, or the acknowledgment and identification of your sources.

In this chapter, you'll learn how the **rhetorical art of imitation**—the process by which we all learn to write, compose, speak, and produce texts—differs from the theft of others' ideas, which is called **plagiarism**. We'll discuss intellectual property and why it is important to respect the work of others, and you'll acquire strategies for avoiding unintentional plagiarism. Finally, we'll provide a means of understanding the process of constructing in-text and end-of-paper citations, and we'll explain the logic of MLA, APA, CSE, and Chicago documentation styles.

Rhetorical Imitation and Intellectual Property: Understanding Plagiarism

In ancient times, **rhetorical imitation**, or the practice of taking after others, was a celebrated form of instruction. Students would copy a speech out word by word, studying the word choice, organization, rhythm, and art of the work. Then they would write a rhetorical analysis (as you did in Chapter 1) of the speech to understand figures and tropes, strategies of argument, and organizational choices. Finally, they would use elements of the speeches they studied, including content (words) and form (arrangement), to draft their own speeches. Through this imitation, they learned to be great rhetors. Such imitative exercises helped students learn from models of excellence.

This, too, is your task in your writing class. After analyzing articles and studying argumentative strategies from samples of student writing, at some point you need to move on to create your own text. Yet, in the process, you may wish to refer back to those on whose work you are building. This is where **documentation** comes in—the responsible and correct acknowledgment of your sources and influences.

> "[Imitation was] the bridge between one's reading and writing (or speaking). . . . Students moved from close imitations of their models to looser sorts, using these models increasingly as starting points for longer, more involved compositions of their own making."
>
> —Gideon Burton

Today, it is common to talk about ideas, not just in terms of words and thoughts, but also in terms of **intellectual property**, that is, the ideas that belong to someone else. In this increasingly litigious society, you need to understand when to stop imitation and when to start acknowledging your sources so that you preserve the rights of others and protect yourself as an emerging writer.

Plagiarism—using another person's idea as your own—was not a crime in classical times, according to scholars Peter Morgan and Glenn Reynolds. But with the invention of printing technology, copyright law, and a cultural emphasis on the profitability of intellectual concepts came a concern about taking someone else's ideas—and therefore their earning potential—whether intentionally or unintentionally. Consequently, you find a demand for originality in writing in both academic and professional circles today. These days, in colleges and universities, plagiarism can lead to suspension or even expulsion because the perpetrator is charged with literally stealing the ideas of someone else.

But there is another, even more compelling ethical reason for keeping in mind the principle discussed in Chapter 5—that research is always a conversation with those who came before. As you work with sources, realize that the claims you are able to make are in fact based on the foundation provided by others. Identifying your sources thus becomes a writing strategy that you need to implement out of *respect* for those who have come before you. By acknowledging their names, ideas, and words, you contribute to a body of knowledge, graciously extending thanks to those who have paved the way. Therefore, while there are legal issues related to intellectual property, copyright law, and "fair use" that you need to know about, if you keep the *respect principle* in mind, you will rarely fall into the trap of inadvertently "stealing" someone's work.

Avoiding Unintentional Plagiarism

Plagiarism—or using someone else's ideas without acknowledgement in their original or even altered form—is a serious offense, even if it occurs unintentionally or accidentally. To avoid unintentional plagiarism, or accidentally taking someone else's ideas or words as your own, you might follow two practices.

1. **Always keep in mind that you are contributing to a conversation with other writers**.

   When you are writing a research-based argument using many texts, think of working with sources as responding to people whose works you cite, or quote, as a way of including them in the dialogue. With research papers, you are having a conversation with an entire room of people, introducing each person in turn, and serving as the moderator as well to contributor.

2. **Develop effective ways of note taking while reading through your sources.**

   If you find an interesting quote, don't just underline or highlight it. Copy it into your research log with a notation about how you might use it. Check the quote carefully and be sure to note the source, including complete bibliographic information and page numbers. If you find an intriguing idea, write down the attribution in your research log.

Consider Michael Rothenberg's notations in his research log for a project on the design plans for the Twin Towers Memorial in New York City.

Michael first lists his source. Then he organizes his notes by category (safety). He then copies the source directly and writes down the full name and identifying information for the quote. He'll use this to build ethos in citing this authority within his paper.

Michael repeats this process for his second note. Here he puts the most interesting words in quotation marks and deliberately uses different words in composing his paraphrase of the source.

Source: www.cnn.com/2003/US/northeast/01/12/wtc.skyscrapers/

Category: Safety

"there's no reason to believe the structures that replace the twin towers wouldn't also be targets." CNN? "they're a target forever"—Klemenic, president of an engineering firm Skilling Ward Magnusson Barkshire in Seattle.

Howard Decker, chief curator of the National Building Museum in Washington, DC, said: the other target was the "squat pentagon." He said that shows terrorists choose targets because of their symbolism, not their height. "The desire to build tall buildings is an old one," he said. "The motivations for it are complicated. Commerce. Capitalism. Ego."

Student Writing

See Michael Rosenberg's complete research paper and other selected student research papers.

www.pearsonhighered.com/envision/210

This notion of considering your sources as people, as the cast of characters for your research paper, can help you avoid *unintentional plagiarism*, or the phenomenon that happens when we assimilate all the material we have read and then think that the ideas are our own. This can happen for

many reasons: fatigue, oversaturation of information, poor memory, or sloppy note taking. Regardless of the circumstances, even the unintentional taking of others' ideas can have very serious consequences. Many colleges and universities have plagiarism policies that do not distinguish between intentional and unintentional plagiarism; the act will bring consequences ranging from a failure in the course to expulsion. When Doris Kearns Goodwin, a widely admired historian, was "caught" using the words and ideas of others in a lengthy book that had taken her many years to research and write, she issued an apology that noted her reverence for her sources, suggested that her note taking strategies early in the research process had been less than meticulous, and promised never to let it happen again.

Citing Sources for Downloaded Images and Multimedia

When you integrate visuals or multimedia in your writing, it is not enough to include just the source and provide the citation for it. You need to spend a few moments thinking about issues of copyright and permissions. Whether you are dealing with images or print quotations, you are using materials produced or prepared by another person, and you must give that person credit for the work. In some cases—particularly if you plan to publish your work—you also need to obtain permission to use it. As you browse through catalogs of images, you need to record in your notes the source of each image you decide to use. If you have copied an image from the Web (by right-clicking and choosing "Save Picture As"), you need to note as much of the full source information as you can find: the Website author, the title, the sponsoring organization, the date. If you have found a visual (photograph, chart, ad) from a print source and scanned it into a computer so you can insert it into your essay, you need to list the print source in full as well as information about the original image (the name of the photographer, the image title, and the date). Listing Google as your source is not sufficient; be sure to find the original source and list it in full.

Keep careful track as you locate images, give appropriate credit when you use them in your essay, and ask for permission if necessary by writing the owner of the image.

Understanding Documentation Style

Today, with software programs that can help you format your source attributions into different documentation styles, it may seem confusing or even frustrating to worry about proper documentation style. But realize that different styles are preferred by different communities of writers, as shown in the following table. The format guidelines for each style actually have a rhetorical purpose corresponding to the way that knowledge is constructed for that community. Taking a moment to understand the logic behind the styles will help you practice proper citation without having to look up every instance of how to do it. In the process, you build your *ethos* as a writer by showing that you speak the language of a particular academic community.

Documentation Style	Community of Writers	Defining Features	Purpose of Features	Example
MLA	Modern Language Association (language, literature, writing, philosophy, and humanities scholars and teachers)	Citation begins with author's name (last name first, full first name), then publication information, date, medium of publication (then, if a website, date you accessed it).	Knowledge advances based on individual author's contributions; thus, names are prioritized over dates; place of publication matters for building ethos.	McCloud, Scott. *Understanding Comics.* New York: HarperPerennial, 1994. Print.
APA	American Psychological Association (psychologists and social scientists)	Publication date immediately follows designation of author, multiple authors may be listed (last name and initials), titles are in sentence style (first word capitalized, rest lowercase)	Since knowledge advances based on dated contributions to the field, dates are prioritized; most writing is collaborative, so up to six authors are listed; titles, typically long and technical, are in lowercase.	Bruce V., & Green, P. (1990). *Visual perception: Physiology, psychology, andecology* (2nd ed.). London, England: Erlbaum.
CSE	Council of Science Editors (such as biology and physics)	References include last name and date; often superscript numbers are used	Like APA style, emphasis is on knowledge advancing through studies and scientific research; a heavily cited style of writing	[1]Goble, JL. Visual disorders in the handicapped child. New York: M. Dekker; 1984. p. 265.
Chicago	University of Chicago (business writers, professional writers, and those in fine arts)	Sources are listed as footnotes or endnotes and include page numbers	Knowledge is incremental, and readers like to check facts as they go along	[2]Scott McCloud, *Understanding Comics* (New York: HarperPerennial, 1994), 33.

For the purposes of this chapter, we focus on MLA style because the writing we've been discussing in this book belongs to disciplines in the humanities. The different styles, methods of organization, modes of argumentation, and conventions for writing in the social sciences, sciences, business, and fine arts communities are not covered in this book, but you can find links to resources through the *Envision* Companion Website for Chapter 7.

In-Text Citations: Documentation as Cross-Referencing

Documentation is not intended to be some surreptitious way to check up on you; rather, it is part of the research dialogue. The idea is that readers might be inspired enough by your research and your use of materials to want to read some of your sources themselves. In this way, documentation functions as a *road map* for your audience to locate the source—both in your bibliography and in the library or online. Accordingly, the central purpose of in-text documentation is to point readers clearly and explicitly to the list of sources at the end of the paper. We call this *cross-referencing*.

Let's take a look at a citation in Michael Rothenberg's paper on the Twin Towers. We call this an **in-text citation** or reference because it occurs within the body of his paper. MLA style always places such references inside parentheses to set them off from the rest of the writing. Look at how the last name and page number of the citation in parentheses point the reader directly to the author's name in the "Works Cited" list.

. . . the Twin Towers were so enormous that together they encased a staggering 11 million square feet of commercial space (Czarnecki 31).

* * *

Works Cited

Bravman, John. Personal interview. 13 May 2003.

Bruno, Lisa D. "Studio Daniel Libeskind." *Baltimore Sun.*

Baltimore Sun, 6 Nov. 2002. Web. 1 June 2003.

Czarnecki, John E. "Architects at the Forefront as They Show Ground Zero Aspirations." *Architectural Record* Nov. 2002: 31–50. Print.

Notice that Michael has alphabetized the list by authors' last names, which corresponds to MLA style documentation which places author names as most important. Readers need only scan down the page to look for the last name of the source cited earlier. This makes it very easy, and once you understand that this **cross-referencing logic** governs all documentation rules, you can begin to understand how to document a wide range of sources—even new multimedia sources for which there are no set rules of citation.

For instance, Michael needed to document several quotes he obtained from a temporary PDF document posted on the Website of a city review board. By understanding documentation as *cross-referencing*, here's what Michael wrote:

In particular, they required a memorial that would include both history and memory "such as the Libeskind's below-grade 'ground zero' space," as well as a proposal "that returns a much-lamented presence to the skyline" like Libeskind's tower, and finally, a plan that develops the site in the context of the community (Hutton 3, 12).

* * *

Works Cited

Hutton, Ernest, ed. *Evaluation of Innovative Design Proposals. New York: New Visions*. N.p. 13 Jan. 2003. Web. 25 May 2003.

As you can see, the word within the parenthetical documentation sets up a *cross-reference* to the first word listed in the "Works Cited" list at the end of the paper. This makes it easy to compose a very concise reference within the paper and easy to find that reference at the end of the paper. If there is no author to put in your parentheses, begin with the first word of the source entry on the Works Cited page. Here is an example from Tanner Gardner's paper on the globalization of the NBA, where he quotes an article from the journal *The Economist*. Many of the articles in this journal are collectively written, so no authors are named.

Student Writing

Read Tanner Gardner's complete paper on globalization and the NBA
www.pearsonhigheredu/envision/215

In this case, Tanner uses the first words of the title. See how the cross-referencing logic of MLA style helps readers find the source in the Works Cited list at the end of the paper:

> The relationship between Nike and basketball is actually reciprocal, as their promotions actually promote basketball internationally by providing publicity for the sport. ("The Yao").
>
> * * *
>
> Works Cited
>
> "The Yao Crowd." *Economist* 9 Aug. 2003: 55. Print.

Tanner used the same technique in other parts of his paper when referring, for instance, to a website with acknowledged author.

Using Notes for Documentation

Although MLA style relies primarily on in-text citations and a final bibliography—unlike Chicago style, which uses primarily footnotes or endnotes—sometimes you might need to include a note. You'll use notes, for example, when you want to include extra explanatory information but don't want to break the flow of your argument.

Following are two notes from Michael's paper. In the first case, he wanted to define some of the key terms of his argument, but he felt it would be intrusive to pause and explain his terms within the paper itself.

> [1]Those in the public who influenced the design of the new World Trade Center include all of those concerned with the project and not just New York citizens. However, even though the majority of these motivated individuals live in New York, they represent every state and many nations. Hence, the collective group of citizens in the worldwide community who are interested in this project are referred to as "the public" throughout this document, but this phrase should be understood to include primarily New York citizens.

In the second case, he wanted to add more information from his research log, but again he felt it would break the flow of his argument. In this case, he was able to include direct quotations and statistics from his research; this built his *ethos* and allowed interested readers to learn more about the subject. Notice that he included the source for his research again through the cross-referencing system. A reader would only have to scan down to the *O* section of his bibliography to find the full source for this citation.

> [2]Five thousand people from the New York area participated in a two-week in-depth discussion starting on July 20, 2002. According to their Website, "This historic gathering—called 'Listening to the City'—gave participants an opportunity to help shape the redevelopment of Lower Manhattan and the creation of a permanent memorial to the victims of 9/11." At this gathering, the 5,000 committed individuals responded to many questions and polls. Of the respondents, 60% thought that new towers should be built at least as tall as the originals, 71% thought that adding a "major element or icon" to the skyline was "very important," and 87% thought it was "important" or "very important" to add something unique to the skyline (Online Dialogues).

In addition to providing explanatory information, notes can also point readers to a list of sources you would discuss or include if you had space to do so. In Michael's case, he wanted to discuss mammoth architectural designs more broadly but did not have the space in his paper to do so. His solution was a note pointing the reader to a source on this topic, which happened to be another paper he had written. This note would also be the place for a list of sources about this tangential topic.

> [6]See my paper, "The Two Towers," on the Petronas Towers as the world's tallest, February 2003.

Typically, such notes are formatted as **endnotes**, appearing at the end of your paper, before the bibliography. **Footnotes**, which appear at the bottom or foot of the page, would again break the flow of the argument. But ask your teacher for specific guidance about your own paper.

MLA-Style Works Cited Lists

You've seen how documentation works as a *cross-referencing system*, in which the in-text citation within parentheses points the reader directly to the source in the bibliography. In MLA style, the bibliography is called a **Works Cited** list because it refers explicitly to the works (or sources) you have cited (or quoted) in your paper. Sometimes a Works Cited list is accompanied by another section called a **Works Consulted** list, which names all the other sources you may have read and studied but did not actually quote from in your final revision.

Realize that a reference page is a moment of *ethos* building as well: by listing both works *cited* and works *consulted*, you demonstrate your research process and new knowledge. You also invite your readers to explore the topic in depth with you.

Documentation for Print and Online Sources

MLA style follows a particular logic in ordering information for a citation. Consult the "At a Glance" box and the table below to begin to understand this system. You might also study the list of examples provided in this chapter, but realize that sometimes for less conventional sources (e.g., Facebook wall posts) you may need to improvise the format based on your understanding of MLA style.

Realize that while the latest MLA Handbook suggests that you include a URL only when your instructor requires it, you should always keep track of the URL in your notes or research log. The authors of this book consistently ask their students to include URLs for online sources.

LOGIC OF MLA STYLE

Satrapi, Marjane.	*Persepolis: The Story of a Childhood.*	New York: Pantheon, 2004. Print.
List the author's name first, by last name. If there are multiple authors, include them all, following the order listed on the publication.	The title comes next. For books and films, italicize the title. For shorter pieces (such as articles, TV shows, songs, etc.), put the title in quotation marks with the larger publication (the collection of essays, TV series, or album) italicized.	Last comes publication information: place, publisher or company, date, and medium of publication. For shorter pieces, include the complete range of page numbers, followed by a period. For shorter online articles, list the medium of publication (Web) followed by a period. For online texts, conclude with the date of access.
If there is no author, use the publishing organization (if available) or jump next to the title.	If you need to refer to the title for in-text citations (and there is no author), use the first few keywords only.	

Single-Author Book

> Satrapi, Marjane. *Persepolis: The Story of a Childhood*. New York: Pantheon, 2004. Print.

Multiple-Author Book

> Andrews, Maggie, and Mary M. Talbot, eds. *All the World and Her Husband: Women in Twentieth-Century Consumer Culture*. London: Cassell, 2000. Print.

Introduction, Preface, Foreword, or Afterword in a Book

> Gerbner, George. Foreword. *Cultural Diversity and the U.S. Media*. Ed. Yahya R. Kamalipour and Theresa Carillia.

New York: State U of New York P, 1998. xv–xvi.
Print.

Cohen, Mitchell, and Dennis Hale, eds. Introduction. *The New
Student Left*. Boston: Beacon Press, 1967. xvii–xxxiii. Print.

Article in an Anthology

Boichel, Bill. "Batman: Commodity as Myth." *The Many Lives of
the Batman*. Ed. Roberta Pearson and William Uricchio.
New York: BFI, 1991. 4–17. Print.

Article from a Journal

Roberts, Garyn G. "Understanding the Sequential Art of Comic
Strips and Comic Books and Their Descendants in the
Early Years of the New Millenium." *Journal of American
Culture* 27.2 (2004): 210–17. Print.

Article from a Popular Magazine Published Monthly

Maney, Kevin. "The New Face of IBM." *Wired* July 2005. Web. 18
August 2005.

Sontag, Susan. "Looking at War." *New Yorker* 3 Jan. 2003: 43–48.
Print.

Article from a Newspaper

Cowell, Alan. "Book Buried in Irish Bog Is Called a Major Find." *New
York Times*. New York Times, 27 July 2006. Web. 31 July 2006.

Article from a Database

Chun, Alex. "Comic Strip's Plight Isn't Funny." *Los Angeles Times*
27 Apr. 2006, home ed.: E6. *LexisNexis*. Web. 4 May 2006.

Article from a Website

Yagoda, Ben. "You Need to Read This: How *Need to* Vanquished
Have to, *Must* and *Should*." *Slate*. Washington Post
Newsweek Interactive, 17 July 2006. Web. 20 July 2006.

Note that for this and all other online sources, the most recent MLA Handbook states "You should include a URL as supplementary information only when the reader probably cannot locate the source without it or when your instructor requires it." **(MLA, p 182)**

Anthology

Herndl, Carl G., and Stuart C. Brown, eds. *Green Culture*.
Madison: U of Wisconsin P, 1996. Print.

Anonymous Article

"Hillary's American Dream." *Economist* 29 July 2006: 32.
Print.

Definition

"Diversity." *American Heritage Dictionary of the English
Language*. 4th ed. Houghton, 2000. Print.

"Greek Mythology." *Wikipedia*. Wikimedia Foundation, 16 April 2010.
Web. May 5, 2010.

Letter to the Editor

Tucker, Rich Thompson. "High Cost of Cheap Coal." Letter.
National Geographic July 2006: 6–7. Print.

Letter or Memo

Greer, Michael. Letter to the authors. 30 July 2006.
Print.

Dissertation (Unpublished)

Li, Zhan. "The Potential of America's Army: The Video Game as
Civilian-Military Public Sphere." Diss. Massachusetts
Institute of Technology, 2004. Print.

Government Publication

United States. Census Bureau. Housing and Household Economic
Statistics Division. *Poverty Thresholds 2005*. US Census
Bureau, 1 Feb. 2006. Web. 20 May 2006.

Interview

Tullman, Geoffrey. Personal interview. 21 May 2006.

Cho, Ana. Telephone interview. 4 June 2005.

Email

> Tisbury, Martha. "Re: Information Overload." Message to Max
> Anderson. 27 Mar. 2008. E-mail.

Online Posting

> Shelly, Ayla. "Visual Rhetoric, Girls, and Ads." *GrlChatSpot*.
> Google. 5 Nov. 2006. Web. 10 May 2010.

Chat Room Discussion or Real-time Communication

> Zhang, Zhihao. "Revision Suggestions." *Cross-Cultural Rhetoric*
> *Chat Room*. Stanford U. 25 May 2006. Web. 5 June 2008.

Tweet or Twitter feed

> @CarsonDaly. Web log post. Twitter.com. 10 April 2010. Web.
> 15 May 2010.

Facebook post

> The White House. "Spurring Innovation, Creating Jobs."
> Facebook.com. 5 August 2009.
> Web. 13 February 2010.

Documentation for Visual, Audio, and Multimedia Sources

Because many of the materials you may work with fall into the category of innovative text produced by new technologies—such as Webmovies, Flash animation, Weblogs, three-dimensional images, storyboards, sound clips, and more—you need to learn how to construct a citation that provides as much detail as possible about the text. Even citing interviews and surveys can be tricky for some because the format does not match conventional books or articles. Just follow the logical steps for citing print and online sources, developing a rubric that works to offer as much information as possible. The key is consistency and adhering as closely as possible to the logic of MLA style.

Photograph or Visual Image

Golden Gate Bridge, San Francisco. Personal photograph by the author. 23 June 2004.

Goldin, Nan. *Jimmy Paulette & Misty in a Taxi, NYC*. 1991. Photograph. San Francisco Museum of Modern Art, San Francisco.

Sherman, Cindy. *Untitled Film Still*. 1978. Museum of Modern Art. *The Complete Untitled Film Stills of Cindy Sherman*. Web. 7 July 2006.

Advertisement

Nike. "We Are All Witnesses." Advertisement. *Nikebasketball*. 3 Jan. 2006. Web. 15 June 2006.

Film

Beyond Killing Us Softly: The Impact of Media Images on Women and Girls. Dir. Margaret Lazarus and Renner Wunderlich. Prod. Cambridge Documentary Films, 2000. Film.

"A Brief History of America." *Bowling for Columbine*. Dir. Michael Moore. United Artists, 2002. *Bowling for Columbine*, n.d. Web. 13 June 2006.

YouTube

Wesch, Michael. "A Vision of Students Today." YouTube. 12 Oct 2007. Web. 31 March 2010.

Comic Strip or Editorial Cartoon

Wilkinson, Signe. Cartoon. *San Francisco Chronicle*. 1 June 2010: A13. Print.

Pastis, Stephen. "Pearls before Swine." Comic strip. *Comics.com*

18 Apr. 2006. Web. 16 May 2006.

Entire Internet Site

Cartoonists Index. MSNBC, n.d. Web. 4 Nov. 2005.

Individual Webpage from an Internet Site

Stevenson, Seth. "Head Case: The Mesmerizing Ad for Headache

Gel." *Slate*. Washington Post Newsweek Interactive,

24 July 2006. Web. 25 July 2006.

Personal Homepage

Corrigan, Edna. Home page. *Ednarules*. N.p., n.d. Web. 24 Oct.

2005.

Cover (Magazine, book, CD, etc.)

Adams, Neil. "Deadman." *Comics VF.com*. Comics VF, 1978. Web.

23 Oct. 2005.

Television Program

"The Diet Wars." *Frontline*. PBS, 2004. Web. 16 Aug. 2006.

Computer Game

Infinity Ward. *Modern Warfare 2*. Activision. 2009. Playstation 3.

Second Life. Your World. Linden Labs, n.d. Web. 7 May 2006.

Screen Shot

"Star Wars Galaxies." Sony Online Entertainment, n.d. Web. 5 Feb. 2005.

Radio Essay

Ydstie, John. "Book Marketing Goes to the Movies." *Morning*

Edition. Natl. Public Radio. 18 July 2006. Radio.

Sound Clip or Recording

Reagan, Ronald. "The Space Shuttle *Challenger* Tragedy Address."

28 Jan. 1986. *American Rhetoric*. Web. 5 Mar. 2006.

Class Lecture

> Connors, Fiona. "Visual Literacy in Perspective." English 210B.
>
> Boston U. 24 Oct. 2004. Lecture.

Speech

> Rheingold, Howard. "Technologies of Cooperation." Annenberg
>
> Center for Communication. U of Southern California,
>
> Los Angeles. 3 Apr. 2006. Speech.
>
> Jobs, Steve. Commencement Address. Stanford U.,
>
> Palo Alto, 12 June 2005. *iTunes U*. Apple. Web.
>
> 27 July 2006.

Painting

> Warhol, Andy. *Self Portrait*. 1986. Andy Warhol Museum,
>
> Pittsburgh. *The Warhol: Collections*. Web.
>
> 3 Aug. 2006.

Map

> *Hong Kong Disneyland Guide*. Map. Disney, 2006. Print.

Performance

> *Phedre*. By Racine. Dir. Ileana Drinovan. Pigott Theater,
>
> Memorial Hall, Stanford, 10–13 May, 2006.
>
> Performance.

Student Writing

See Stephanie Parker's full research paper and other student research papers using MLA style.

www.pearsonhighered.com/envision/224

Student Paper in MLA Style

Stephanie Parker's research paper focuses on how digital communities, such as Soompi (a Korean pop culture website), have transformed ideas of racial identity. She worked with a wide range of both print and electronic sources in her project.

Parker 1

Stephanie Parker

Dr. Christine Alfano

PWR 2 Cultural Interfaces

7 December 2008

Soompi and the "Honorary Asian": Shifting Identities

in the Digital Age

Every morning at 7:00 AM, Norwegian James Algaard turns on his computer and joins Soompi IRC: a chatroom for members of a Korean Pop Culture discussion forum. James' daily entrance into the chatroom is enthusiastically greeted by online acquaintances who know him as <SeungHo>, a connoisseur of Korean Hip Hop and a collector of limited edition sneakers. Seungho Lee was born in South Korea, but was adopted by a Norwegian family; websites like Soompi are his only connection to Korean culture. Thousands of miles away in Los Angeles, it is 10:00 PM when I, an American with a strong interest in Asia, join the same chatroom to spend time with Seungho and thirty other "Soompiers," people from around the world who have come together to form a strong and tight-knit online community. The chatroom itself [. . .] is visually mundane— a window that gradually fills with text as different users type, but Soompi IRC is an organic and multicultural part of cyberspace where people communicate in English, Korean, Mandarin, Cantonese, Spanish, Norwegian, Swedish, Vietnamese, Japanese, Tagalog, and French about every topic imaginable, 24 hours a day.

We Soompiers are representatives of "Generation I"—we have grown up with the Internet and are using it to define

Parker 2

ourselves in a more globalized society (Gates 98). A decade ago, cultural identity for people like Seungho and me was limited by factors like geography, language, and ethnicity; with the emergence of new technology and online communities, we have access to an ever-growing variety of choices for personal expression. Soompi and other cyber communities are at the forefront of a larger movement towards redefining how we culturally relate to one another. This movement will extend past the reach of the Internet and act as a catalyst for cross-cultural interaction and understanding on a level never seen before.

* * *

"This Site is My Life": Soompi Addicts and the Asian Fix

For the past decade, most academic research on cyber culture has focused on the type of social interaction that takes place within the digital medium. Scholars Howard Rheingold, Elisabeth Reid, Amy Jo Kim, and Lisa Nakamura have all helped to build the foundations for the study of online group behavior. But there is also another important part of Internet life that is only beginning to develop with the current generation of web users—how membership in an online group affects a person's self-perception in relation to others in real life. Nessim Watson is a Professor of Communication at Westfield State College, and has devoted years to the study of American mass media and cultural representations. After spending two years participating in and studying an online fan club, he concluded that, "those

Parker 9

youth formed a community which created not only individual benefits for participants but also a group strength" (102). It is those "individual benefits" that should provide the next source of material for research. The strong allegiance to a web-based group is not something that an Internet user logs in and out of—they take this allegiance with them and it influences their decisions and behavior in the real world: their mode of personal expression, their opinions about other groups, and especially their cultural identity.

Soompi is one of the best venues to observe the brand new phenomenon of people gaining a real sense of culture from an online source. According to Quantcast, a free internet ratings site, Soompi.com has 26 million page views per month, with a full 66% accomplished by "Addicts," or users who log on more than once every day ("Traffic Stats . . ."). For them, Soompi is the most convenient place to get their fix of Asian culture. This makes sense, and is in line with a report published in 2001 by the Pew Internet & American Life Project, "Asian-Americans and the Internet: The Young and Connected." According to the study, English-speaking Asian-Americans "are the Net's most active users . . . and have made the Internet an integral part of their daily lives" (Spooner 2). For hundreds of thousands of people in this demographic, Soompi has definitely become an important force in their personal lives and decisions, and in some cases, is the only website visited besides social utilities

Stephanie's page numbers skip to 9 here since we've abridged her paper.

Stephanie cites the page number for the print source from which she took this direct quote. Notice that because she used the author's name earlier in the sentence, she does not need to include it again in her parenthetical citation.

She cites the source for the statistics she uses. Since her source had no author, she refers to it here with an abbreviation of its title, which she places in quotation marks since it is the title of the article. In the works cited, she lists this source by its title as well, so it is easy for the reader to cross-reference.

Even though Stephanie read this as an electronic file, the study was in PDF form and therefore has page numbers that she could refer to in her citations.

Parker 10

This source is a discussion thread from the website that Stephanie is discussing, but for the purposes of citation, she refers to it by its title, just as she would for an article that had no author listed.

like Facebook ("What Would You . . ."). They can use Soompi to build their knowledge of Asian culture, and to form new connections with other people they can relate to around the world. In September of 2008, a discussion topic was posted on the Forums: "What Would You Do Without Soompi?" Certain self-proclaimed "addicts" left replies such as, "I probably wouldn't be so into Asian stuff," and "I would be a lot less knowledgeable about the world" ("What Would You . . ."). For thousands of Soompiers, the Forums are where they learn Asian-specific modes of fashion, style, speech patterns, and other cultural behaviors of expression.

This part of personal development is extremely important in the case of Asian-Americans living in predominantly non-Asian areas, without an "Asian group" of friends to participate in cultural activities with. Prominent scholars in Asian-American studies constantly emphasize the unique relationship between the Asian-American community and New Media, and its power to change traditional ideas about identity, culture, and the potential fluidity of both (Nakamura, *Digitizing Race* 184). Lisa Nakamura recognizes in *Digitizing Race: Visual Cultures of the Internet* that "Interactive media like the Web can question identity while building discursive community in ways that other static media cannot" (184). It allows anyone who wishes to contribute to the evolution of Asian-American culture to effectively "log in" and express their approval, resistance, or

Since Stephanie is working with two different texts written by Nakamura, here she specifies which she is referring to by including the title as well as the author and page number in the citation.

The second time that Stephanie references Nakamura's book, she does not need to include the author or title in the citation since they are exactly the same as in the previous citation.

Parker 11

creativity in the largest Forum on the planet, all while strengthening the bonds of a real community. Daniel Shim relates his own experience: "I was born in Canada in white communities & I grew up to be like them. Soompi has given me knowledge about Asian culture that I would not get from my school or family" (Online Interview). To follow that point further, in her book, Nakamura argues that the Internet provides a Forum for "questioning a rigid and essentialized notion of Asian American 'authenticity'" (185). This is extremely important—the idea of culture being inextricably linked to ethnicity, language, and geographic location becomes irrelevant in the face of rising online communities, the organic and global nature of which forces the issue of what makes a person "Asian," or "American." Since Daniel joined Soompi and began to use the Internet as a tool for personal expression, his popularity online has grown enormously: his YouTube videoblog, in which he comments on events in his daily life and makes fun of Asian stereotypes, has almost 30,000 subscribers and is the 4th most popular comedy blog in all of Canada (Shim, "Shimmycocopuffsss's..."). Without having grown up around many Asian young people, Daniel has been extremely successful in navigating the cultural landscape with the help of his online community, even producing his own ideas about Asian-American identity as a New Media celebrity (see Figure 6). For young people like

Since this is from an interview, there is no page number to cite. However, since Stephanie lists more than one source from Shim in her works cited, here she includes a citation that makes it clear that this quote was taken from her online interview with him.

Stephanie includes a parenthetical reference to Figure 6 to draw her visual evidence into dialogue with her main written argument.

Parker 12

Figure 6. Daniel Shim's parody video, "Wasabi Boy-No Engrish" confronts Asian stereotypes with comedy and has been viewed almost 200,000 times. Author screen shot.

Stephanie once again takes a direct quote from an interview she conducted and so does not cite a page number or author here. The curious reader would look up "Kang" on the works cited and discover that the quote came from a personal interview.

Daniel in Toronto and Seungho in Norway, Susan Kang says that "online is pretty much the only place they feel like they can connect to other Asians." Soompi makes it not only possible, but easy for Asians who live in a non-Asian place to immerse themselves in Asian culture and comment on it—an unprecedented step in the separation of culture and a static location.

Parker 19

Works Cited

Bell, David. *An Introduction to Cybercultures*. London: Routledge, 2001. Print.

Chen, Louie Haoru. Online interview. 16 November 2008.

"Crazy Sale for Korean Fashion." Advertisement. *Yesstyle*. 10 November 2008. Web. 10 November 2008.

Dator, Jim and Seo, Yongseok. "Korea as the wave of a future: The emerging Dream Society of icons and aesthetic experience." *Journal of Futures Studies*, 9:1 (2004): 31–44. Print.

Gates, Bill. "Enter 'Generation I.'" *Instructor*. March 2000: 98. Print.

Gulia, Milena and Wellman, Barry. "Virtual communities as communities: Net surfers don't ride alone." Eds. Smith, Mark A. and Kollock, Peter. *Communities in Cyberspace*. New York: Routledge, 1999. 167–194. Print.

Herring, Susan G. "Questioning the generational Divide: Technological Exoticism and Adult Constructions of Online Youth Identity. " *Youth, Identity, and Digital Media*. Eds. David Buckingham. MIT Press, 2000. 72–95. Print.

Jones, Stephen G. *Virtual Culture: Identity & Communication in Cybersociety*. London: Sage Publications Ltd, 1997. Print.

Kang, Susan. Online interview. 25 October 2008.

Kim, Amy Jo. *Community Building on the Web*. Peachpit Press, 6 April 2000. Web.

Ko, Shu-ling. "GIO looking to take foreign soap operas off prime time TV." *Taipei Times*. 11 January 2006. *AsiaMedia*. 11 January 2006. Web. 20 November 2008.

This works cited represents an abridged version of the much longer works cited that Stephanie included with her full paper.

All the sources in the works cited listed in alphabetical order by author's last name, or, in the cases where there is no identified author, by title.

Stephanie lists a variety of sources here, from academic journal articles, to books, newspaper articles, advertisements, and even online sources such as webpages, YouTube videos, and discussion list postings.

Notice the formatting of the entries: the first line of each entry is flush left, with a hanging indent in the wrapped lines so readers can skim the Works Cited easily.

Parker 20

When there is no author, the title is listed first.

"Korea Wave Hits Middle East." *Dae Jang Geum* 13 December
2005. Web. 1 November 2008.

Lee, HyukMin. Telephone interview. 15 October 2008.

Nakamura, Lisa. *Cybertypes*. New York: Routledge, 2002.
Print.

When an author's name appears more than once, three hyphens (---) stand in for the name in the second and subsequent entries, and the entries by the same author are alphabetized by title.

---. *Digitizing Race: Visual Cultures of the Internet*.
Minneapolis, MN: University of Minnesota Press, 2008.
Print.

Reid, Elisabeth. "Electropolis: Communications and Community
on Internet Relay Chat." Honors Thesis. University of
Melbourne, 1991. Print.

Rheingold, Howard. *The Virtual Community: Homesteading on the
Electronic Frontier*. Addison-Wesley Publishing Company,
1993. Print.

Shim, Daniel. Online interview. 12 November 2008.

---. "Shimmycocopuffsss's Profile Page" YouTube. 27 November
2008. Web. 28 November 2008.

---. "Wasabi Boy-No Engrish." YouTube. 5 March 2008. Web. 28
November 2008.

Spooner, Tom. "Asian-Americans and the Internet: The Young
and Connected." *Pew Internet and American Life Project*.
12 December 2001. PDF file.

Parker 21

"Traffic Stats for soompi.com." Quantcast.com. 1 November
    2008. Web. 1 November 2008.

"Wannabe Asians/Wasians" 1721 Posts. *Soompi*. Started 28 July
    2006. Web. 1 October 2008.

Watson, Nessim. "Why We Argue About Virtual Community: A
    Case Study of the Phish.net Fan Community." Jones
    102–110. Print.

"What Would You Do Without Soompi?, How would your life be
    different?" 95 posts. *Soompi*. Started 1 September 2008.
    Web. 1 October 2008.

"Winter Sonata to be aired in Egypt and Iraq." 5 January 2005.
    Web. 10 November 2008.

Yang, Jeff. "On top of YouTube: Happy Slip, Choi,
    KevJumba." *The San Francisco Chronicle*. 6 June 2008.
    Web. 20 October 2008.

Notice here how in the Watson entry, Stephanie cross-references with the Jones citation above so as not to be redundant.

The Writer's Process

Now that you've learned about the meaning of intellectual property, the dangers of plagiarism, the rhetorical purpose for documentation style, the cross-referencing logic of in-text citations, and the guidelines for MLA Works Cited and Consulted lists, it is time for you to review your own writing. Have you acknowledged all your sources in full? Did you include proper and concise parenthetical attributions in the paper? Does your bibliographic list provide an alphabetized reflection of your research? If so, then you have accomplished a great deal as a writer.

PREWRITING WITH THE *ENVISION* WEBSITE

Visit the *Envision* Website and read Doris Kearns Goodwin's article "How I Caused That Story" from *Time* magazine, January 27, 2002. In this article, Goodwin explains how she unintentionally plagiarized one of her 300 sources; her new technological approach to note taking offers a concrete strategy for preventing this disaster. As a team, develop a "top-ten" list of how to avoid the dangers of plagarism. Write up your answers as a potential article for *Time* magazine and implement these practices into your own work as a writer and researcher.

www.pearsonhigheredu.com/envision/234a

WRITING PROJECTS

1. **Documentation Log:** Develop your own system of note taking to avoid the kind of plagiarism trap that writer Doris Kearns Goodwin fell into.

2. **Peer Review of Citations:** Share your draft paper with a group of peers and have them check to see which sources need citation. Does your paper contain knowledge you must have obtained from a source? If so, you need to acknowledge the source of that knowledge. Do certain passages seem to be common knowledge? If so, you don't need to cite them. What paragraphs could go into notes? What aspects of your paper need more explanation and could use a note?

3. **Writing with Technology:** You might find it helpful to turn to one of the scholarly tools for producing a Work Cited list. These include *Ref Works, End Note,* and *TermPerfect*. You can find links to these tools on the *Envision* Website. Many researchers and scholars depend on these tools, keeping notes right in the program, inserting all identifying information for a source, and then selecting the documentation format needed for their papers. The technology then produces a list in the proper documentation style. You need to double-check the list, but it can save you time.

www.pearsonhighered.com/envision/234b

 Visit www.pearsonhighered.com/envision for expanded assignment guidelines and student projects. Visit www.mycomplab.com for additional general writing and research resources.

Part III

DESIGN AND DELIVERY

CHAPTER 8
Designing Arguments

CHAPTER 9
Delivering Presentations

What a shift in the means of delivery does is bring invention and arrangement into a new relationship with each other.

—Kathleen Yancey

CHAPTER 8

Designing Arguments

Chapter Preview Questions

- What are the best ways to design arguments for specific audiences?
- How can I compose an academic abstract and "bio"?
- What is decorum and how does this rhetorical principle govern document design?
- What techniques can you learn for designing your writing in digital and multimedia formats?
- How do visual arguments work, such as opinion advertisements (or op-ads), photo essays, and Websites?

FIGURE 8.1. The cover of Michael Chaitkin's research essay offers a carefully designed visual argument.

This chapter will give you the expertise to design your work for diverse purposes and audiences. We'll provide specific guidelines for academic essays, including line-spacing, margin size, and other formatting considerations. You'll learn how to write an academic abstract, a short biography (bio), and a cover letter. Then we'll examine hybrid document design in the form of newsletters and brochures before turning to visual arguments, such as op-ads, photo essays, and multimedia projects.

Michael Chaitkin, for example, turned the cover of his research paper into a **visual argument**—a graphic representation of a written argument—that served as a compact visual depiction of his thesis (see Figure 8.1). In his paper, Michael explored the significance of Michelle Bachelet becoming Chile's first elected female president; he contended that although she was the daughter of a convicted traitor who was tortured to death by Chilean dictator Augusto Pinochet, she offered the promise of "healing history's wounds" by bridging the political and cultural gap between fighting communities in Chile. Michael encapsulated this argument visually in many ways: by placing the photograph of Bachelet in the center of his collage; by using a picture of Pinochet as a somewhat oppressive top border for the page; by placing images of the Chilean communities on both sides of Bachelet; and by locating his central research question, in blue, between them. In this way, he carefully and deliberately employed the strategies of invention, arrangement, and style to produce a collage that served both as a cover for his written research paper and as an argument in its own right.

Understanding Document Design and Decorum

Let's return to Alex, our hypothetical student from Chapter 1. Her interest in a Health and Society major led her to write an analysis of anti-smoking advertisements and a research paper on the urban subculture of teenage runaways. She now needs to format her paper for her teacher, and she also is considering submitting it for publication in her college's undergraduate research journal. Moreover, her teacher wants her to convert her paper into a visual argument to appear in a class exhibit. Alex needs to learn appropriate document design for academic audiences, and she wants to explore her choices of media for the visual argument. In each case, she has four key decisions to make: Alex must identify her *argument* (her main point), her *audience* (whom she intends to reach), her *medium* (printed article, abstract, advertisement, photo essay, or multimedia montage), and the specific *form* (the layout and design aspects) for her composition. What governs her choices in each case is a matter of document design strategy, or the choices writers make in formatting their work.

To use terms from classical rhetoric, the decisions you face for document design have to do with **decorum**—a word defined as "appropriateness." In everyday language, someone who exhibits decorum in speaking knows the right kinds of words and content to use given the circumstances and audience. For example, you might swear or whoop in joy at a baseball game, but not on a job interview when talking about how your team won the game. But decorum as a rhetorical principle extends beyond choosing the right words and phrases for the occasion.

In the Roman rhetorical tradition, Cicero separated decorum into three levels of style that he assigned to different argumentative purposes. Cicero defined the *grand style* as the most formal mode of discourse, employing sophisticated language, imagery, and rhetorical devices; its goal is to move the audience. He considered *middle style* less formal than grand style but not completely colloquial; although it uses some verbal ornamentation, it develops its argument more slowly in an attempt to persuade the audience by pleasing them. The final level, *plain style,* mimics conversation in its speech and rhythms, aiming to instruct the audience in a clear and straightforward way. By adding decorum to our rhetorical toolkit, we can make decisions about how to design documents. As demonstrated in the "Levels of Decorum" table below, we can attend to argument, audience, medium, and form by understanding the *level of style* for a particular occasion. Like our classical counterparts, we must understand our rhetorical situation and use a style that best suits the circumstance.

LEVELS OF DECORUM

Level	Characteristics	Example: Written Argument for an Antismoking Campaign	Example: Visual Argument for an Antismoking Campaign
Grand or high style	Ornate language; formal structures; many rhetorical devices	Academic paper to be published in a scholarly journal	An antismoking advertisement in the *Journal of the American Medical Association*
Middle style	Some ornamentation; less formal language; argument is developed at a leisurely pace	Feature article or editorial column to be published in the campus newspaper	A photo essay or collage for a school exhibit about effects of smoking or lung cancer
Plain or low style	The least formal style; closest to spoken language; emphasis on clarity, simplicity, and directness	Weblog post on family experiences with cigarette's harmful effects	A Website devoted to the physiology and psychology of nicotine addiction

For the rest of this chapter, we'll look at various models for document design, examining the way in which we need to adjust our choice of style according to the formal and rhetorical demands of each situation.

Understanding Academic Writing Conventions

From the perspective of decorum, the conventional academic essay falls under either grand or middle style, depending on the preferences of your audience. If your instructor asks you to compose a formal written paper, you will definitely be writing in grand style.

In addition to mastering the content and using grand style for your word choices, you also need to follow the accepted format for designing your essay, as shown in the "At a Glance" box.

An entire scholarly community has reached consensus on format conventions for academic papers, so that everyone knows what information will be provided where. It's similar to the convention of every car in the United States having the steering wheel on the left; the convention fosters a set of shared expectations designed to promote consistency, order, and ease of use.

But there's a deeper *purpose* for these academic-writing conventions. Most have to do with a rhetorical relationship, the fact that people (your instructor and your peers) will be reading your paper, and these reviewers need ample space to provide written comments. By double-spacing your document and providing 1-inch margins on all sides, you leave room for reviewers to comment on lines or paragraphs. You put page numbers and your name in the upper-right corner to enable reviewers to keep track of whose paper it is and to easily refer to your writing by page number in closing comments. The rationale for stapling or clipping is to keep your pages from getting lost.

AT A GLANCE

Characteristics of Academic Writing in Grand Style

- Language should be more sophisticated than ordinary speech
- Use formal structures to organize your paper, including:

  A complete introduction containing your thesis

  A transition paragraph predicting your argument

  Clear subsections for each part of your argument

  A substantial conclusion

AT A GLANCE

Key Elements of Academic Document Design

- Double-space all pages.
- Provide 1-inch margins on all sides.
- Number pages at the top right; include your last name.
- Use subheads to separate sections.
- Staple or clip the paper together.
- Use in-text citations to acknowledge research sources.
- Use endnotes or footnotes for additional information.
- Include a list of references at the end.
- For specific examples of documentation, see Chapter 7.

AT A GLANCE

Including Visuals in a Paper

- Does your paper focus on a visual topic, such as the analysis of ads or films? If so, you probably want to include images or screen shots as evidence and as primary materials to analyze in your writing.
- Does your paper rely on images, such as political campaigns from billboards or Websites, as supporting evidence for your thesis? If so, include images of these materials in your paper.
- If you simply insert an image without comment, readers will skip over it. Make sure you describe its relevance in the text near the image.
- Include a caption with the figure number and a brief description.
- Provide the complete image source in your bibliography.

Integrating Images in Academic Writing

You might want to include visuals in your research paper for many reasons. If, for instance, your topic concerns hybrid cars, you might want to insert a technical diagram to explain the car's mechanics to readers. If you are analyzing advertisement campaigns for hybrid cars, your argument would benefit from showing readers an example through a strategically integrated image. But realize that randomly inserting a picture into your paper does not serve the *purpose* of using images rhetorically in an academic argument. Instead, you need to integrate visual texts into your document design in a rhetorically effective manner.

Carefully consider your strategy of arrangement and the *placement* of your images: Will you put them in an appendix? on your title page? on a separate page? on the same page as your written argument? Each decision is both a stylistic and rhetorical choice. An image placed in an appendix tends to be viewed as *supplementary*, not as integral to an argument; an image on a title page might act as an epigraph to set a mood for a paper, but it is less effective as a specific visual example. If you want to use your images as *argumentative evidence*, you need to show them to your readers as you analyze them; therefore, placing them beside the words of your argument will be most successful.

Once you have determined the placement that best serves your rhetorical purpose, you need to insert the image effectively. Like a quotation, an image cannot be dropped into a text without comment; it needs to be **signposted**, or connected to your argument through deliberate textual markers. You can accomplish this by making explicit **textual references** to the image—for example, "shown in the image at the right" or "(see Figure 3)"—and by taking the time to explain the rhetoric of the image for readers. Just like words quoted from a book or an interview that you might use as evidence, visual material needs *your interpretation* for readers to view it the way you do. Your analysis of its meaning will advance your argument by persuading readers to see the image as you do, and in the process, readers will pause to contemplate the evidence rather than skip over it.

Moreover, it is crucial to draft a **caption** for the image that reiterates the relationship between the point you are making in the paper and the visual evidence you include. In a paper Albert Thomas wrote about the popular sport of *capoeira*, a form of Brazilian martial arts that resembles dancing, he included a still image from the film *Ocean's 12* and wrote an effective caption.

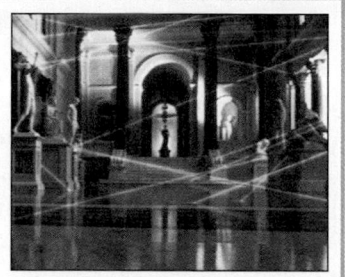

Figure 1. Vincent Cassel's character in *Ocean's 12* uses *capoeira* to evade this laser grid.

Albert includes a still shot as visual evidence in case his readers haven't seen the film.

His caption includes a figure number, the name of the person and the text (the film), as well as a link to his argument: "Cassel's character . . . uses *capoeira* to evade this laser grid."

A less effective caption would have simply named the film.

Remember, however, that what is most important is the analysis of the image you include in the body of your paper; don't hide the meaning of the image in the caption. Captions should be concise, but they should not do the work of the written argument.

Design of Academic Papers

A page from student Allison Woo's paper on Asian-American female stereotypes in contemporary cinema provides an example of both effective academic writing conventions and effective placement and captioning of visuals (see Figure 8.2). Since Allison's project analyzed female stereotypes in two films, *Tomorrow Never Dies* (1997) and *Payback* (1999), she decided to include two images as evidence. Rather than relegating these pictures to an appendix, Allison positioned them in the paper with the text wrapped around it, making the visuals an integral part of her arguments.

Allison's caption lists necessary information—figure numbers, descriptive titles, names of the actresses and films, and the years of release—as well as the sources for the images. Moreover, by paraphrasing the written argument, the caption paraphrases the central point of Allison's paragraph. Through this successful union of words and images, Allison constructs an academic argument effectively and persuasively.

Allison's last name and the page number are in the upper-right corner.

She indents the first line and double-spaces the text.

By embedding the images in the paper, Allison makes readers pause to analyze them as evidence—the way readers would study a poem or a quoted line from a book.

She arranges the visuals so they are in dialogue, reproducing the comparison that is the purpose of her paragraph. In this way, the two figures function effectively as visual evidence for her argument: the striking similarity in pose, costume, and demeanor between actresses Lucy Liu and Michelle Yeoh substantiate Allison's points about the prominence of the "Dragon Lady" stereotype in popular American films.

Woo 9

Meanwhile, the Dragon Lady images of sexuality are equally prevalent in film today. In *Tomorrow Never Dies* (1997), Asian actress Michelle Yeoh plays a seductive Chinese spy, who simultaneously flirts, manipulates, fights, and plays with her costar, James Bond (played by Pierce Brosnan). Screenwriter and novelist Jessica Hagedorn lists Yeoh's character as an archetypical Dragon Lady. Dressed in tight jumpsuit in her favorite color of corruptible black, Yeoh's character double-crosses, connives, and seduces her way through the movie, and it is always unclear whether she is good or evil.

Figs. 8 and 9. Michelle Yeoh in *Tomorrow Never Dies*, 1997 (left); Lucy Liu in *Payback*, 2002. (right). Their common characterization, dress, hairstyle, weaponry, and "dangerous" sexuality illustrate the way Hollywood repackages the same stereotyped characters in different movies.

Bond eventually conquers all, winning sexual access to the Asian woman. In *Payback*, Lucy Liu's character Pearl also double-crosses both sides.

Although she only appears in a few scenes, most of them show her seductively whispering a few lines of sexual prompting. Achieving almost orgasmic pleasure from sexually manipulating and dominating men, she thrives in her sexuality and moral corruption. Even Caucasian movie critic Sam Adams recognizes Pearl as a stereotypical "Dragon Lady," as she makes sexual advances on the hero (Mel Gibson) and the villains

---

FIGURE 8.2. In this excerpt from her paper, "Slaying the Dragon," Allison Woo showcases visual and verbal arguments working together.

Tools of Design for Academic Audiences

In addition to the research paper, you might choose to compose supplemental pages, such as a cover page containing an academic *abstract* and research *bio*—a brief biography of the author. We'll discuss these aspects now so you can add them to your toolkit of writing strategies.

Composing an Abstract

The **research abstract** is a professional academic genre designed both to present the research topic and to lay out the argument. Abstracts differ depending on the disciplinary audience and the purpose of the writing: When applying to academic conferences in the humanities, for example, academics often must write abstracts that predict the paper's argument, research contribution, and significance, while writers in the sciences or social sciences typically write abstracts *after* the paper has been completed to serve as a short summary of the article. You will encounter abstracts when you begin searching for research articles; they often precede a published paper or accompany bibliographic citations in online databases.

Abstracts can range from a few sentences to a page in length, but they are usually no longer than two paragraphs. The key in writing an abstract is to explain your argument in one brief, coherent unit. As you compose your abstract, you will need to make several rhetorical decisions.

To understand how your answers to the questions listed in the "At a Glance" box will shape your writing, let's consider three student abstracts that each correspond to a different level of decorum, use varying levels of specificity, and implement diverse means of constructing a research persona.

■ Molly Cunningham, for her abstract on her paper "Illuminating the Dark Continent: Hollywood Portrayals of Africa," writes in the *grand style* of decorum: she uses complex academic terms and a sophisticated vocabulary, including terminology from her discipline of postcolonial anthropology. In three complex sentences, she conveys her theoretical approach to analyzing film, names the films, and provides her thesis before ending with a statement of broader significance.

AT A GLANCE

Writing an Abstract

Plan to write one or two paragraphs about your paper, working through these questions:

- What level of decorum or style do you wish to use?
- How will the style predict the tone of your paper and establish your persona as a researcher?
- Do you want to use "I"?
- How much specificity should you include from the paper?
  - ▪ Do you want to list the concrete examples you analyze in your writing?
  - ▪ Do you want to give an overview of your argument?
  - ▪ Should you name sources you use in making your argument?
- How can you be both brief and engaging?

- Laura Hendrickson's abstract for her paper titled "Plastic Surgery Among Women in South Korea" uses the *middle style* of decorum by combining the use of "I" with specific terms from her research, such as "Neo-Confucian ideals." She identifies her topic—observations about plastic surgery in Korean female role models—and makes a claim about it—that surgery represents a projected Western standard of beauty.
- David Pinner relies more heavily on *plain style* for his abstract on copyright and the Creative Commons movement (see below). His abstract includes contractions, avoids excessive display, and is written in the first person.

Notice the clear, direct style that avoids excessive display or ornamentation.

The use of the contraction *can't* and first person mark this as plain style.

The somewhat informal concluding statement of purpose resists providing a fully developed argument.

> Since the rise of Napster and mp3s, the battle for intellectual property control of artistic works has exploded. Restrictive measures by the RIAA and MPAA threaten to take control of creative works away from both users and creators, to the point where people can't even control the data on their computer. However, a new alternative has emerged: Creative Commons, a copyright license designed for flexibility, readability and ease of use. In my project, I examine the way that Creative Commons is changing the nature of artistic collaboration in a world where art is increasingly created and distributed through electronic means.

Shaping Your Bio

While the abstract offers a concise statement of the argument, the **bio** is a concise paragraph that explains the persona of the writer to the intended audience. The bio functions to persuade readers of the writer's depth of knowledge or connection to the topic. Usually, the bio describes the writer's credentials, interests, and motivations for engaging in research work. Molly Cunningham's bio for her paper on Hollywood depictions of Africa follows this model, resembling the polished "About the Author" paragraph that you might find at the back of a book on the topic or in the headnote of an academic article:

🖱 **Student Writing**
See research abstracts and student bios in a variety of styles.
www.pearsonhighered.com/envision/245

> Molly Cunningham is a sophomore planning to double major in Cultural and Social Anthropology and English. After spending time in East Africa, she has become interested in exploring cultural definitions of the orphan within the community and family in light of postcolonialism as well as the AIDS pandemic. She is currently planning a summer research project in Botswana to do ethnographic research on this topic. Cunningham is also interested in the politics of humanitarian aid and the interplay between community and international donors. Involved in fundraising for a Kenyan orphanage, she hopes to deconstruct the meanings and attitudes that shape the nature and determine the amount of foreign aid going into Africa. She has utilized this research project to expand her thinking on this topic while learning to convey her findings to wider audiences.

Molly names specific qualifications and experiences she has had that make her an authority in this area.

She ends the bio with her future plans in this area of research that suggest her pursuit of a "research line" or academic path of scholarly inquiry.

If you are writing a bio to accompany a research proposal you may feel that, at this point in your project, you have no authority on the topic. Keep in mind that as you explore your sources, you will become more knowledgeable about your topic and be able to contribute to dialogue about your area of research. Thus even at an early stage of your research, you can use language, tone, and style to construct a sense of ethos. Look, for example, at David Pinner's bio:

> David Pinner is a sophomore at Stanford University majoring in physics. His father came from a traditional copyrighted background, while his mother's family had long been in the public domain. Being raised in a multilicensed household was difficult, but thanks to the work of Creative Commons and other copyleft organizations, his situation is finally being recognized by the general public. He enjoys electronic media, sailing, playing music, and Stickin' it to The Man. He is a dues-paying member of the Electronic Frontier Foundation (www.eff.org) and releases his blog under an Attribution-NonCommerical-ShareAlike v2.0 Creative Commons license.

When formatting your own bio, you might decide to include a photograph of yourself. Remember to select your picture carefully, with attention to its rhetorical impact. Many students who choose to write a traditional bio like Molly's opt for a formal photograph such as a school portrait; other students, like David, might choose a more candid or humorous picture to complement the tone of their bios. One student, when writing about online gaming communities, even created a Photoshopped portrait of herself standing next to her onscreen avatar identity to represent the two perspectives she was bringing to her research. As you can tell, the picture works in conjunction with the bio not only to construct a persona for the writer but also to suggest that writer's rhetorical stance.

Combining Visual and Verbal Design Elements

The visual rhetoric of a page matters to an audience: from the paragraph indents to the margins and double-spaced lines, to the rhetorical placement of images—all these design decisions are ways of conveying your level of decorum and your purpose to your specific audience. When we say "first impressions," we often mean how well a writer meets the conventions anticipated by the audience.

When your audience allows you to combine visual and verbal elements, you can produce *a hybrid composition* such as a feature article for a magazine, a newsletter aimed at a community audience, or an online article for diverse readers. Research has shown that in such texts, readers tend to focus on the visual part of a text first, before the words. Whether it's a news article, a traditional academic paper with a visual, or a multimedia collage, the visual grabs the attention first. Perhaps the images in this book engage your interest more immediately than the prose. Indeed, according to Adbusters, an organization devoted to cultural criticism and analysis, the visual part of any page is noticed significantly more than any text on the same page. Adbusters uses this finding to provide advice for creating ads, but we can apply the insight to written compositions combining visual and verbal elements.

Figure 8.3 provides a useful diagram for understanding the way readers process information, showing that 70 percent of readers notice visuals and 30 percent pay attention to headlines; much farther down on the attention-grabbing scale are the body, subheads, and the signature. Knowing this, consider the importance of visuals as you approach designing your own hybrid compositions. As for your headline—second in importance to viewers—follow a suggestion from Adbusters: "The most important thing to remember here is that your headline must be short, snappy

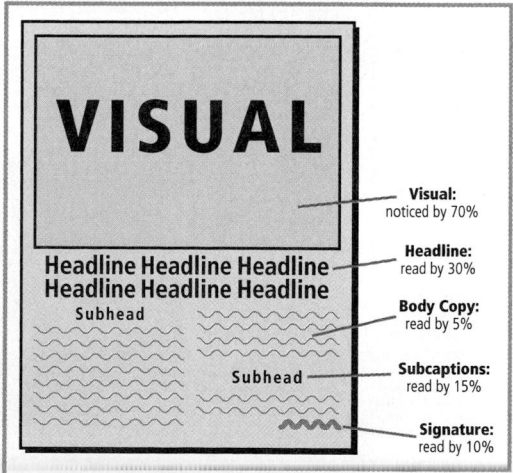

FIGURE 8.3. A graphic representation of what readers notice most on a page: visuals grab attention most.

and must touch the people that read it. Your headline must affect the readers emotionally, either by making them laugh, making them angry, making them curious or making them think." Clearly, headlines work through rhetorical appeals: you need to think carefully about which appeal—pathos, ethos, or logos—would provide the most effective way to engage your audience.

Let's look at the design decisions Ashley Mullen made in formatting her writing project on the topic of police brutality. She created a newsletter that featured a cover story in which she arranged words around a powerful image.

In designing this text, Ashley took into account not only the argument she sought to make but also, as Figure 8.4 makes clear, the choices of layout, placement of images, font size, color, and overall design. Her painstaking care with the design of this text is evident in the power of her finished product. Inside the newsletter, Ashley selected several photographs—each functioning as an individual argument—as a graphic way of representing the additional points she wanted to make on the issue: each photo anchored her writing and complemented the diverse perspectives she crafted. We can see here how visual rhetoric functions as a powerful tool of argument for her hybrid composition; it complements her careful attention to style through her word choices, imagery, expressions, and argument for each position. You might do the same in your writing through formatting

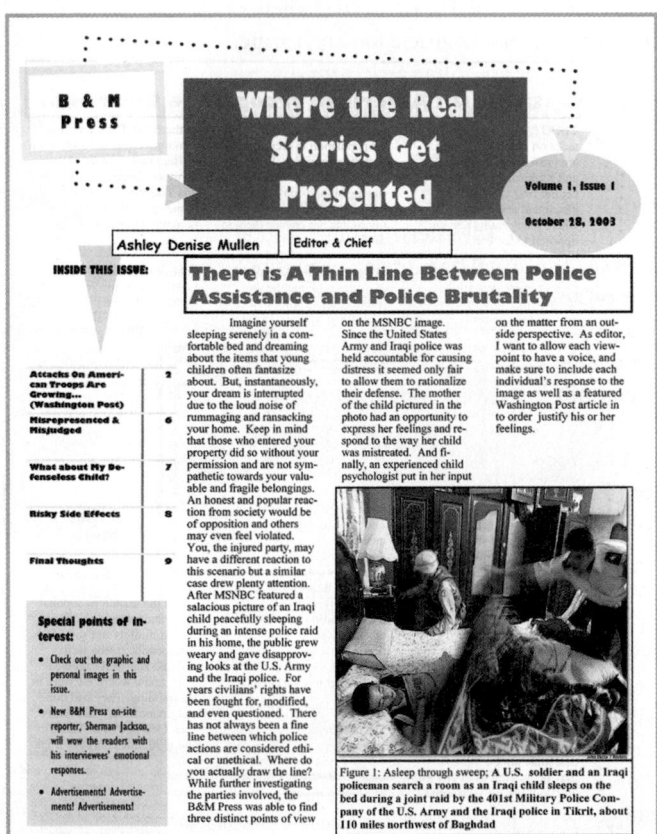

FIGURE 8.4. Design of Ashley Mullen's hybrid composition.

your work in newspaper columns or as a magazine feature article, Website, or personal letter.

Designing Arguments for Public Audiences

Although Ashley Mullen designed her hybrid composition for an academic audience (her class), she could have easily decided to share this writing project with a community group, a public service organization, or a student group dedicated to social change. Often we call such projects **service-learning** or **community service** projects because they combine learning (or writing) with service to the community. The writing you do for this type of class project is likely to be produced for a nonacademic audience, including a nonprofit agency, a city council, or members of an outreach group.

For these writing projects, you might be asked to produce a grant letter, a newsletter article, a fact sheet, a brochure, or even a Website. Such projects benefit both the nonprofit organization and the members it serves; in addition, it provides you with experience producing the kinds of texts you'll be asked to write throughout your professional career.

Let's take a look at the design strategies employed in community service writing projects, which are often multilayered, just like many of the professional projects you might encounter outside the university setting. That is, you might be asked to develop not just one flyer, pamphlet, or poster but rather a series of interconnected texts; thus, design becomes a more complicated process of connecting diverse documents according to purpose and audience.

For example, as part of a service-learning project for a non-profit Open Space organization, Jonathan Denby and Chris Fedor created a poster advising visitors to the local baylands to refrain from feeding the wildlife. As Figure 8.5 shows, the poster draws the audience in through the pairing of its provocative headline ("You are killing us with your kindness!") with a seemingly innocuous picture of a hand feeding bread to a duck. The incongruity of word and image moves the reader to the bolded question "HOW?", and then down into the bottom of the poster that outlines different elements of the argument. Although they used a vertical structure (we read from top down), Jonathan and Chris deliberately distributed the key components across the bottom of their page, using clear subheads to anchor their points and guide their readers

> Community-based writing—whether it is practical or academic—is *writing for real*. It engages tangible issues, uniting thought and action, and it calls for new approaches to writing.
>
> —Carolyn Ross and Ardel Thomas, *Writing for Real*, 17

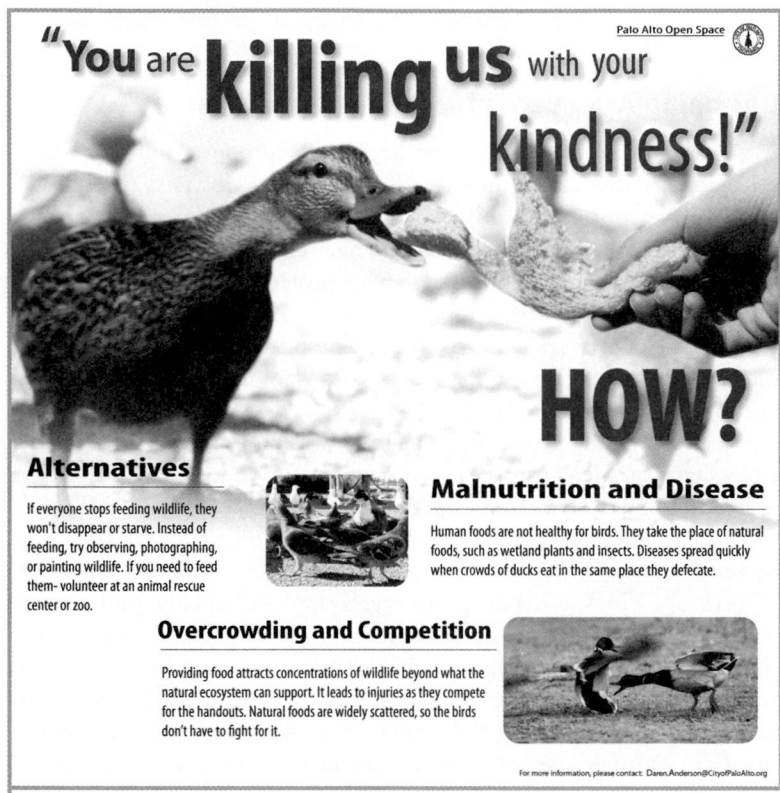

FIGURE 8.5. Jonathan Denby and Chris Fedor's poster for Palo Alto Open Space.

through their claims. Notice also the strategic use of subsidiary images to reinforce their points both as visual evidence and as pathos appeals. Referring back to Figure 8.3, we can see that much of the success of this poster lies in Jonathan and Chris's understanding of how to effectively design a visually-based argument.

Keep in mind that community service writing projects are often multi-layered, just like many of the professional projects you might encounter outside the university setting. That is, Chris and Jonathan might have been asked to create a website or newletter article to accompany their poster; or for a similar assignment, you might be asked to develop not just a single pamphlet or flyer, but rather a series of interconnected texts. In such situations, design becomes a more complicated process of connecting diverse documents according to purpose and audience.

Formatting Writing for Audiences

Let's look now at a purely verbal or written example of formatting writing for online audiences before we move to the visual arguments in the next section. In the following reading, the author employs many of the elements from the "At a Glance" box on document design that appeared earlier in the chapter. The selection includes a title, subheads, references, and a reference list at the end. But notice how the written argument has been changed or translated into a *hybrid composition* to meet the expectations of the online reading audience.

WHAT'S WRONG WITH THE BODY SHOP?
—a criticism of 'green' consumerism—

REFERENCED VERSION—all the facts and opinions in the London Greenpeace A5 'Body Shop' leaflet validated. Note: most references are given just by way of example.

The Body Shop have successfully manufactured an image of being a caring company that is helping to protect the environment [1] and indigenous peoples [2], and preventing the suffering of animals [3]—whilst selling 'natural' products [4]. But behind the green and cuddly image lies the reality—the Body Shop's operations, like those of all multinationals, have a detrimental effect on the environment [5] and the world's poor [6]. They do not help the plight of animals [7] or indigenous peoples [8] (and may be having a harmful effect), and their products are far from what they're cracked up to be [9]. They have put

The title is in plain style and all capital letters, with the subtitle in lowercase. This font decision makes it appealing to online readers.

The numbers correspond to notes and sources at the end. These notes are *hyperlinked*, so readers can jump there easily while reading on the Web.

themselves on a pedestal in order to exploit people's idealism [10]—so this leaflet has been written as a necessary response.

Companies like the Body Shop continually hype their products through advertising and marketing, often creating a demand for something where a real need for it does not exist [11]. The message pushed is that the route to happiness is through buying more and more of their products. The increasing domination of multinationals and their standardised products is leading to global cultural conformity [12]. The world's problems will only be tackled by curbing such consumerism-one of the fundamental causes of world poverty, environmental destruction and social alienation [13].

FUELLING CONSUMPTION AT THE EARTH'S EXPENSE

The Body Shop have over 1,500 stores in 47 countries [14], and aggressive expansion plans [15]. Their main purpose (like all multinationals) is making lots of money for their rich shareholders [16]. In other words, they are driven by power and greed. But the Body Shop try to conceal this reality by continually pushing the message that by shopping at their stores, rather than elsewhere, people will help solve some of the world's problems [17]. The truth is that nobody can make the world a better place by shopping.

20% of the world's population consume 80% of its resources [18]. A high standard of living for some people means gross social inequalities and poverty around the world [19]. Also, the mass production, packaging and transportation of huge quantities of goods is using up the world's resources faster than they can be renewed and filling the land, sea and air with dangerous pollution and waste [20]. Those who advocate an ever-increasing level of consumption, and equate such consumption with personal well-being, economic progress and social fulfillment, are creating a recipe for ecological disaster [21].

Rejecting consumerism does not mean also rejecting our basic needs, our stylishness, our real choices or our quality of life. It

The article uses argumentative subheads, as might an academic paper. They convey points of argument being made in the article. Moreover, they keep readers interested.

is about creating a just, stable and sustainable world, where resources are under the control of local communities and are distributed equally and sparingly—it's about improving everyone's quality of life. Consuming ever more things is an unsatisfying and harmful way to try to be happy and fulfilled. Human happiness is not related to what people buy, but to who we are and how we relate to each other. LET'S CONSUME LESS AND LIVE MORE!

Notice how the article uses all CAPS to draw the online reader's attention and even begins a new section with a two-word question.

MISLEADING THE PUBLIC

Natural products? The Body Shop give the impression that their products are made from mostly natural ingredients [22]. In fact like all big cosmetic companies they make wide use of non-renewable petrochemicals, synthetic colours, fragrances and preservatives [23], and in many of their products they use only tiny amounts of botanical-based ingredients [24]. Some experts have warned about the potential adverse effects on the skin of some of the synthetic ingredients [25]. The Body Shop also regularly irradiate certain products to try to kill microbes—radiation is generated from dangerous non-renewable uranium which cannot be disposed of safely [26].

* * *

CENSORSHIP

As the Body Shop rely so heavily on their 'green', 'caring' image, they have threatened or brought legal action against some of those who have criticised them, trying to stifle legitimate public discussion [46]. It's vital to stand up to intimidation and to defend free speech.

Some sections are very short, a common feature in online writing, where information is "chunked" into accessible packages.

WHAT YOU CAN DO

Together we can fight back against the institutions and the people in power who dominate our lives and our planet. Workers can and do organise together to fight for their rights and dignity. People are increasingly aware of the need to think seriously about the products

The article uses direct address, the pronoun *you*, to engage readers. This design strategy again indicates the use of the plain style.

For more information, contact:
London Greenpeace
5 Caledonian Road
London N1 9DX, UK.
Tel/Fax 0171 713 1269
Tel 0171 837 7557
E-mail: lgp@ envirolink.org

The "More Information" column above is an online design version of the bio; the contact information gives readers more knowledge of the persona while building ethos and authority.

Since these notes are positioned far down on the page, they can go into more detail because they assume that only very interested readers will be accessing this part of the composition.

we use, and to consume less. People in poor countries are organising themselves to stand up to multinationals and banks which dominate the world's economy. Environmental and animal rights protests and campaigns are growing everywhere. Why not join in the struggle for a better world? London Greenpeace calls on people to create an anarchist society—a society without oppression, exploitation and hierarchy, based on strong and free communities, the sharing of precious resources and respect for all life. Talk to friends and family, neighbours and workmates about these issues. Please copy and circulate this leaflet as widely as you can.

REFERENCES

1. See "Fuelling Consumption" paragraphs in the leaflet and associated references.

2. See "Exploiting Indigenous Peoples" paragraphs in the leaflet and associated references.

3. See "Helping Animals?" paragraph in the leaflet and associated references.

4. See "Natural products?" paragraph in the leaflet and associated references.

10. [Numerous publications, statements, advertisements, etc. by the Body Shop.] For example, the company's Mission Statement (1998) says that they are dedicating their business "to the pursuit of social and environmental change" and are trying to ensure that their business "is ecologically sustainable, meeting the needs of the present without compromising the future."" For us, animal protection, human rights, fair trade and environmentalism, are not just fads or marketing gimmicks but fundamental components in our holistic approach to life of which work and business are a part" [Gordon Roddick (Chairman) quoted in 1996 *Body Shop* publication "Our Agenda".] "I'd rather promote human rights, environmental concerns, indigenous rights, whatever, than promote a bubble bath" said Anita Roddick (the *Body Shop*

founder and Chief Executive) [speech at 'Academy of
Management', Vancouver (Aug 95).]

Back to 'Beyond McDonald's—Retail' Section

London Greenpeace Press Release
WWW Body Shop FAQ
London Greenpeace reply to Body Shop statement
A5 version of 'What's Wrong With The Body Shop'

From a design perspective, the final series of links for future reading signifies one of the great benefits of writing in a digital environment.

As you can tell from this article, the same strategies of design that
shape academic research papers also apply to other modes: what is most
important in each is a consideration of *purpose, audience,* and *argument.*
Think about how readers will interact with your writing—whether as a
print copy handed in for comments (in which case you double-space and
follow academic guidelines); as a newsletter (in which case you might
open with a powerful image, lay out the writing in columns or boxes, and
use an interesting page size); or as a hybrid piece to be read on the Web
(in which case you include hyperlinks, single-space, create shorter chunks,
and use font strategically).

Designing Visual Arguments

In essence, *visual arguments* are compact multimedia texts that exist as independent creations, such as op-ads, photo essays, Websites, and montages.
We can understand these texts through the levels of decorum (outlined earlier in the chapter): someone surfing the Web might find the student
Website dedicated to family members who died from smoking cigarettes
(our plain-style example); a person browsing through departmental publications might encounter a student's photo essay about the effects of smoking (our middle-style example); or a visitor looking at an exhibit case in a
library might see op-ads created by a Writing and Social Issues class and find
in this work powerful pieces of visual rhetoric (our grand-style example).

When you construct a visual argument—whether generated for your research project, as a new argument about a issue, or as an assignment for your class—you have the opportunity to experiment with many forms of media to make a powerful argument. You can apply strategies for inventing, arranging, and producing the design of an innovative visual argument that will persuade viewers to agree with your message.

Keep in mind, however, that each medium structures information in a distinct way. A photo essay is set up differently than a Webpage, just as a Webpage is set up differently than a magazine advertisement. Therefore, part of creating a powerful visual argument lies in identifying your chosen medium's conventions of structure and style and adjusting the form of your argument—its layout, design, style, and organization of information—to be the most appropriate choice for your project.

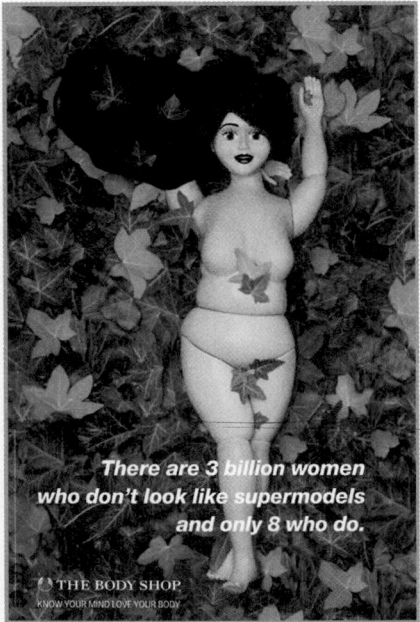

There are 3 billion women who don't look like supermodels and only 8 who do.

THE BODY SHOP
KNOW YOUR MIND LOVE YOUR BODY

FIGURE 8.6. This Body Shop opinion advertisement relies on a powerful visual argument to shock readers into questioning concepts of beauty.

Crafting an Op-Ad

The **op-ad,** or **opinion advertisement**, is one of the most concise forms of visual argument. Most op-ads promote an opinion rather than a consumer product. Many nonprofit organizations, special interest groups, and political parties find the op-ad a particularly effective way to reach their target audiences. Like all ads, the op-ad is a compact persuasive text, one that uses rhetorical appeals to convey its message. In addition, like other types of ads, an op-ad may rely partially on written text, but it tends to work through the visual components of its argument.

In Figure 8.6, for instance, the op-ad makes its point through a strategic combination of visual and verbal elements. The Body Shop has crafted an innovative image that communicates a powerful message: the realistically proportioned doll, set in a confident, casual pose against a natural background of ivy, produces a strong counterstatement against standards of body image in the mass media that promote exceptional thinness for feminine beauty. The words, "There are 3 billion women who don't look like supermodels and only 8 who do," are arranged to reinforce the visual argument of the doll's curvy body. The image creates an argument based on pathos, while the statistics draw on logos. The design of the op-ad thus works through visual and verbal strategies to make people think twice about body image. The tiny words under the Body Shop name and logo accentuate and confirm the argument of the image: "Know your mind love your body." In this way, the op-ad uses the way readers attend to information on a page: image first, headline second, caption third.

In many ways, the figure of the heavyset Body Shop doll evokes Barbie; op-ads often rely on this rhetorical strategy—**parody**, or the use of one text's formal properties to subvert the meaning of the original and make an independent argument. We can see the power of this strategy in Figure 8.7, a spoof ad from Adbusters. In this example, the parody ad invokes the popular Absolut Vodka ad series with some key differences: the iconic Absolut Vodka bottle has been transformed into a circle of chairs for an AA meeting; and the caption and taglines now reflect the AA agenda.

FIGURE 8.7. This Alcoholics Anonymous op-ad parodies the design of the familiar Absolut Vodka ads.

To understand how to compose your own op-ad, let's look at the process by which one student, Carrie Tsosie, constructed her visual argument. After writing an effective research paper that presented the dangers of allowing uranium mining on or near Navajo reservations, Carrie decided to reformulate her argument as an op-ad to reach a larger audience. Her initial considerations were her visual format and her headline—two elements of her ad that underwent some revision. She explained:

> My first idea was to have an image of a deformed lamb because then the audience would see what radiation poisoning can do. I wanted to use the phrase "Stop mining before it starts," but it seemed like that phrase was overdone, and I don't think that my audience could really relate to the deformed lamb because they do not know how important it is to some Navajo people and their lives. (Tsosie, reflection letter)

Alternative Energy for Whom?

25% of U.S. power will be produced from 75 million lbs. of uranium taken from Navajo lands.

However, most homes on the Navajo Reservation are without electricity.

Dinè Citizens Against Ruining our Environment

FIGURE 8.8. Carrie Tsosie's op-ad uses visual juxtaposition and a strong headline to make its argument against U.S. mining practices.

As shown in her completed op-ad (Figure 8.8), Carrie decided against the pathos-based image of a sick animal.

She opted instead to feature different human environments through her strategic choices of images. In addition, rather than base her ad on a strong imperative such as "Stop Mining," she chose to soften her voice and reach her audience by asking them to question their assumptions about alternative energy. In her final op-ad, she composed a heading with the provocative question "Alternative Energy for Whom?" and then followed the words with a striking visual argument. It is here, in the image, that we find the main work of argumentation. Carrie combined an image from the urban landscape with a stereotypical image from the reservation to produce a striking effect, using what we call *visual juxtaposition*, or the combination of multiple images, as a rhetorical device to call attention to the discrepancy between these ways of life and inform readers about her critique.

AT A GLANCE

Designing an Op-Ad

- Decide on your purpose (to inform, to persuade, to move to action).
- Identify your audience.
- Know your argument.
- Determine which appeals to use (pathos, logos, ethos).
- Select key images for your ad.
- Write your print text; decide how it will function in relation to your image(s).
- Draft a gripping headline to complement your image.
- Experiment with layout—arrangement, image size, organization of text—to arrive at the most effective design.

Producing a Photo Essay

Although op-ads offer a concise, forceful argument, you may wish to develop your points more thoroughly than one page allows or use visual space to show the range of material with which you've been working. If so, consider the **photo essay**—a text in which photographs, rather than print text, convey the central argument. In a word-based essay, verbal text takes priority, and images are typically used as supplements. In a photo essay, by contrast, the visual either collaborates with the verbal or becomes the *primary mode* of representation and persuasion.

As a genre, the photo essay first emerged in 1936 with the launching of *Life* magazine, whose mission statement was "to see life; to see the world." Over the 63 years it remained in print, *Life* hosted many of America's most famous photo essays, covering a range of topics from the space race to the Vietnam War, the civil rights movement, and rock and roll. But the photo essay can assume many different forms and use diverse media: it could be a series of documentary photographs and articles about southern sharecroppers published together in book form, such as Walker Evans's and James Agee's *Let Us Now Praise Famous Men* (1941); it could be a book-length photo essay that juxtaposes images with first-person narratives, such as Lauren Greenfield's *Girl Culture* (2002); it could be a striking 27-page color spread in a magazine, such as William Albert Allard's "Solace at Surprise Creek" in the June 2006 issue of *National Geographic*; or it could even be an online arrangement of captioned photos, such as *A Rescue Worker's Chronicle*, created by paramedic Matthew Levy. In each case, the photographs and written text work together, or the images themselves carry the primary weight of the argument.

Today electronic photo essays are essential conveyers of important events, a result of Internet news sources like CNN.com, Time.com, and MSNBC.com, which routinely publish photo essays as "picture stories" on their Websites. Such texts are composed of a series of images and words that work together to suggest an argument about a person, event, or story. Each electronic photo essay typically contains (1) a photo, (2) an accompanying caption, (3) an audio option, and (4) a table of contents toolbar that allows readers to navigate through the images. The result is an electronic text that maintains many structural similarities to print text: it offers readers a clear sense of progression from beginning to end while investing its argument with the rhetorical force of multiple media (word, image, sound).

The Early Years	War photography has advanced much since its inception in 1848 during the Crimean War. However, in our media obsessed society it is easy to forget the reason why war photography is necessary. What good could possibly come from the images of death and destruction?	World War I
Despite the advantages of real time media, war photography can still profoundly touch us. Whether it be a picture of the bodies after Gettysburg, or of a haggard soldier half buried in a flooded trench, or of a German soldier taunting an elderly Jew, or of a Vietnamese girl running from her burning village, or of an emaciated POW in a Serbian concentration camp, these images etch deeply into our psyche. Their permanence is unmistakable.	1848—1945	In highly propagandized wars like the Civil War, World War I, and the Vietnam War images of suffering soldiers and civilians revealed to a naïve public what war is really about. These images show that glory, honor, truth, and valor do not exist in the savage frontlines.
The Vietnam War	Most importantly, however, war photography can reveal to us the crimes committed under the pretense of war. After World War II, horrifying images of the Holocaust insured that the world would never forget the crimes committed during war. And in the Balkans, the work of a few brave photojournalists would shed light on a hidden Holocaust.	The Balkans

FIGURE 8.9. Ye Yuan's "Looking Through the Lens" photo essay with the rollover graphic activated.

Let's now consider how one student, Ye Yuan, created an online photo essay that uses a dynamic format to give readers control over the way they view the information and the way the argument is assembled.

Figure 8.9 demonstrates this reader-oriented dynamic. The arrangement of information, though it follows a roughly left-to-right, top-to-bottom organization, also opens up the possibility of browsing this photo essay in a less rigidly determined fashion. As you might expect, clicking on a bolded title takes you to a series of sequential images from that time period, offering structure to this broad discussion of war photography. At first glance, this arrangement might seem to rely on a traditional hierarchy of image and word, with the pictures serving as a secondary layer to the word-based introduction. Yet as soon as the reader begins to interact with this photo essay, moving the mouse across the page, this illusion is dispelled. Each bolded title contains a rollover graphic, so that when the reader moves the mouse over the words, a representative image appears. This dynamic relationship between word and image suggests a conjunction of meaning between the two; cooperation between the visual and the verbal is designed to "hook" and move the reader to the next level of the photo essay.

At the subsection level (shown in Figure 8.10), the reader finds a carefully chosen image that represents war photography from that historical period. Here, the photographs function as the arguments, because the heading remains constant for each subsequent image; the pictures change, but the print remains the same.

Documenting the Unspeakable

"The Final Solution" drawn out by the Nazis called for the total extermination of the Jews living in Germany and occupied Europe. This picture like most taken of the Holocaust were taken by German photographers employed by the Propaganden Kompanien. This picture shows a Jewish scholar about to be executed by a German SS officer.

1 2 3 4 5

FIGURE 8.10. One of Ye Yuan's linked pages in his photo essay. Each link contains a single photograph with an explanatory caption.

The photo essay works best if you have a topic that can be effectively argued through an accumulation of visual evidence presented as a sequence of images. Keep in mind that designing a photo essay is like drafting a research paper: you may take pages of notes, but the task of crafting the argument involves sifting through information, deciding between relevant and irrelevant materials, and arranging the most powerful evidence in your finished product. Remember to shape your photo essay around your argument through carefully made rhetorical choices about purpose, audience, and medium.

Composing a Website

If you decide to move your project online and produce a Website, your readers will then encounter your visual argument as **hypertext**, or a series of interlinked Web pages. Hypertext authors construct a framework for an argument through the **homepage** (the site's introduction), the **navigation scheme** (the site's organizational structure), and the contents of individual pages, offering both internal and external links designed to guide readers through the various levels of argument and evidence. In effect, a *hypertext argument* is produced by the collaboration between the author's direction and the readers' participation; in this way, the rhetorical situation of a Website as a visual argument becomes literally interactive, with readers playing an active role in the construction of meaning.

This dynamic determines the argumentative structure for TheTruth.com's Crazyworld page (see Figure 8.11), accessible through TheTruth.com's archives of past pages. The site's target audience might be young people inclined toward smoking. But by appearing on the Internet the site conveys its argument to the broader public, using the carnival motif to suggest what a "crazy world" we live in, where tobacco companies continue to sell—and consumers continue to buy and smoke—cigarettes that contain chemicals like arsenic, benzene, and cyanide. The site's primary *level of decorum* is plain style: through simple language, the carnival metaphor, and engaging visuals, the

> ### AT A GLANCE
>
> ### Designing a Photo Essay
>
> 1. Decide on the argument or thesis for your project.
>
> 2. Categorize your images, arranging them within the theme groups.
>
> 3. Organize them into different configurations: by chronology, theme, and subject.
>
> 4. Draft written text in the form of headings, captions, and paragraphs.
>
> 5. Determine your layout by experimenting with ways of formatting the words and images.

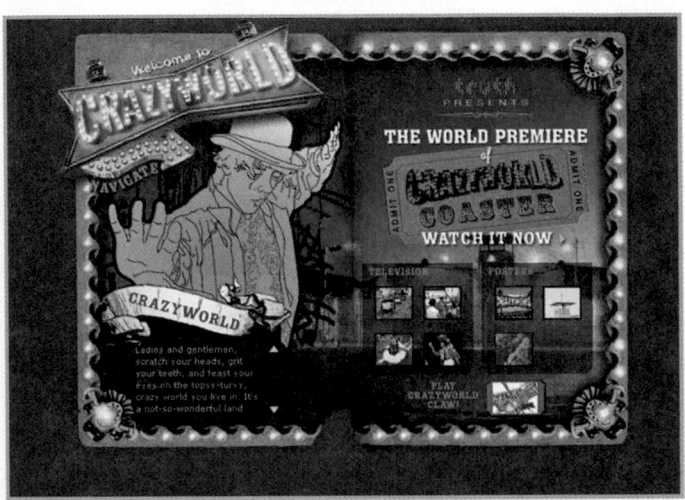

FIGURE 8.11. The Crazyworld homepage demonstrates multiple strategies of effective Website composition.

Website seeks to persuade viewers of the dangers of tobacco usage to both smokers and nonsmokers. This draws readers into the site, where they encounter the more explicitly argumentative indictments of Big Tobacco in the site's subsidiary content pages that reveal statistics, interviews, and indictments of cigarette companies.

The power of this visual argument lies in the flexibility of its design, which allows the audience to explore its many features. Although it resists relying on the sort of linear development typically found in paper texts, it still offers readers a variety of structured and clearly delineated pathways into its central arguments against Big Tobacco. On the surface, the site presents striking graphics and a visual *menu bar*, consisting of links to different aspects of the site. However, its primary *navigation toolbar*, the list of links that provide direct access to the interior of the Website, is actually hidden beneath the clown image. The toolbar only appears when the viewer rolls the mouse over the word *Navigate*, placed beneath the curved arrow that points at the clown. This Website, then, has been composed as a highly interactive piece of digital writing. There is no "right way" to navigate this site, and the writers are able to reach a wide audience and convey a powerful argument about the dangers of smoking.

The process of authoring your own Website may seem daunting at first. However, in many ways drafting text for the Web resembles

AT A GLANCE

Essential Elements for Composing a Website

- Decide on your target audience.
- Select your content and main argument.
- Determine your purpose (to teach, persuade, or move to action).
- Compose your level of decorum.
- Design your site organization, navigation, and layout.

drafting the complex argument of a long research paper: in both cases, you need to identify the necessary elements of your composition, and then you need to follow a process of careful planning and organization.

In designing your Website, you will need to account for three levels of information: a *homepage* at the **primary level** (which will serve as the introduction to your site); a *series of topic pages* at the **secondary level** (which will contain both content and, sometimes, links to further, more specialized subtopic pages); and the *subtopic pages* at the **deep level** (which will contain content and perhaps even more links). Although most sites contain only one home page, some use a **splash page**—often featuring a single provocative quote, a flash animation, or gripping image—that functions as a hook or **gateway** to a more substantive introductory homepage. There is no limit on the number of topic and content pages you can include; you should determine the scope of your project and number of pages based on your assessment of how to make your argument most effectively.

In terms of design, composing a Website resembles the process of outlining a research paper. Yet there are important differences between digital writing and writing for print readers. For a Website:

- *Chunk* your information—or divide it into manageable parts.
- *Strive for consistency* of theme, font, and/or color throughout your site; avoid visual clutter and ineffectual use of images.
- Think about the *relationship between the words and images.*
- *Consider creating* a *template,* or visual precedent, that establishes the key elements for the rest of the site, much as an introduction in a written paper often sets the style and conventions for the rest of the argument to follow.

Let's look at a sample web project on the visual rhetoric surrounding the 1963 March on Washington. The design was intended to encourage readers to engage with the primary texts within the framework of a researched argument.

The homepage for this site (Fig. 8.12) models the composition of the entire project. The most striking element is the photograph, used here to underscore the author's argument. (The photograph is taken from Wikimedia Commons, a repository for public domain photographs, showing the author's careful attention to copyright regulation; since a webpage is a type

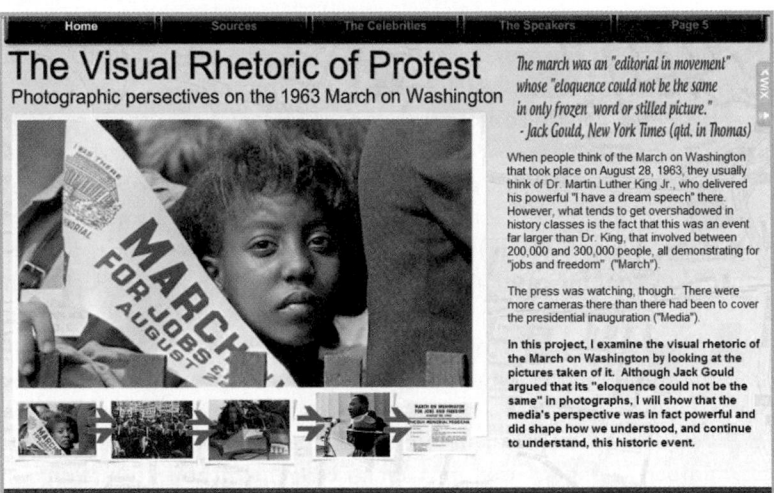

FIGURE 8.12. This project on the 1963 March on Washington uses a carefully designed website as its medium.

of publication, you should not use copyrighted images in public websites.) Notice the way the homepage

- pairs image with text;
- uses a quote (in blue) as an epigraph for the page;
- explicitly states its argument in bold;
- meticulously cites its sources (with parenthetical, hyperlinked references to the Sources page).

On the subpages, the author supports her researched argument through reference to secondary sources and analysis of the primary texts. For instance, on the "Celebrities" page, she analyzes photographs of Joan Baez, Bob Dylan, Harry Belafonte, Sammy Davis Junior, and Charlton Heston. The homepage also demonstrates the site's attention to organization. The tabbed menu at the top is duplicated by the visual menu below, where each subpage is assigned a representative image. Color is used strategically in both instances (white font; yellow border) to help the viewers locate themselves in relation to the larger structure of the argument.

As you compose your own Website as a visual argument, be sure to consider **usability**—how user friendly your hypertext is and how accessible to users with disabilities. Even a site with professional design and a state-of-the-art graphic interface is ultimately ineffective if the audience cannot navigate it. You can test your Website for usability through the resources available on the *Envision* Website. Learning to write with attention to diverse readers will make you a more rhetorically savvy and effective communicator.

Making a Multimedia Montage

In this last section, we'll introduce you to writing projects such as visual collages, multimedia mixes using audio and video, hand-painted murals, self-produced films, startup magazines, and more. We'll call these texts **multimedia montages** because they involve the combination of numerous media (images, sound, writing, digital elements, and more) and because they often consist of nonlinear collections of evidence; the argument occurs in the project as a whole. Although the term *montage* is taken from film studies and refers to a sequence of still images, we'll extend it to refer to any combination of diverse media elements. The key to designing multimedia montages lies in understanding not only your audience, argument, medium, and form but also the purpose for the project.

> ## AT A GLANCE
>
> ### Designing a Website
> - Draft a header; consider including an image in it.
> - Map a logical organization for your site to help readers find information easily and understand your purpose and argument.
> - Include a navigation tool either below the title or at the left margin.
> - Develop clear content using words and images.
> - Be consistent in using color, imagery, and font; avoid jarring color combinations or visual clutter.
> - Be strategic in your use and placement of images
> - Link to subpages and external sites.
> - Provide a feedback link for comments.
> - Include a "last updated" feature note.
> - Test your site for usability—both in terms of its general user friendliness and its accessibility to users with disabilities.
> - Use user-friendly online tools (such as Wix, Wordpress, or PBWorks) to help design your site.

Consider Yang Shi's decision to construct a visual collage based on his purpose. He began his project with the goal of creating a print photo essay on the subject of Mao Zedong's political impact on China, but he soon found that the photo essay's linear structure seemed to suggest a single definitive interpretation of Mao's influence. Since Yang was interested in exploring the complexity and contradictions inherent to the issue, he found the graphic possibilities of a visual collage preferable since this format allowed for a dialogue between simultaneous, competing images. By

Student Writing

Read Yang Shi's reflection letter concerning his design decisions.

www.pearsonhighered.com/envision/266

juxtaposing and intertwining numerous images from 1960s China, Yang Shi created a powerful, complex argument about the causalities of Mao's Cultural Revolution. Yang recognized that in a collage he could not only exploit the power of numerous images but also crop and arrange those images for rhetorical purpose. Accordingly, he created an overtly chaotic layout, one that he felt reflected the lack of focus of the Chinese Cultural Revolution (see Figure 8.13).

Despite the initial impression of randomness, however, there is an underlying order to Yang's collage: from the portrait of Mao heading the page, to the patriotic children surrounding him, to the statistics at the bottom, and finally to the outline of China as a faint red background at the poster's center in front of the protestors, all the visual elements structure the text's visual argument. In one sense, China encompasses all these representations—struggles and tragedies, ideals and victories. Yet the collage's inclusion of Mao's choice of political imagery—the propaganda drawings of

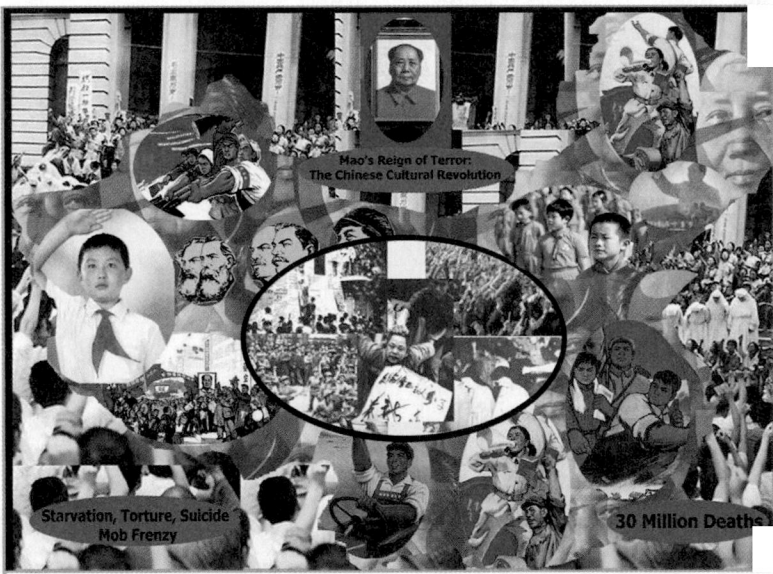

FIGURE 8.13. Yang Shi's photo collage about Mao Zedong and the Chinese Cultural Revolution.

happy workers—suggests that Mao undermined his own anti-West stance by "marketing" himself along the same lines as traditional Western advertising. In this way, Yang's strategic use of the collage form produces a powerful statement through a careful arrangement of images and color.

Think carefully about your purpose, your argument, your audience's familiarity with the topic, the organization of your materials, and the media available to you as you design your own multimedia montage.

- KiYonna Carr paired a sequence of historical and contemporary photographs with her own voice-over narration to create a self-timed slideshow about the enduring legacy of slavery on African-American women's self-image.
- Derrick Jue used a short-film format for an argument about Iraq war protests, arranging a slide show of news photographs showing the war, protest demonstrations, and politicians speaking about the war and adding a soundtrack—the song "Wake Me Up" by Evanescence. The rapid succession of images paired with stirring music provokes an emotional reaction, without need for verbal commentary.
- Jessica Vun used a tactile collage—a handsewn fabric "manners" book—to give readers a "feel" for gender roles in the 1800s.
- Allison Smith stained her own drawings with tea to suggest age for a project on Margaret Sanger's battle for legalized birth control.
- Madeline Wright used Google Maps to create a final visual argument for her project on Intelligent Design versus evolution in Texas education, using the geographic interface to support her claim that intelligent design prospers in small towns and rural areas (see Figure 8.14).
- Lauren Dunagan used a 14-foot hand-painted graffiti mural to make an argument about the power of graffiti as a medium for social protest and self-expression.

In all of these cases, the student carefully considered how to use a non-traditional medium (a model, a stained historical document, a mural) to create a rhetorically effective argument. The range of persuasive possibilities presented here suggests the ways writing has changed over time—and how it continues to evolve with the advent of new writing and composing technologies. From Weblogs to interactive multimedia exhibits and collaborative hypertext projects, the way we understand language, argument, and persuasion continues to evolve.

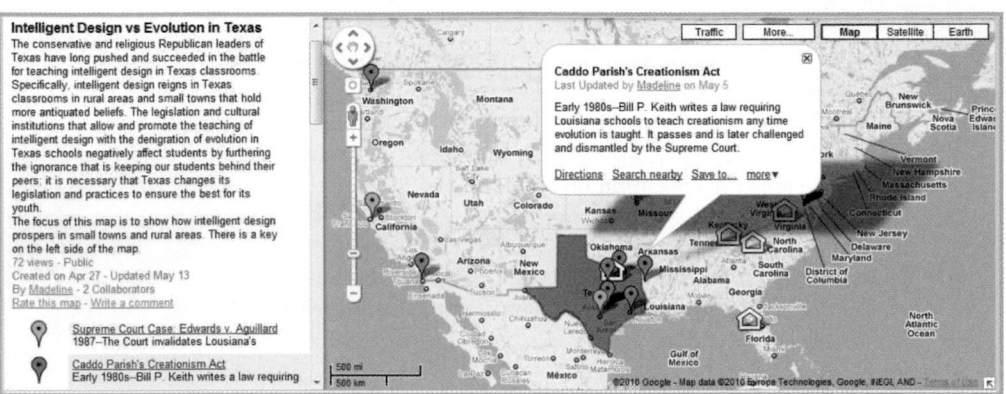

FIGURE 8.14. Madeline Wright used Google Maps to compose her visual argument for her research project.

With the ever-changing face of modern media, you have an increasing number of choices for designing arguments with purpose, power, and creativity.

The Writer's Process

In this chapter, you've learned how writing offers an opportunity to experiment with designing and producing your texts in ways that meet your purpose and match the expectations of your audience. Often this means knowing, understanding, and adhering to conventions set forth by a community of scholars, readers, or writers. This is the case for the document design of your research paper, cover page, abstract, and bio. At other times, this means exploring innovative approaches to design in multimedia contexts. It is also the case for the document design of hybrid compositions and visual arguments. All modes of design depend on your rhetorical expertise in choosing a level of decorum, in knowing what strategies best work for your situation, in deciding on your medium and your format, and then in having these choices support your purpose in designing your work. By examining academic essays, op-ads, photo essays, Websites, and multimedia montages, you have seen that the rhetorical principles of audience, argument, form, and purpose carry across diverse media. It's time now for you to make your contribution. Write out your brainstorming ideas, and begin to design your own argument.

PREWRITING CHECKLIST
Focus on Analyzing Design in Arguments

❏ **Argument:** What is the topic and the argument? What evidence is used to support the argument? What is the rhetorical stance and point of view on the topic? What role does verbal, visual, or multimedia play in persuasion in this text? Are words and images complementary or does the argument work primarily through one means?

❏ **Audience:** Whom is the argument intended to reach? What response seems to be anticipated from the audience? sympathetic? hostile? concerned?

❏ **Medium:** Is the medium used appropriate for the argument and its target audience? What type of interaction does the medium create with its audience?

❏ **Form:** What are the specific characteristics of the medium? Consider layout, images, style, font. How are these elements organized?

❏ **Purpose:** What is the purpose in presenting the argument to the audience in this design? To move them to action? inform them? teach them? What type of decorum or style (grand, middle, or plain) is used to realize this purpose?

PREWRITING WITH THE *ENVISION* WEBSITE

Perform a rhetorical analysis of several Websites: first, using the link from the *Envision* Website, look at "Error 404," a parody Webpage created during the U.S. war with Iraq; then compare http://www.whitehouse.org, a parody site, with the official White House site. How does the parody site use rhetoric, organization, style, and decorum to produce an argument? Working collaboratively, draft a sample homepage that makes the same argument as the parody page but without using parody. What rhetorical choices did you make in designing your page?

www.pearsonhighered.com/envision/269

WRITING PROJECTS

1. **Design Elements to Accompany Your Final Revision:** Write an abstract and bio for your final research paper. Check that you have adhered to proper academic document design. Now compose a one-page op-ad featuring the argument from your research project. The op-ad should combine both images and written elements. Keep in mind those elements important to successful advertising, including consideration

of audience and purpose; use of space, color, and image; strategies of development; and an appropriate hook. Indicate in a written note the intended audience (who would read it) and context (what magazine or newspaper they would read it in) for your ad. Post all your documents online as a showcase of your work as a writer and researcher.

2. **Visual Argument:** Create a photo essay based on the argument from your research paper or as part of an independent project. The images you use in your photo essay may be from your paper, or you can use a completely new set, particularly if you did not use images in your paper. Your argument may mirror that in your research paper, or you may focus on a smaller portion of your overall argument. The style, arrangement, medium, and rhetorical strategies of your photo essay should match your audience and your purpose. Include written text in your photo essay strategically. Once you have finished, write a one-page reflection on the strategies you used in this project.

3. **Multimedia Argument:** Transform your written essay into an electronic format that uses audio strategically as part of the text's persuasive power. You can match your images to a recorded argument. Alternatively, combine visual images with a soundtrack. Pick your music carefully, and time each image to match a particular mood or moment in the music or select music to match the sequence of your images. If you are transforming a paper essay into an electronic audio version, feel free to modify your organization, arrangement, text selection, and even treatment of images to accommodate this shift in medium. Once you have finished, write a one-page reflection on how the shift in medium affected your argument.

 Visit www.pearsonhighered.com/envision for expanded assignment guidelines and student projects. Visit www.mycomplab.com for additional general writing and research resources.

CHAPTER 9

Delivering Presentations

Chapter Preview Questions

- How can I transform a written argument into a presentation?
- What are the branches of oratory, and how do they shape my presentation options?
- When should I use a speech, a poster session, PowerPoint, or a live performance? What rhetorical choices shape my decision?
- How can the canons of memory and delivery help my presentation?

You've finished your written argument. You've submitted it to your instructor according to proper academic conventions and maybe you have even translated it into a hybrid composition or visual argument. But sometimes you are asked to do more: to present your argument to an audience in the form of a "live" presentation. Both academic and public audiences call for oral or multimedia presentations on occasion, and you need to develop skills and strategies for designing and delivering presentations to take advantage of these opportunities. In this chapter, we'll learn from famous writers and speakers, such as Barack Obama, whose keynote speech at the 2004 Democratic National Convention catapulted him to the forefront for the 2008 presidential race. Obama's rhetorical strategies in this speech laid out the basic themes of his campaign—"[T]here's not a liberal America and a conservative America; there's the United States of America. There's not a black America and white America and Latino America and

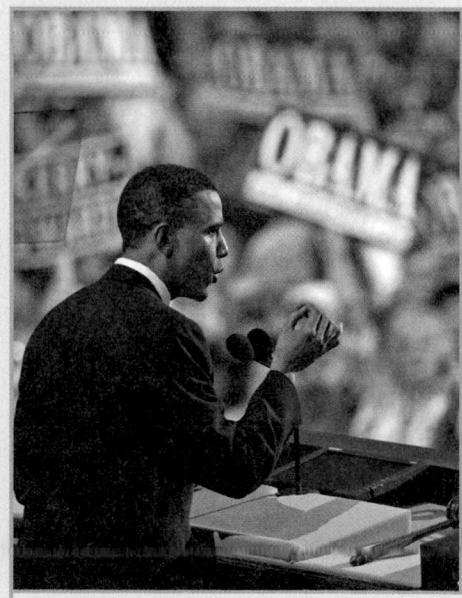

FIGURE 9.1. Barack Obama delivers his argument at the 2004 Democratic National Convention.

Asian America; there's the United States of America"; "Do we participate in a politics of cynicism or a politics of hope?"—and offered a powerful argument for hope and unity. But his presentation did not derive solely from his written script. As the image in Figure 9.1 suggests, it was the convergence of well-crafted language, passionate delivery, and deliberate gesture that combined to produce a memorable moment in American history.

You might look to Obama and other orators as models for effective presentation strategies as you prepare to shape your writing for oral delivery. As you approach drafting your presentation, take time to explore the many possibilities available to you for this act of effective communication. You will need to base your decisions for picking certain presentation strategies on a solid rhetorical foundation, and to do so, you need to understand the *branches of oratory* as well as how to apply them to particular occasions. In this chapter, you'll learn effective strategies for selecting the appropriate branch of oratory for your rhetorical situation, for translating your written argument into a multimedia presentation, and for scripting and designing a memorable and effective delivery of your argument.

Understanding the Branches of Oratory

As you draft, design, and deliver a compelling presentation, classical rhetoric may provide ways of understanding the needs of your specific writing situation—your own purpose, audience, and persona. Today we turn to rhetoric to shape any verbal or visual argument, but rhetoric originally evolved as a technique in classical Greece for teaching people how to speak both eloquently and persuasively in public. Classical rhetoricians such as Aristotle divided oratory into three **branches** based on time, purpose, and content.

- **Judicial** or **forensic discourse** involves defending or accusing and deals with the past. Think of this as oratory about right and wrong. *You might employ judicial oratory to argue about a past action in debate team, or moot court or law school, using verbal arguments as well as charts, graphs, photos, and other visual evidence arranged and designed to persuade your audience.*

- **Deliberative** or **legislative discourse** concerns politics or policy and typically argues for or against specific actions that might take place in the future. Think of this as oratory about what is benefical or harmful. *You might employ deliberative oratory to exhort or dissuade an audience in promoting the launch of your own business, the development of a new software, or a plan for a fund-raising trip. Your presentation might include memos, a financial plan, and specifications concerning the worthiness of the enterprise; you might employ PowerPoint slides, charts, images, prototypes, models, and animation to support your argument.*

- **Epideictic** or **ceremonial discourse** generally deals with the present. Think of this as oratory about praising or blaming. *You might employ ceremonial oratory in a senior thesis, a company report, an advertising campaign, or even a political party statement designed to praise (or blame) a candidate.*

BRANCHES OF ORATORY: CONTEMPORARY EXAMPLES

Judicial or forensic discourse— involves accusing or defending	**Deliberative or legislative discourse—** designed to argue for or against specific actions	**Epideictic discourse—** involves praise or blame
Johnny Cochran's 1995 defense of O. J. Simpson represents a notable instance of forensic discourse when Cochran used powerful visual and verbal rhetoric to clear O. J. Simpson of murder charges.	In his documentary film *An Inconvenient Truth* (2006), Al Gore employs deliberative discourse to advise the audience of the necessary steps for reducing the future impact of global warming.	Eulogies, such as the speeches delivered at Senator Edward Kennedy's funeral in 2009, are a typical form of epideictic discourse in that they center on praising and celebrating people's lives.
Notice the way Cochran makes his point visually by slipping on gloves that had been used in the crime to underscore his point "If it doesn't fit, you must acquit."	*An Inconvenient Truth* features Gore giving a series of lectures, many of which are rendered more powerful by carefully chosen background images and striking photographs.	Although colleagues told funny stories about Ted Kennedy, their remarks were celebratory and their demeanors somber and respectful.

As you can tell, although the branches of oratory may be unfamiliar in theory, we see them in practice all the time, from your instructor's PowerPoint lecture defending the inclusion of "intelligent design" in high school science curricula (forensic) to a club member's report about the success of their community outreach program (epideictic). Since strategies differ from one rhetorical branch to another, you'll find it helpful to assess which branch best addresses the demands of your particular situation.

Audience, Purpose, and Persona

The branches of oratory are only one of the resources from classical rhetoric that writers draw on in crafting successful presentations. Concepts such as attention to *audience, purpose,* and *persona,* which we've discussed in relation to written texts, are key elements for oral rhetoric as well. For instance, consider how attention to purpose, audience, and persona determines the presentations shown in Figures 9.2 and 9.3. Notice rock star Bono's trademark sunglasses as he presents his views to world leaders at the Davos economic forum in Figure 9.2. Compare this to Steve Jobs and his very rehearsed presentation at Mac World 2008, where he stands in his predictable black turtleneck and jeans, gesturing emphatically to underscore his point. In each case, the speaker has chosen presentation strategies—including words, expression, dress, props, and persona—to fit the audience and purpose of his rhetorical situation. Keep this in mind when you need to design a presentation, select words and visual material, and practice a form of delivery that is specific to the rhetorical situation. In each case, you can carefully construct your presentation to be a powerful visual and verbal argument.

FIGURE 9.2. U2 leader Bono addresses world financial leaders at the annual symposium in Davos, Switzerland.

Consider the many kinds of presentations you encounter as part of your academic experience. Do you attend lectures on specific topics, with a single speaker standing at a podium and delivering a verbal argument? Have you been an audience member for a formal academic panel, where multiple speakers take turns presenting arguments, sometimes providing handouts to the audience or using a projection screen to convey their ideas? Or is your most frequent presentation experience the PowerPoint lecture, in which the speaker provides a point-by-point map of the material, includes images related to the subject matter, and sometimes posts a copy of the slides on a Website for future reading? Although these presentations might differ in format, they are similar in that all are designed to meet the needs of their particular audience and rhetorical situation.

FIGURE 9.3. Steve Jobs, Apple CEO, presents a new product at MacWorld 2008.

In your own work, you may find yourself presenting to your class, to a larger academic audience as part of a conference panel, to college administrators or a university forum, or even to a public audience. In each case, you'll have many choices to make. You can start determining the possibilities for your own presentation by using focusing questions such as those found in the "At a Glance" box on the next page, designed to help you identify your audience, purpose, and persona.

As the final point in the "At a Glance" box suggests, most presentations today include strategically chosen visual texts—what we used to call "visual aids"—that in fact perform a crucial rhetorical function: they collaborate with words to convey the speaker's argument. A photo of extensive crop damage can provide *evidence* in an environmental science lecture, and a chart can communicate economic trends to an audience quickly and effectively. Sometimes, moreover, visuals provide a stronger message than or even contradict the verbal component of the speech. A presenter might use a visual text ironically—for instance, showing a slide listing statistics that refute an opponent's argument or providing an emotional appeal while conveying information in a flat tone of voice. In these ways, visual texts communicate powerful arguments that you can use as part of your overall presentation.

AT A GLANCE

Identifying Your Audience, Purpose, and Persona

1. **What format will my presentation take** (purely oral speech, multimedia slideshow, interactive drama, etc.)?

2. **Who is my audience?** What do they know or not know about this topic already? How receptive will they be to my material?

3. **What is my purpose?** What do I hope to accomplish? What is my ultimate goal with this presentation?

4. **What branch of oratory does my presentation represent?** Is it designed to defend or accuse? To argue a position or policy? To celebrate or condemn?

5. **What persona do I want to convey** to my audience (knowledgeable, friendly, impassioned, concerned, expert, peer, etc.)? How do I visualize myself as a presenter?

6. **What kind of tone do I want to use** in my presentation (fun, serious, informative, sarcastic, concerned, alarmed, practical, etc.)?

7. **What supporting materials do I plan to use** in my presentation (quotes from research, photographs in a PowerPoint slide or on a handout, film or commercial clips, graphs, charts, posters, etc.)?

Transforming Research into a Presentation

Whether you are a student preparing for an in-class presentation or a polished public-speaker, creating a compelling oral argument involves a process of planning, scripting, revision, and rehearsal. Figure 9.4 provides us a glimpse into this composition process; shown here are President Obama's handwritten edits of his September 9, 2009, speech to Congress about health care reform. Through consultation with his speech writers, the President carefully crafted word choice, sentence structure, example, and organization to produce a compelling polemic on the need for nationalized health care.

Like the President in this example—who drew on a vast corpus of research, statistics, and examples in producing this speech—when composing your presentation, you will need to consider how to best transform your research into a form meant for oral delivery. This process can be quite challenging; you need to take into account scope, content, and style. If you have 15 written pages of argument, this would probably take 40 minutes or more to read out loud. But of course, you would certainly not choose to simply read your written paper; writing meant to be read silently differs from writing meant to be read out loud. Only in certain academic circles is there a preference for complex, written prose as a formal presentation style. In most cases, audiences desire clear, conversational speech that is easy to follow. To achieve this goal, you need to think about transforming your research argument from one kind of writing to another—from writing for readers to writing for listeners. You'll also need to cut down the sheer amount of material you can convey and think about ways to present it in an interesting, memorable way. You can accomplish all these goals through a process of *selection, organization,* and *translation.*

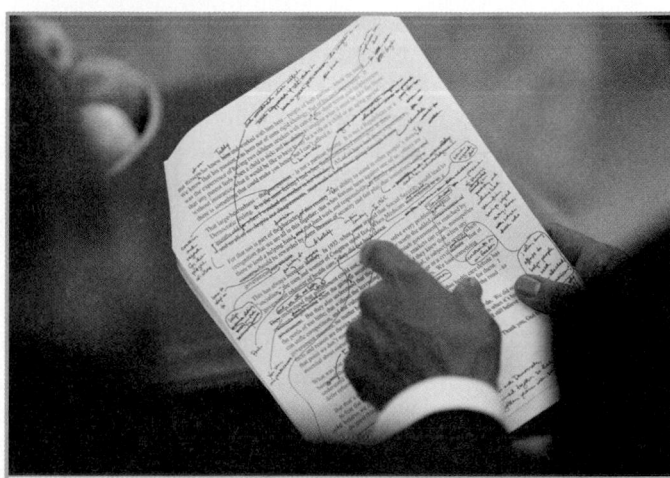

FIGURE 9.4. President Barack Obama's speeches are the product of a careful process of drafting and revision, as is apparent in this picture of the President's annotated speech for a September 9, 2009, address to a joint session of Congress.

Selection

Always plan for a shorter presentation time than what you actually have allotted. Most of us speak for longer than we realize; so if you are planning material for a 10-minute presentation, aim for 8; a 15-minute presentation, aim for 12; a 5-minute presentation, aim for 3. One way to keep your time frame manageable is to select a subset of material to present. That is, if your written argument comprises three main areas, plan to cover only one in your presentation. Also, if you plan on speaking extemporaneously (or improvising), be sure that you build this into your schedule for your presentation. Finally, remember to be as selective with your visual evidence as you are with your overall information; if your research relies heavily on images, charts, or graphs, be sure to carefully consider which to include in your presentation. You might opt to use only the most powerful images, or you might decide to center your presentation on a single case study or example and therefore feature only those materials relevant to that narrower focus.

You should find the focusing questions in the "At a Glance" box helpful for moving through the process of selection for your project. Question 1 will help you identify the crux of your presentation. This may be your thesis, but it may also *not* be your thesis. That is, in the course of writing your paper, you may have found that what really matters most is the need to raise awareness about an issue, the need to publicize potential solutions to a problem, or the need to advocate for a particular research agenda. Question 2 will help you narrow your project to a few points designed to convey your project's significance to the audience. Question 3 will help you confirm your purpose and begin to translate your main point into a medium that will persuade your audience: do you want to raise awareness, rally support, propose a change, offer new insights, or suggest avenues of future research? You need to select your materials with these goals in mind.

AT A GLANCE

Questions for Focusing Your Argument

1. What matters most about this project?
2. What two or three points can I make to convey my answer to the above question?
3. What do I want my audience to walk away thinking about when I am done?

Organization

As you move through the process of transforming your research into an oral presentation, you have an opportunity to **reorder** your written argument to meet the needs and expectations of a listening audience. You might, for instance, begin with your conclusion and then convey the narrative of your research. Or you might want to show your visual evidence first, ask questions, and then provide your thesis at the end. In other words, you don't need to create your presentation as a miniature version of your written talk. Be innovative in your choice of organization; think about what structure would be the most effective for your audience.

To help with this process, create a flowchart, outline, or block graphic of each element of your presentation. Don't forget your opening "hook" and closing message as you work on organizing your presentation. Try matching each component to a minute-by-minute schedule to make sure that you are within time limits. And finally, consider creating a **visual outline** by drawing or pasting in images next to your verbal cues to show how and when you will use visual rhetoric as a part of your presentation. Looking at a section of Tommy Tsai's presenta-tion outline (see Figure 9.5) for his oral presentation on World War II pro-paganda, we can see that he carefully paired the words he intended to speak (on the right) with the slides he would show to his audience (on the left). In this way, he could clearly map the relationship between the visual and verbal elements of his presentation, creating a strong underlying organization for his argument. The key here is to see the presentation as its own genre of writing and draft a text that meets the needs of both your audience and your purpose.

FIGURE 9.5. Tommy Tsai's presentation outline strategically juxtaposed the oral script with the visual evidence he would present in his slides. Note that he includes a blank slide.

Student Writing

See design and content plans for several student presentations.
www.pearsonhighered/envision/279

AT A GLANCE

Key Questions to Shape Your Organization

- **How can I "hook" my audience?** What would be an effective way to open my presentation? Should I appeal to emotion? to reason? Should I establish my authority as a researcher? What parts of my research would help me do so?

- **What strategies can I use to organize my presentation?** Narration? Example? Cause and effect? Problem-solution? Process? Definition? Which strategies would be most useful for conveying my argument clearly and effectively to my audience?

- **What main points do I want to use as the centerpiece** of my presentation? Do I want to focus on a single case study or on multiple examples?

- **At what point do I want to present my thesis?** Do I want to start with a question or line of inquiry and then end with my argument in my conclusion? Or do I want to start strong with my thesis within the first moments of my talk and then prove it with evidence?

- **How do I want to close my presentation?** Do I want to conclude by summing up my points or by pointing to the future or further implications? Do I want to end with a call to action or with a provocative question? What strategy would create the greatest impact on my audience?

Translation

The final step of the transformation is to translate your writing from text meant to be read to text meant to be heard. This is more important than it may first appear. Think about presentations you've attended where the speaker read from a script without looking up or changing the inflection of his or her voice. If you sat down and read that same speech, you might have found it interesting; however, listening to the material presented in that way, you probably found yourself bored, confused, or both. The point here is that there are important differences between these types of writing, and you need to carefully *translate* your research into a form accessible to your listening audience.

The extent to which you modify your writing as you draft your script depends on your audience and purpose; for instance, if you were trying to persuade your college administrators to endorse a new recycling policy (an example of deliberative discourse), you would adopt a different style and mode of speaking than if you were accusing that same administration of inattention to the recycling issue at a student council meeting (an example of forensic discourse). However, in general, there are some steps you can take to facilitate the translation process.

- **Examine the length of your sentences,** the complexity of your prose, and the sophistication of your diction. Most listeners find shorter sentences, specific language, and clear transitions and prose structures important for understanding oral discourse.
- **Avoid jargon** and define any terms with which your audience might not be familiar.
- Consider adding explicit **signposting**— verbal "signs" that indicate the steps of an argument or the structure of your presentation. More often than not, listeners need more explicit signposting than do readers of papers.

Listeners also respond to humor, direct address, concrete examples, and even questions. These strategies are designed to directly engage your audience's attention. As you write your script, annotate your written copy with places where you pause, emphasize words, look up, or laugh. Also include reminders of when to point to visuals or advance your slides.

Transformation in Action

Let's take a close look at how one student transformed her written research paper into a multimedia research presentation. As we saw in Chapter 4, Susan Zhang wrote a research proposal on the photo manipulation of media images. After finishing the written proposal, she was asked to present her proposal orally to her class. What follows is the written script for her presentation; as you read through it, you may want to reference her original proposal (see pages 126–131) in order to appreciate the way she transformed her written argument into an oral presentation.

Hi everyone, my name is Susan, and before I begin, a little bit about me.

[cue slide: "About Me"]

Last summer I vacationed with my family in Australia, and that was the beginning of my interest in photography, as you can see. **[cue animation: Mom & me]** And I had a really great time taking pictures of wildlife there, including this one of a duck. **[cue animation: duck]** Well actually that was all a lie. I've never been south of the equator, and that picture of my mom and me is grafted onto the background of Sidney harbor, and that duck is a digital rendering of the animal.

This prompts some unusual questions. If I can pass off a digitally altered photograph as real, why can't others, such as the news and the media for example? Can we trust the pictures that we see in the news?

[cue slide: title slide]

And that brings us to the topic of my proposal, which is titled "Little Photoshop of Horrors? Digital Manipulation of Media Images."

Let's start by looking at some examples.

[cue slide: OJ] This photo is from 1994 when O. J. Simpson was arrested. *Newsweek* kept his mugshot unaltered, while *Time* darkened the color of his skin. Minority groups protested that this made him look darker and more menacing and therefore presumed his guilt. The photographer claimed that he was only going for a more artful, more compelling image.

Note how Susan has references to her slides.

Her language is casual and low style. She even uses humor.

Her explicit signposting helps the audience follow her argument.

[cue slide: Martha Stewart] This is the *Newsweek* cover released last year when Martha Stewart was released from prison. The caption is "Martha's Last Laugh: After Prison, She's Thinner, Wealthier and Ready for Primetime." This may be true, but the slim body pictured is not in fact hers.

[cue slide: Walinski]

This photo was taken in 1994, which is when a British soldier was photographed pointing a gun at an Iraqi citizen. It is actually a composite *[cue animation: original photos]* of these two photos. The photographer later apologized and was fired.

[cue slide: "Introduction"]

What happened? Before digital imaging, people trusted photography to be an honest medium. A photographer and his camera were deemed the unbiased purveyor of reality. How has the capacity for photo manipulation affected the credibility of photos in media? Some hypotheses I have are: **[cue animation: point one]** has it led to a loss of credibility due to more powerful image-editing techniques, or **[cue animation: point two]** has it led to increased credibility due to the evolution of stricter standards?

[cue slide: "Perspectives"]

Some perspectives I plan to take are number one historical. **[cue animation: historical]** I intend to look at photo manipulation before digital imaging to look at whether people doctored photos then and whether the guidelines are stricter then versus now. **[cue animation: public]** Also, I plan

She uses rhetorical questions and cuts down the length and complexity of her prose in order to convey her argument effectively to her audience.

to look at the public response to digital manipulation. For example, where is the line drawn? Sometimes when the doctoring is obvious, it could be interpreted as social satire or commentary; however, if it's subtle, people could perceive this as perception. Also, how easily can people recognize altered images? **[cue animation: photographer]** And for the photographer's point of view, what are some of the reasons for our digitally manipulated photographs. Could it be out of respect for the privacy of the subject, or for the sensibilities of the audience? Also, what are the guidelines and the various contexts in which they may apply?

[cue slide: "Methods"]

Some methods that I'll use for my research include books. **[cue animation: books]** I'll start with a kind of general approach to ethical photojournalism. Some books I have include *The Burden of Visual Truth: The Role of Photojournalism in Mediating Reality* and also some books on digital image ethics. I also plan at looking at **[cue animation: databases]** online databases to find some examples of digital image ethics and photo manipulation, some articles on recent controversies over altered photos, authoritative opinions by photojournalists and photographers, and some examples of how their public responded to the incidents.

[cue animation: Websites] And also I'll look at some other Websites such as news and media sites online and some smaller photojournalism sites to see how they address image

The ample use of "I" works well in her presentation to convey a confident research persona.

She invokes specific examples in her script to make her talk persuasive.

> authenticity and to see if they label their images as illustrations or as genuine photographs. And finally I'll look at online guidelines. The National Press Photography Association has a Website for a digital code of ethics, for example.
>
> **[cue slide: "Summary"]**
>
> In summary, we find digital imaging has made photo manipulation easier and perhaps more prevalent. For example, you could use aesthetic touch-ups, graft parts of pictures onto others, and even construct a picture entirely from scratch. As a result, there's a lot of public skepticism over the reliability of the images. So my proposal is to explore to what extent this skepticism is really justified.

Her strong and compelling conclusion provides an effective ending to her script.

Reading through Susan's proposal, we can see the effective ways in which she transformed her proposal for oral delivery.

Selection: Although she focused on a single pair of images in her original proposal, Susan used a series of current, recognizable examples of photo manipulation to persuade her audience in her presentation, including some photographs she "altered" herself. She also condensed her sources section and eliminated her timeline altogether, taking into account what information would most interest her listeners.

Organization: Susan's organization in the latter half of her presentation resembles that found in her proposal in moving through methods, to sources, to conclusion. However, her introduction is completely reworked, designed to better capture the attention of a listening—and viewing—audience.

Translation: Throughout, Susan simplified her language and moved to a more colloquial tone that matched the very colloquial introduction she used to hook her audience. Compare, for instance, the final line of her oral presentation with this one, which served as the final sentence for her proposal: "A closer look at the occurrences of digital manipulation today, as regulated by the evolving guidelines of photojournalism, could reveal to what extent such skepticism is warranted." In her presentation, the language is much more direct, clear, and succinct. It is tailored to a listening audience.

Considering Strategies of Design

As you can tell from Susan Zhang's presentation, careful translation can be the key to communicating your argument powerfully and persuasively. Her combination of personal example, a series of persuasive case studies, a strong voice, clear structure, and solid delivery all combined to create a compelling presentation. What other presentation models might you consider?

- Jessica Luo centered her talk about the media coverage of the Tiananmen Square uprising in 1989 on photographs from both Chinese and European presses. She created pairs to demonstrate the arguments made through photos by each media organization. Jessica wanted to move a mainly American student audience into caring about an incident that happened in China more than 20 years ago. Thus, she decided to transform her "objective" writer's voice into a personal narrative and used rhythmic, repetitive terms that explained the rhetorical significance of each image.

- For a project on land mines, Stewart Dorsey showed two PowerPoint presentations side by side on large projection screens. He stood between the two screens to suggest that his argument offered a feasible compromise between polarized camps.

- Max Echtemendy used a mixture of media and interactivity in his research presentation on fantasy violence. First, he set up a table showing horror novels, DVD boxes, articles in magazines, music videos, and many other examples of "fantasy violence all around us." Then he asked students to complete a brief questionnaire, and he worked with their answers as he discussed the key elements of his argument. He ended by showing a clip from *The Lord of the Rings* and asking for audience response.

- Tom Hurlbutt, exploring the implications of Internet surveillance, created a dynamic PowerPoint presentation that linked to Websites, asked students to log on to Amazon, and revealed code that showed their search history from previous class sessions. In this way, he integrated graphic effects in a rhetorically purposeful way.

- Eric Jung, for a presentation on art and technology, transformed the classroom into a twenty-second-century museum, complete with "exhibits" of technologically produced art. He assumed the role of museum guide and gave the class a "tour" of the exhibit, concluding with a "retrospective" lecture about the early twenty-first-century debate over how digital media changed popular conceptions of art.

These innovative projects suggest the many effective ways to use strategies of selection, organization, and translation to design the most intriguing, powerful, and appropriate presentation for your purposes.

COLLABORATIVE CHALLENGE

Take 10 minutes to brainstorm the design possibilities for your presentation. Complete the following questions:

1. What format will your presentation take?
2. What materials do you plan to use in your presentation?
3. What might be a potential outline for your presentation?

Now peer review your responses with a partner. Have each person suggest changes, new ideas, and alternative ways of designing the presentation. You might also use this time to begin practicing the presentation. Finally, to get a sense of how your presentation will change according to your audience, consider how your answers would change depending on whether you presented to a class audience or a group of friends in the dorm, a review panel at a company, or a potential employer. Experiment to find the most effective ways to design your presentation.

Using Visuals Rhetorically

Presentations can vary greatly in their design and delivery. At times, you may be asked to deliver an exclusively *oral presentation*, in which you make your argument without the use of any visuals. We are most familiar with this form of public speaking: great civil rights leaders, peace activists, and political leaders rarely cue up a PowerPoint slide to make their points.

Yet, even the shortest talks can be augmented by strategically chosen visual texts that enhance the persuasiveness of an argument. For your own assignments, you will probably be given the option of using visuals in your presentations, so it is important that you develop strategies for doing so effectively—that is, with rhetorical purpose.

Writing for Poster Sessions

Posters communicate arguments both verbally and visually. The presentation style is used most frequently in the sciences, where **poster sessions** are common at conferences and large conventions. Visitors walk through exhibit halls where hundreds of posters are on display, stopping to read those that interest them and often requesting copies of the complete research paper. If you plan on pursuing a science major, you might want to ask your instructor if a poster presentation is acceptable to report research findings.

To create posters, researchers select salient points from their work and organize the content into short summaries with complementary visuals. The goal of a poster presentation is to produce a visual-verbal display that conveys the research accurately, engagingly, and concisely. Figures 9.6 and 9.7 show examples of award-winning student posters from a Stanford University student research symposium. While clearly the authors of these posters designed them differently, both share certain features:

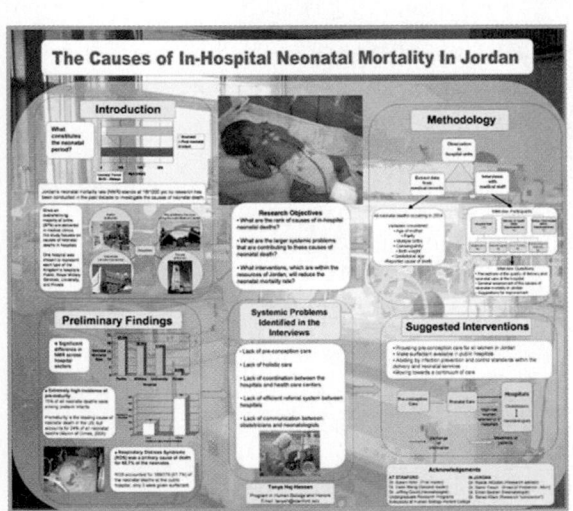

- Bold headings offering clear titles that are easy to read from a distance
- Clear, vertical hierarchies for information
- Concise written content paired with compelling images

FIGURE 9.6. Tanja Haj-Hassan won awards for this poster, displayed at the 2005 Stanford Symposium for Undergraduate Research in Progress.

Both posters are designed to engage the interest and understanding of their audience.

FIGURE 9.7. Co-researchers Carlos Ortiz and Jonathan Hwang transformed their research into this award-winning poster for the 2005 Stanford Symposium for Undergraduate Research in Progress.

AT A GLANCE

Guidelines for Creating Posters for a Poster Session

- Make sure your poster is readable from a distance; size your fonts accordingly.
- Put the poster's title, authors, and academic affiliation at the top.
- Avoid visual clutter; consider using white space to offset various elements, including tables, figures, and written texts.
- Arrange materials in columns not rows.
- Avoid long passages of texts; rely primarily on visual persuasion.
- Always check with the conference organizers for their specific guidelines.

For more detailed advice, go to the *Envision* Website. www.pearsonhighered/envision/289.

Writing for Multimedia Presentations

In today's increasingly high-tech environment, multimedia presentations have become very popular in both academic and professional contexts. There are a range of options available to today's presenter; PowerPoint, Keynote, or Prezi slideshows; film or audio clips; screencasts; projection of digital images; even live Web browsing. Many factors will influence your choice of multimedia support, including your access to technology, the capabilities of the room in which you are presenting, the requirements of your presentation assignment, and your own technological expertise. However, any time you consider incorporating multimedia into a presentation, be sure to keep in mind the following: these multimedia components are *secondary* to your argument. Start by planning what to say, and then choose the rhetorical tools that will help you craft the most powerful presentation.

Working with Slideshows

For many presenters, the default tool for presentations is PowerPoint. In fact, commonly we overhear students saying, "I have to give a Power-Point" rather than "I have to give a presentation." The first step in constructing a successful slideshow—whether using PowerPoint, Keynote, Prezi, or other slide software—is to remember that you need to prioritize your argument, not fonts, templates, design, and graphics.

This is a rule clearly observed by dynamic presenters, from Steve Jobs to Lawrence Lessig, who successfully integrate slides into their presentations. Increasingly, they have moved away from text-heavy slides filled with bullet lists of information, to a more visually dynamic, minimalist style that balances text with image and that serves as visual evidence (some might even say visual punctuation) to their oral argument.

If you are composing a slide-based presentation, think strategically about how to use those slides to your best advantage. Will you use them to analyze primary sources (images, film clips, information graphics)? To structure your argument, outlining claims and subclaims? To reinforce key terms or concepts? To showcase definitions or key quotations? To feature an in-depth case study or example? To move your audience emotionally through *pathos* or appeal to their intellect through compelling data? Keep in mind, too, that it's not just what slides you create that matters; it's how you use them.

Morgan Springer, for instance, felt that using a map in his slideshow would strengthen his argument on self-determination in Kosovo and East Timor. Having selected one, he customized it to his argument by coloring in red those countries experiencing political wars and military dictatorships. As a final touch, after presenting that slide to the audience, he used the slide animation to circle the two countries that he was going to focus on in his own particular project (Figure 9.8).

Similarly, Natalie Farrell had her audience in mind while working with her materials for a project on Yucca Mountain. She wanted the class to guess at the power of a projected nuclear disaster on Yucca Mountain before shocking them with the actual numbers, so she created slides with blanks left in the list of statistics (Figure 9.9). After a moment of audience participation where she invited them to verbally fill in the blanks, she then moved to a slide that revealed the true statistics (Figure 9.10).

Student Writing

See Morgan Springer's complete presentation as well as examples of other multimedia slideshows.
www.pearsonhighered.com/envision/291

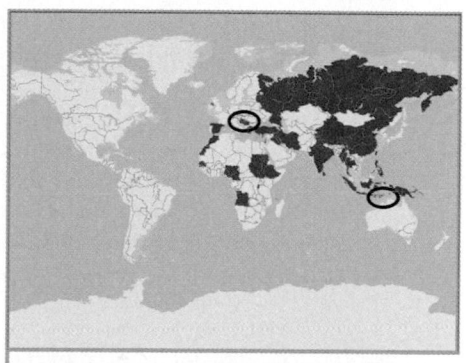

FIGURE 9.8. One of Morgan Springer's map slides from his PowerPoint presentation on self-determination in Kosovo and East Timor.

Scary facts

When full, Yucca Mountain Will be _____ more radioactive than the bomb dropped on Hiroshima

FIGURE 9.9. Natalie Farrell's presentation titled "Yucca Mountain and Nuclear Waste: Gambling with the Future of the Human Race," slide 5.

Scary facts

When full, Yucca Mountain Will be _1,400,000_ more radioactive than the bomb dropped on Hiroshima

FIGURE 9.10. Slide 6, in which Natalie dramatically fills in the blank

AT A GLANCE

Writing an Effective Slide-Based Presentation

- Use purposeful visuals, not clip art.
- Plan to spend time discussing the images you use as visual evidence.
- When using a film or audio clip, be selective in how much to show so it doesn't overwhelm your presentation.
- Don't put too much text on each slide or rely too heavily on bullet lists.
- Use slide animation to stagger the amount of information you share with your audience.
- Keep fonts consistent in style, size, and color to avoid distracting the audience.
- Break complicated ideas into multiple slides.
- Consider using clear, interesting headers to help visually structure your argument.
- Tie your slides together with a visual theme, motif, or template that, if possible, reflects the tone or content of your topic.
- Include sound effects and animation rhetorically rather than for flair or flash.
- Give a handout with full quotations or complicated information graphics as necessary.

Find more detailed advice on the *Envision* Website. www.pearsonhighered/envision/292.

For his project, Frank Li decided to embed a screenshot of Yahoo's Fire Eagle press release in his slideshow. However, previewing it, he realized that although the image created a significant visual impact, it was too text-heavy for the audience to read. To solve this problem, he used his slide software to highlight a key quote from the text (Figure 9.11), so his audience would have the benefit of both the primary source and the quotation.

Conversely, Alex Bleyleben's use of slides is notable for his understanding of when *not* to use them. In his presentation about global activism, Alex projected a series of images of the slaughter of the endangered black rhino. To capitalize on the momentum of this pathos appeal, Alex dramatically turned the screen after quickly showing a series of gruesome pictures so as to shift the

FIGURE 9.11. Frank Li pulls out a key quote from his primary source on his slide.

audience's attention back to his own presence at the podium as he delivered the key points of his argument.

These examples suggest many purposeful, rhetorical ways of writing for slide-based presentations that move beyond just using the slides to visually record your notes. Rather, they succeed in what cultural critic Stephen Shugart deems is the necessity of "transforming the concept of PowerPoint from 'presenting at' into 'a way of promoting discussion' or to use it in unconventional ways to create more effective learning situations."

Beyond the Slideshow

As with all arguments, in deciding how to compose your presentation, you should begin with your purpose and your audience and then design your text to meet your needs. In some cases, that will mean shutting off your slideware and looking into alternate ways to leverage the power of multimedia in your argument. Let's look at some of the innovative ways in which some students used multimedia to support their oral argument:

In her presentation "Redefining the Essay," Caroline Chen embedded audio clips from her interview with rhetoric scholar Andrea Lunsford into her slideshow, reinforcing the key points from their discussion by transcribing select phrases onto the slides for the audience to read as they listened to the audio.

Max Oswald, for his presentation on the effects of technology on modern life, adopted a very unconventional approach. He composed the first eight minutes of his talk as a YouTube-style video, complete with spliced scenes and dramatic camera angles, to make his point about the distancing effect of technology (Figure 9.12). Then, as shown in Figure 9.13, for the final three minutes of his presentation, he turned off the video and delivered his conclusion in person, dramatically underscoring his argument about the difference between technologically-mediated and live encounters.

FIGURE 9.12. Max Oswald created a YouTube-type video as the core of his presentation about the distancing effects of modern technology.

FIGURE 9.13. At the end of his presentation, Max underscored his argument by stopping the video and delivering his conclusion live.

During a presentation on the political applications of Twitter, Luisa Russell took her audience to Venezuelan President Hugo Chávez's Twitter page, pointing out his growing number of followers, then performing a rhetorical analysis of the content of his feed. At the end of the presentation, she then refreshed her screen, pointing to the updated number of followers as a way of emphasizing for her audience the currency of her topic and Twitter's ever-increasing significance as a political platform.

Rather than browsing the internet live during her presentation, Rose Emerson used screen capture software to record a segment of gameplay from *Modern Warfare 2*. She then played the footage in the background as she delivered her argument about hypermasculinization and hypermilitizarization in video games, pausing the recording at pre-designated moments so she could approach the screen and point out key elements to support her argument. She timed her presentation carefully so that she moved toward her conclusion during a particularly brutal moment of the gameplay that culminated in her character's death, delivering her final lines as the screen capture froze on the final image of battle's bloody aftermath.

AT A GLANCE

Delivery with Multimedia

- Practice your timing; experiment with the way you introduce and analyze the media that you present.
- Make eye contact; look at your audience, not the screen.
- If you are using slides, try not to read off them; prepare a separate script to create a dialogue with your audience.
- Always practice a multimedia presentation at least once before giving it live, especially if you are using slides with animations, or film or audio clips.

Choosing Methods of Delivery

As you can tell, the way you present your visual materials is just as crucial as drafting content for that presentation. In other words, after *selection, arrangement,* and *design* of materials, you need to think about ways of *delivering* the presentation. But why is delivery so important? Won't the content carry the persuasiveness of the presentation? If the writing is good, won't the delivery be good? Indeed, the writing must be skillful; the selection, organization, and

AT A GLANCE

Some Fundamental Elements of Delivery

- *Stance or posture:* also called embodied rhetoric
- *Gesture:* use of hands to communicate information
- *Voice:* pitch, tone, loudness, softness, and enunciation
- *Pacing:* of words, visuals, and argument
- *Rhetorical appeals:* use of logos, pathos, ethos
- *Visuals:* slides, posters, graphics, handouts
- *Embodied visuals:* not only stance but dress, appearance, mannerisms
- *Style:* elements such as repetition, allusion, metaphor, stories, personal narrative, jokes, and pauses

translation of your argument into an appropriate, audience-centered design are crucial for your success. But you also need to attend to *how* you communicate your argument to your audience. In other words, you need to involve those last two canons of rhetoric, *memory* and *delivery.* In brief:

- **Memory** entails both memorizing one's argument to communicate it to the audience and evoking memorable phrases.
- **Delivery** concerns strategies of presenting your argument to an audience.

We know that memory was crucial for rhetoricians before the invention of the printing press. Speakers would memorize phrases, stories, and histories to pass down from generation to generation. Significantly, this process occurred through a form of visual organization called an **architectural mnemonic technique**, a method in which you associate a phrase to a room or a part of a house so that as you look around during your presentation you receive visual clues to trigger your memory.

As you think about strategies of presentation, you might want to try memorizing key parts of your speech through this technique by creating a visual map of your script. Also, attend to the way your audience will remember your words, and choose your examples, your diction, and your pacing accordingly. In this way, memory leads naturally into delivery, the last canon of rhetoric.

When asked which three of the five canons of rhetoric he considered most significant, the Greek orator Demosthenes replied, "delivery, delivery,

> "[The rhetorician Cicero described mnemonic technique as] a set of visual images like the rooms of a house, which can be associated with the items in a long speech"
>
> —William Covino and David Joliffe (67).

> Delivery, as one of the five canons of rhetoric, deals primarily with the effectiveness of a speech's presentation. Oral communication, combined with variations in the presenter's voice and body movements, comprises the delivery of speech. The speaker's ability to manipulate auditory and visual techniques enables him/her to effectively convey his/her argument to the audience.
>
> —Kelly Ingleman

delivery." In other words, so crucial is this fifth canon that it can supersede the rest. One core aspect of the canon of delivery is the *sound* of the presentation: how speakers use tone of voice, pacing, strategic pauses, or changes in volume or inflection to make their arguments memorable and effective.

Embodied Rhetoric

If you think of some of the most prominent speakers of recent history— Barack Obama, Ronald Reagan, former Congresswoman Barbara Jordan— you probably can hear in your head the rhetorically powerful ways they used the sound of language itself. You can likewise prepare yourself for effective oral delivery by annotating your script to indicate places where you will pause, emphasize a key word, or use the strength of your voice to underscore a point. Written cues like this can help you to deliver a memorable, moving, and convincing oral argument.

However, it is not just the *sound* of delivery that affects the persuasiveness of an oral presentation but the *look* of that presentation as well. How many times have you seen a talk in which the speaker dressed up to make a point or used the rhetoric of his or her body to persuade the audience? This form of presentation is a genre we call **embodied rhetoric**, a presentation in which the body becomes a visual means of communicating the message. In most presentations, you employ the power of embodied rhetoric through the clothes you wear, how you stand, the voice you choose, and even how you hold the materials you use to convey your argument. When Liz Kreiner delivered her presentation on sexual assault on campus, for instance, she made very strategic decisions about her embodied rhetoric: to emphasize the seriousness of her subject, she dressed conservatively and stood absolutely still at the podium as she recounted the disturbing stories of date rape that she had uncovered during her research. Her somber demeanor, reinforced by her serious tone of voice, produced an extremely powerful rhetorical moment (see Figure 9.14).

FIGURE 9.14. During her presentation on sexual assault on campus, Liz Kreiner opted against using multimedia, relying instead on her voice and embodied rhetoric to convey the seriousness of her subject.

In most cases, we see embodied rhetoric at work through gesture. Often, when we think about the term *gesture* in relation to public speaking, we think of very overt or intentional hand motions that public speakers make for emphasis, like that made by Jake Palinsky in

FIGURE 9.15. In his presentation on recent developments in stem cell research, Jake Palinsky used gesture deliberately to help his audience understand a scientific diagram.

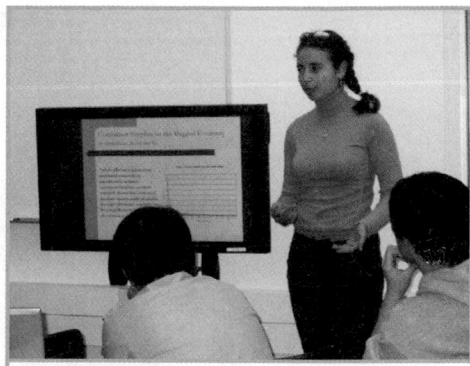

FIGURE 9.16. In a moment of explanation, Alina Lanesberg uses a subtle gesture to emphasize her point and draw her audience into her argument.

Figure 9.15, in which he directs the audience's attention by gesturing to the diagram he is describing. Our eyes follow his finger to focus on the part of the diagram he is explaining at that moment.

The gesture is a careful rhetorical move: it has purpose and works effectively as a strategy of communication. Sometimes gestures in public speaking seem less carefully composed, such as the one in Figure 9.16. Here we see the speaker in midsentence, her hands opened as if in an involuntary accompaniment to her words. But notice how the open palm, extended toward members of the audience, invites them to listen; it is tilted down to allow words to travel and open the space between the speaker and the audience. This subtle instance of embodied rhetoric invites the listeners into the argument and demonstrates a moment of explanation and connection.

Although we all use gestures without realizing that we do, we can in fact train ourselves to use the rhetoric of the body more carefully, and even strategically, as an integral part of our overall presentation design. Your purpose in using gestures as part of a presentation should be to harness the power of the body effectively to communicate ideas. Therefore, as you draft and deliver your presentation, remember that your *entire* body—from body language to clothes, posture, expression, and gestures—participates in communicating your ideas and information.

Analyze the gestures used by one of the most famous public speakers, Martin Luther King Jr. (see Figure 9.17 and Figure 9.18). Write a brief analysis of the suggested meaning and purpose of each gesture, describing each of the images as you make your argument. Then select the words you might match to the gesture. This exercise will help you explore strategies to use in your own presentations.

FIGURE 9.17. Martin Luther King Jr. gesturing at a press conference.

FIGURE 9.18. Martin Luther King Jr. emphasizes his point at a mass rally in Philadelphia, August 4, 1965.

> Winston Churchill could never have stirred the British public as he did were it not for the grave, serious, and controlled tone of voice that he employed in his radio speeches. His faith in the allied powers rang out in stentorian cadences that by their very vibrations instilled belief in the masses. His message was often cliché, but his delivery was never anything but spellbinding. Had he had a feeble voice, perhaps Germany would have fared better.
>
> —Dr. Gideon Burton

Practicing Your Presentation

Speakers like Martin Luther King Jr. dedicate much of their time to practicing their delivery. Similarly, two ideologically opposed political figures, Adolf Hitler and Winston Churchill, relied extensively on practice to develop their delivery.

- Hitler incessantly recorded himself speaking and using hand gestures, then would watch the films over and over again, selecting the motions that he felt were most powerful. Next, he would practice that form of delivery—the tone of voice, the pacing, the bodily stance, and the hand gestures—until he felt it was perfect. Finally, he would destroy the recordings so that no one would know how carefully he practiced. The practice made his delivery seem natural and his power seem real.

- Churchill used voice alone to persuade the British public to withstand the waves of Nazi attacks night after night in the bombing of Britain. Over the radio wires, his practiced and powerful words—delivered with the perfect amount of confidence and encouragement—helped the British persevere during those dark days.

These examples reveal the power of practice in strengthening delivery and its capacity to persuade audiences. Likewise, you should incorporate repeated practice into the process of drafting and revising your presentations. As with any assignment, your argument will benefit from peer review, so consider performing a "dress rehearsal" for a friend or roommate to get his or her feedback on the clarity of your ideas, your use of multimedia or visual aids, and the effectiveness of your delivery. Better yet, become your own peer reviewer by filming your "dress rehearsal" and then critiquing your performance. Sometimes, by becoming a member of the audience yourself, you can see how to revise your presentation into a truly powerful oral argument.

Anticipating Problems and the Question-and-Answer Session

As you practice your presentation, don't forget to consider problems that might arise, such as faulty technology, a bored or confused audience, or even hecklers. To troubleshoot technology, visit your room and test out your equipment in advance. Make sure you have backup for the technology: save your work on a CD or memory stick, or email it to yourself. But remember, even if your practice session goes smoothly, bring handouts in case your PowerPoint slides don't work, and be prepared to talk without technology if necessary. Also, be ready to cut down or extend the length of your talk by indicating on your script places you might pause or points you might discuss in more detail. Realize that the more comfortable you are with your material, the more you can adapt on the spot to the needs of your audience.

Successful adaptation includes handling the question-and-answer session well; this part of a presentation, usually located at the end, serves as the final opportunity to clarify your argument and convince your audience. A successful presenter anticipates and, in some cases, even sets up the framework for the question-and-answer session. For instance, during his presentation on Marilyn Manson, Ben Rosenbrough realized he didn't have time to develop the link he saw between Elvis Presley and Manson in his formal presentation and so he made only a passing reference to the connection, hoping that the audience would be intrigued and ask about it after his talk. When they did, he advanced his PowerPoint beyond his conclusion slide to one documenting these connections in a powerful way. His surprise preparation for the question-and-answer session made his presentation design exceptionally successful. Similarly, you can anticipate what questions your audience might have by delivering your presentation to a peer group member, seeing what questions your presentation generates and even practicing trial responses. Consider having some new evidence, a stunning visual, or even a handout prepared to answer a question that you hope might be asked after your presentation.

Documenting Your Presentation

Design. Delivery. Practice. What is left? After all your hard work on your presentation, you probably want to leave some kind of trace, a written artifact, or a form of textual memory of the presentation. **Documentation**—*some form of written or visual evidence of your presentation's argument*—is the answer. Documentation serves an important rhetorical function: to inform and persuade. This might take the form of a **handout** that provides additional information in the form of an annotated bibliography, a summary of your key points and thesis, visual rhetoric from your presentation, references for further reading, or a printout of your PowerPoint presentation. You should put your contact information on it so the audience can ask you further questions.

Documentation might also consist of a **text** or **script** for your presentation. This can either be the annotated printout of your PowerPoint presentation, a full speech, or a typed set of notes in outline form with placeholders for your slides or media aids such as shown in Tommy Tsai's visual outline (see Figure 9.5). More innovatively, you might document your presentation with a **creative take-away** that reflects a key aspect of your presentation. Consider Wendy Hagenmaier's handout for her project on media coverage of the bombing of Hiroshima and Nagasaki (see Figure 9.19). The cover of the *New York Times* from

Student Writing

See Courtney Smith's handout, designed to accompany her presentation on Palestinian female suicide bombers, as well as other presentation take-aways.

www.pearsonhighered.com/envision/300

August 1945 is attached to a small candle; Wendy's caption reads, "Light this candle in remembrance of how the August 1945 atomic bombings of Hiroshima and Nagasaki have been remembered by Japanese and American photojournalists. The 'flashes' of its flame will serve to remind you that photojournalistic coverage is often an attempt to shape collective national memory and that remembrance is subjective." Another student, Falco Pichler, presenting his research finding on Nike marketing strategies, created a "backstage pass" to what he called the "Nike Show" and invited students to read his paper online. Aaron Johnson, presenting his research on media representation of athletes who take performance-enhancing drugs, made a mock subscription card with the title "Sports Exaggerated" as creative documentation for his presentation (see Figure 9.20). Using Photoshop, he embedded a cover of *Sports Illustrated* into the subscription card and listed the main points of his argument as "advertising points" for his presentation. Notice his complete contact information at the bottom of the card.

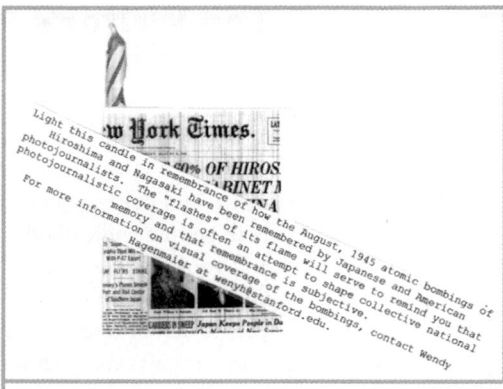

FIGURE 9.19. Wendy Hagenmaier's creative handout on the 1945 atomic bombings of Hiroshima and Nagasaki.

These examples begin to show the range of creative documentation strategies you might pursue as the final part of your presentation. Taking the lead from Aaron, you might even craft an interactive visual take-away such as a graphic montage, a minibook, or other forms of visual argument. The importance of such texts—whether conventional prose handouts or compelling visual creations—lies in their power to make your presentation memorable, convincing, and engaging. So consider your strategies for documentation as carefully as you design your entire presentation.

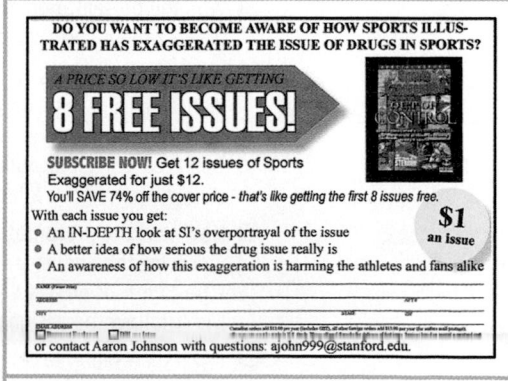

FIGURE 9.20. Aaron Johnson's creative presentation take-away for his research project on *Sports Illustrated*.

The Writer's Process

In this chapter, you have explored possibilities for presentations; learned how to convert a written argument into a spoken, visual, multimedia presentation or performance; and worked through the different ways of writing for oral, poster, and PowerPoint presentations. Recall the strategies of design, arrangement, and delivery you have learned, and keep in mind the importance of both gesture and embodied rhetoric as ways of communicating your message and your purpose to your particular audience. Finally, as you begin to craft your own presentation, remember the old adage, "practice makes perfect." Peer review and revision are as important to your presentation as collaboration on drafts and revision are to your written work. They enable you to anticipate problems and harness your creativity as you shape your ideas into a memorable, moving, and persuasive form of rhetorical communication.

PREWRITING CHECKLIST

Focus on Analyzing Presentations

❏ What is the presenter's purpose? To inform? persuade? instruct? motivate? initiate discussion? Did the presentation successfully accomplish that purpose?

❏ What is the presenter's relationship to the topic he or she discussed? Is the presenter an expert? a novice? fairly well informed?

❏ Was the presentation appropriate for the audience? Consider language, organization, and explanation of technical or specialized concepts.

❏ Did the speaker present him- or herself as an authority instructing the audience? as a peer sharing information? Did the presenter make eye contact (indicating a direct relationship with the audience) or simply read from a prepared text (indicating a focus on the material rather than the audience)? How did this affect the structure and style of the presentation?

❏ How was the presentation structured? Was an outline or summary provided for the audience to follow? Was this done orally, on the board, in a handout, or on a slide? Was the development of the argument clear? Did it follow the designated structure?

❏ Did the presenter take into account the audience's reaction? For instance, did he or she notice some confusion in the audience and pause to explain a difficult point?

❏ How did the presentation begin? Did the presenter use any effective oral or visual devices to "hook" the audience? Was there a clear conclusion?

❏ Were the main points clearly developed? How was the scope of the presentation? Was there too much information? too little?

❏ Did the presenter use word choices appropriate to the occasion, audience, and subject matter? Were the sentence structures too complex (as if to be read silently) or more colloquial (as if to be read aloud)? Did the presenter project his or her voice enough? Did he or she speak slowly and clearly or rush through the material?

❏ Did the presenter use any formal devices—figurative language, deliberate repetition, literary allusions?

❏ Consider the presenter's embodied rhetoric. Did he or she stand or sit? remain stationary, or move around? Did the presenter use gestures, facial expression, or even costume to add to the rhetorical effect of the argument?

❏ How did the presenter use visuals? Did he or she show slides, bring in posters, write on a blackboard, distribute handouts, engage in role-playing, pass around books, or bring in material evidence for the presentation? Were the visual components rhetorically purposeful or did they seem an afterthought?

❏ If the presenter used posters, were they clear and accessible to the audience? Did they stand alone as arguments, or was their meaning only clear in conjunction with the oral presentation? Were the words large enough to read from a distance? Did the poster avoid visual clutter? Did it contain a clear title and use information graphics effectively?

❏ If the presenter used a slide program such as PowerPoint, was the visual design of the slides effective? Did the slides have a unity of theme, color, and layout? Did the presenter avoid visual clutter on the slides? How much text was on each slide? Were placeholders used for emphasis or pacing? Were there innovations in the slideshow, such as using dual screens, animation, or embedded clips or Internet links? Were these effective or distracting? Did the presenter speak to the computer screen rather than the audience? Did the presenter's body block the screen, obscuring the slides?

(*continued*)

> ❏ If the presenter used the blackboard or whiteboard, did he or she write clearly and legibly? Were the notations on the board purposeful? Did the presenter block the board, making it difficult to read?
>
> ❏ If the presenter used technology, were there any technical difficulties? Did the presenter overcome them smoothly (for instance, having a backup plan), or have a difficult time recovering from the glitch, perhaps because of relying more heavily on technology than on the force of argument?
>
> ❏ Did the presenter finish within the allotted time? How did he or she handle the question-and-answer session?

PREWRITING WITH THE *ENVISION* WEBSITE

Compare the very different styles of two speeches, both given by women, both concerning human rights, but presented to very different audiences and by very different personas: Eleanor Roosevelt's speech entitled "Adoption of the Declaration of Human Rights," delivered December 9, 1948, in Paris, France; and a speech by Cher (played by Alicia Silverstone) from the movie *Clueless* (1995) on "Whether all oppressed people should be allowed refuge in America" (both linked through the *Envision* Website). Look at the written versions of their speeches as you listen to them talk. What characteristics of the spoken word does each piece of writing share? How are they different?

www.pearsonhighered.com/envision/304

WRITING PROJECTS

1. **Field Research on Presentation:** As part of the necessary preparation for writing your own presentation, conduct field research in the form of observing three public speeches, presentations, or oral/multimedia arguments. If possible, take a camera with you and document your observations of each kind of presentation. Type up a brief rhetorical analysis on the delivery, rhetorical strategies, and effectiveness of each one. Then indicate what strategies you plan to use in your own presentation. These presentations can include lectures in any of your classes, speakers visiting campus or your dorms, or the practice presentation of a member of your class.

2. **Formal Presentation:** Create and deliver a timed presentation of your research argument for your class (ask your instructor for the precise time limit). You should

include the appropriate media (visual rhetoric, PowerPoint slides, Websites, movie clips, performative or interactive aspects). In addition, the oral delivery of your presentation might include a handout that you distribute to the class to provide information—for example, an annotated bibliography, a summary of your key points and thesis, visual rhetoric from your presentation, references for further reading, or a printout of your PowerPoint presentation—formatted in the proper manner (or in a creative way if that works for your presentation) with your complete contact information on it. Also compose a script for your presentation. This can either be the annotated printout of your PowerPoint presentation, a full speech, or notes in outline form (with placeholders for your slides or multimedia). Include references in the text or script of your presentation to any materials you use (handouts and printouts of multimedia).

3. **Collaborative Presentation:** Work in groups of two to four to design and deliver a presentation to the class. You might want to divide the tasks of selecting material, brainstorming strategies of presentation, and designing your visual materials. Will you take turns speaking throughout the presentation, or will each person be responsible for a distinct segment of the presentation? Will one person write the script, another person deliver it—perhaps from memory—while a third creates the slides? Choose the strategy that best suits your audience and your purpose. Don't forget to practice together, and when your group is presenting, look at the others who are speaking to keep the class's attention focused on your group presentation.

4. **Community Writing Presentation:** Either in groups or individually, design your presentation for a specific community audience. What happens if you present your research project on performance art to a group of politicians, to school administrators, to the theater department? Think about how your message can reach a broader audience in this way. What if your project is on the educational poster campaign to prevent the spread of AIDS? After you design one presentation for your writing class, rewrite it to meet the audience expectations of a not-for-profit organization, an international amnesty meeting, or an urban center continuing education class.

 Visit www.pearsonhighered.com/envision for expanded assignment guidelines and student projects. Visit www.mycomplab.com for additional general writing and research resources.

Works Cited

CHAPTER 1

Aristotle. "Rhetoric." *The History and Theory of Rhetoric.* By James A. Herrick. Boston: Allyn & Bacon, 1998. Print.

Diamond, Matthew. "No Laughing Matter: Post-September 11 Political Cartoons in Arab/Muslim Newspapers." *Political Communication* 19 (2002): 251–72. Print.

Holkins, Jerry. "The Hipness Threshold." *Penny-Arcade.* Penny Arcade Blog, 12 Mar. 2004. Web. 22 June 2006.

Marchetto, Marisa Acocella. *Cancer Vixen: A True Story.* New York: Knopf, 2006. Print.

Marlette, Doug. "I Was a Tool of Satan." *Columbia Journalism Review* (Nov./Dec. 2003): 52. Web. 22 June 2006.

McCloud, Scott. *Understanding Comics.* New York: HarperPerennial, 1993. Print.

Villanueva, Victor Jr. *Bootstraps: From an American Academic of Color.* Urbana, IL: National Council of Teachers of English, 1993. Print.

CHAPTER 2

Bowen, Laurence, and Jill Schmid. "Minority Presence and Portrayal in Mainstream Magazine Advertising: An Update." *Journalism and Mass Communications Quarterly* 74.1 (2004): 134–46. Print.

Stevenson, Seth. "You and Your Shadow." *Slate.com.* Slate, 4 Mar. 2004. Web. 7 June 2006.

Twitchell, James B. *Adcult USA.* New York: Columbia UP, 1996. Print.

---. "Listerine: Gerard Lambert and Selling the Need." *Twenty Ads That Shook the World.* New York: Three Rivers Press, 2000. 60–69. Print.

CHAPTER 3

Booth, Wayne. *The Rhetoric of Fiction.* Chicago: University of Chicago Press, 1961. Print.

Curtis, James. "Dorothea Lange, Migrant Mother, and the Culture of the Great Depression." *Winterthur Portfolio: A Journal of American Material Culture* 21 (Spring 1986) 1–20. Print.

Dunn, Geoffrey. "Photographic License." *San Louis Obispo Times.* San Luis Obispo (CA) Times, 17 Jan. 2002. Web. 11 June 2006.

Ephron, Nora. *Scribble, Scribble: Notes on the Media.* New York: Knopf, 1978. Print.

Frank, Robert. *The Americans.* New York: Grove Press, 1959. Print.

Gottesman, Jane. *Game Face.* NewYork: Random House, 2001. Print.

CHAPTER 5

Zimbardo, Philip G., Ann L. Weber, and Robert L. Johnson. *Psychology: Core Concepts.* 4th ed. Boston: Allyn & Bacon, 2003. Print.

CHAPTER 6

Blast, Joseph. "Gorgeous Propaganda, Frightening Truth." *Heartland Perspectives.* Heartland.org, June 2006. Web. 11 June 2006.

Lamott, Anne. *Bird by Bird: Some Instructions on Writing and Life.* New York: Anchor, 1995. Print.

Rasch, David. "How I Write Interview." *Stanford Writing Center.* Stanford University, 17 Nov. 2003. Web. 17 Nov. 2003.

Schulte, Bret. "Saying it in Cinema." *U.S. News and World Report.* U.S. News, 28 May 2006. Web. 20 April 2010.

CHAPTER 7

Chicago Manual of Style. 16th ed. Chicago: University of Chicago Press, 2010. Print.

American Psychological Association. *The Concise Rules of APA Style.* Washington, DC: American Psychological Assoc. 2009. Print.

Cone, Justin. "Building on the Past." JustinCone.com. n.d. Web. 27 June 2006.

Modern Language Association. *MLA Handbook for the Writers of Research Papers.* 7th ed. New York: Modern Language Association, 2010. Print.

American Psychological Association. *Publication Manual of the American Psychological Association.* 6th ed. Washington, DC: American Psychological Association. 2010. Print.

Council of Science Educators. *Scientific Style and Format: the CSE Manual for Authors, Editors and Publishers,* Seventh Edition. Reston, VA: Council of Science Educators in cooperation with the Rockefeller University Press, 2002. Print.

CHAPTER 8

Adbusters Culturejammer Headquarters: Journal of the Environment. Web. <http://www.adbusters.org>.

Agee, James. Foreword. *Let Us Now Praise Famous Men.* Boston: Houghton Mifflin, 1969. Print.

Allard, William Albert. "Solace at Surprise Creek." *National Geographic* (June 2006). Print.

Cicero. *De Inventione.* Trans. H. M. Hubbell. Cambridge, MA: Loeb Classical Library, 1949. Print.

Greenfield, Laura. *Girl Culture*. San Francisco, CA: Chronicle Books, 2002. Print.

Levy, Matthew. "A Rescue Worker's Chronicle." University of Maryland Baltimore County. November 2001. Web. 9 June 2010.

Ross, Carolyn, and Ardel Thomas. *Writing for Real: A Handbook for Writing in Community Service*. New York: Pearson Longman, 2003. Print.

CHAPTER 9

Burton, Gideon. *Silva Rhetoricae: The Forest of Rhetoric*. Humanities. Brigham Young University. Updated 26 February 2007. Web. 9 June 2010.

Ingleman, Kelly. "Delivery." *Rhetoric Resources at Tech*. Georgia Institute of Technology. Web. 20 October 2006.

Credits

Images

Page 1: Abhed Omar Qusini/Reuters. 2: © 2009 Nate Beeler, Washington Examiner, and PoliticalCartoons.com.

Figure 1.2: The Advertising Archives.

Figure 1.3: AP/Wide World Photos.

Figure 1.4: © Tribune Media Services, Inc. All Rights Reserved. Reprinted with permission.

Figure 1.8a, Figure 1.8b: Excerpted from Cancer Vixen. © 2006 MARISA ACOCELLA MARCHETTO. Cartoonist Marisa Acocella Marchetto tells the story of her triumph over breast cancer in her celebrated memoir Cancer Vixen (Knopf) www.marisamarchetto.com.

Figure 1.15: © 2009 Nate Beeler, Washington Examiner, and PoliticalCartoons.com.

Figure 2.2: Courtesy of RUSK PROFESSIONAL HAIRCARE.

Figure 2.4: © Chevron Corporation and used with permission.

Figure 2.5: The Procter & Gamble Company. Used by permission.

Figure 2.6: Courtesy of Volkswagen of America, Inc.

Figure 2.7: The Advertising Archives.

Figure 2.8: General Motors Corp. Used with permission. GM Media Archives.

Figure 2.9: Courtesy of Ford Motor Company.

Figure 2.10: Alyssa J. O'Brien, 2006.

Figure 2.11: Image courtesy of The Advertising Archives.

Figure 2.13: Image Courtesy of The Advertising Archives.

Figure 3.1: AP/Wide World Photos.

Figure 3.2: Margaret Bourke-White/Time & Life Pictures/Getty Images.

Figure 3.3: Library of Congress.

Figure 3.4: Library of Congress.

Figure 3.5: Todd Heisler/Polaris Images

Figure 3.6: Bettmann/Corbis.

Figure 3.7: "Triathlon Start" Harvey's Lake, Pa., 1994. Photograph by Mark Cohen.

Figure 3.8: "By a Nose" Philadelphia, Pa. Norman Y. Lono, 1980.

Figure 3.9: "Girl on a Swing" Pitt Street, NYC, 1938. Photograph by Walter Rosenblum.

Figure 3.10: AP/Wide World Photos.

Figure 3.12: Courtesy of Deseret Morning News Archives.

Page 86: AP/Wide World Photos.

Figure 3.13: Abhed Omar Qusini/Reuters.

Figure 3.14: Courtesy Boston Herald.

Page 105: TM & Copyright © 20th Century Fox. All rights reserved/Courtesy Everett Collection.

Figure 4.1: Patrick Broderick/Modern Humorist.com.

Figure 4.2: Hoover Institution Archives Poster Collection.

Figure 4.3: Courtesy National Archives 513533.

Figure 4.4: Courtesy National Archives 516102.

Figure 4.5: Courtesy National Archives 514597.

Figure 4.7 top right: Library of Congress.

Figure 4.7 bottom right: The Art Archive/Musee des 2 Guerres Mondiales Paris/Dagli Orti.

Figure 4.7 bottom left: Image Courtesy of The Advertising Archives.

Figure 4.7 top left: Courtesy National Archives 513533.

Figure 4.8 top right: Library of Congress.

Figure 4.8 bottom right: The Art Archive/Musee des 2 Guerres Mondiales Paris/Dagli Orti.

Figure 4.8 bottom left: Image Courtesy of The Advertising Archives.

Figure 4.8 top left: Courtesy National Archives 513533.

Figure 4.9: Library of Congress.

Figure 4.10: Courtesy of Micah Ian Wright & AntiWarPosters.com.

Figure 4.11: © 2003-WHITEHOUSE.ORG.

Figure 4.12: Courtesy of Steve Horn.

Figure 4.13: Courtesy of Micah Ian Wright & AntiWarPosters.com.

Page 119: Office of Global Communications. http://www.psywarrior.com/afghanleaf08.html.

Page 121: Courtesy of National Archives 513533.

Figure 5.1: ArcticNet-NCE/Time & Life Pictures/Getty Images.

Figure 5.2: Cover text only from SCIENCE Vol. 311, No. 5768 (24 March 2006). Reprinted with permission from AAAS. Photo. Nevada Wier/Corbis.

Figure 5.3: Time & Life Pictures/Getty Images.

Figure 5.4: Steve Bronstein/The Image Bank/Getty Images.

Figure 5.5: Rocket Blitz from the Moon by Chesley Bonestell. Bonestell Space Art.

Figure 5.6: Time & Life Pictures/Getty Images.

Figure 5.9: Stem Cells, March 2006 cover © AlphaMed Press.

Figure 5.10: Courtesy of the Yale Scientific Magazine.

Figure 5.11: © Vincent Chen 2009.

Figure 6.1: Courtesy of Universal Studios Licensing LLLP.

Page 241: Warner Bros./Photofest.

Figure 6.3 top: TM & Copyright © 20th Century Fox. All rights reserved/Courtesy Everett Collection.

Figure 6.3 middle: TM & Copyright © 20th Century Fox. All rights reserved/Courtesy Everett Collection.

Figure 6.3 bottom: TM & Copyright © 20th Century Fox. All rights reserved/Courtesy Everett Collection.

Figure 6.4: © Lions Gate/Courtesy Everett Collection.

Figure 6.5: © Paramount/Courtesy Everett Collection.

Figure 7.1: Building on the Past by Justin Cone.

Page 235: AP/Wide World Photos.

Figure 8.1: Courtesy of the author.

Pages 241, 242 left: Danjaq/Eon/UA/Keith Hamshere/The Kobal Collection.

242 right: Paramount/Icon/Andrew Cooper/ The Kobal Collection.

Figure 8.6: Reproduced with the kind permissions of The Body Shop International, plc.

Figure 8.7: Courtesy www.adbusters.org.

Figure 8.6: Courtesy of the author.

Figure 8.13: Courtesy of the author.

Figure 9.1: AP/Wide World Photos.

Page 273 left, right: AP/Wide World Photos.

Page 273 center: Paramount Classics/Photofest

Figure 9.2: Reuters/Stefan Wermouth/Landov.

Figure 9.3: AP/Wide World Photos.

Figure 9.4: Official White House Photo by Pete Souza.

Figure 9.17: Bettmann/Corbis.

Figure 9.18: Topham/The Image Works.

Text

"Do No Harm: The Coalition of Americans for Research Ethics." Screen shot from http://www.stemcellresearchy.org/. Reprinted by permission Do No Harm: The Coalition of Americans for Research Ethics.

Ephron, Nora. "The Boston Photographs." Reprinted by permission of International Creative Management, Inc. Copyright © 1978 by Nora Ephron.

Gottesman, Jane. Screen shots from the online version of *Game Face*, found at http:// washingtonpost.com/wp-srv.photo .onassignment.gameFace/. Reprinted by permission of Game Face Productions.

Marlette, Doug. "I Was a Tool of Satan." Reproduced from *Columbia Journalism Review*. November/December 2003. © 2003 by *Columbia Journalism Review*.

NIH Stem Cell linformation hosted by the National Institute for Health of the U.S. government. (http://stemcells.nih.gov)

Schulte, Bret. "Saying it in Cinema." www.usnews.com/usnews/newsarticles/ 060605/05warming,b,htm, © 2006, in U.S. News.

Stevenson, Seth. "You and Your Shadow: The ¡Pods are mesmerizing. But does your ¡Pod think it's better than you?" Reprinted by permission from *Slate*. 3/2/2004 Issue.

TheTruth.com. "Crazyworld" screen shot from http://www.thetruth.com. Reprinted by permission of the American Legacy Foundation.

"What's Wrong With the Body Shop." from the Beyond McDonald's pages at http://www.McSpotlight.org

Index